The Great War and America

THE GREAT WAR AND AMERICA

Civil-Military Relations during World War I

NANCY GENTILE FORD

In War and in Peace: U.S. Civil-Military Relations
David S. Heidler and Jeanne T. Heidler, General Editors

Praeger Security International
Westport, Connecticut · London

Library of Congress Cataloging-in-Publication Data

Ford, Nancy Gentile, 1954–
   The Great War and America : civil-military relations during World War I /
   Nancy Gentile Ford.
     p. cm. — (In war and in peace : U.S. civil-military relations, ISSN 1556–8504)
   Includes bibliographical references and index.
   ISBN-13: 978–0–275–98199–0 (alk. paper)
  1. World War, 1914–1918—United States. 2. Civil-military relations—United States—
   History—20th century. 3. World War, 1914–1918—Social aspects—United States.
   4. United States—Social conditions—1865–1918. I. Title.
   E780.F67 2008
   940.3'1—dc22   2007043243

British Library Cataloguing in Publication Data is available.

Library of Congress Catalog Card Number: 2007043243
ISBN-13: 978–0–275–98199–0
ISSN: 1556–8504

First published in 2008

Praeger Security International, 88 Post Road West, Westport, CT 06881
An imprint of Greenwood Publishing Group, Inc.
www.praeger.com

Printed in the United States of America

∞

The paper used in this book complies with the
Permanent Paper Standard issued by the National
Information Standards Organization (Z39.48–1984).

10 9 8 7 6 5 4 3 2 1

To Miranda, I am honored to call you daughter

Contents

Series Foreword   ix

Preface   xi

Acknowledgments   xiii

1. The Preparedness Movement: America Reevaluates Its Military   1

2. Drafting and Training Citizen-Soldiers: New Civil-Military Relations   27

3. Mobilizing Public Opinion and Suppressing Dissent: Civil-Military Cooperation and Conflict   51

4. Over There: Science, Technology, and Modern Warfare   71

5. Demobilization and Reemployment: The War Department Steps In   93

Documents   117

Notes   145

Selected Bibliography   169

Index   177

Series Foreword

No other aspect of a nation's political health is as important as the relationship between its government and military. At the most basic level, the necessity of protecting the country from external and internal threats must be balanced by the obligation to preserve fundamental civil liberties. The United States is unique among nations, for it has successfully maintained civilian control of its military establishment, doing so from a fundamental principle institutionalized in its constitution and embraced by its citizens. The United States has thus avoided the military coup that elsewhere has always meant the end of representative government and the extinguishing of individual freedom. The American military is the servant of citizens, not their master.

This series presents the work of eminent scholars to explain as well as assess civil-military relations in U.S. history. The American tradition of a military controlled by civilians is venerable—George Washington established it when he accepted his commission from the Continental Congress in 1775—but we will see how military leaders have not always been sanguine about abdicating important decisions to those they regard as inexperienced amateurs. And while disagreements between the government and the military become more likely during wars, there is more to this subject than the institutional arrangements of subordination and obedience that mark the relationship of government authorities and the uniformed services. The public's evolving perception of the military is also a central part of this story. In these volumes we will see explored the fine line between dissent and loyalty in war and peace and how the government and the armed forces have balanced civil liberties against national security. From the years of the American Revolution to the present, the resort to military justice has always been an option for safeguarding domestic welfare, but it has always been legally controversial and generally unpopular.

The United States relies on civilians to serve as most of its warriors during major conflicts, and civilian appreciation of things military understandably changes during such episodes. Opinions about the armed services transform accordingly, usually from casual indifference to acute concern. And through it all, military and civilian efforts to sustain popular support for the armed forces and mobilize enthusiasm for its operations have been imperative, especially when the military has been placed in the vague role of peacekeeper far from home for extended periods. The changing threats that America has confronted throughout its history have tested its revered traditions of civil-military relations, yet Americans have met even the most calamitous challenges without damaging those traditions. The most successful representative democracy in the world has defended itself without losing its way. We are hopeful that the volumes in this series will not only explain why but will also help to ensure that those vital traditions Americans rightly celebrate will endure.

David S. Heidler and Jeanne T. Heidler,
General Editors

Preface

The traditional interaction between the armed forces of the United States and the larger society significantly transformed during the Great War. To fully understand the art and science of the First World War, one must take into account broader cultural and social issues and examine the interconnection of political, economic, and psychological aspects that affect war and society. Throughout America's participation in the conflict, these aspects directly affected the structure and power of the U.S. armed forces, altered American society, and redefined democracy.

Historically, a complex strain existed between American society and its military, since the armed forces simultaneously represented both a threat to democracy and its ultimate protector. Founding fathers struggled; as they attempted to design a military capable of expanding in defense of the nation, but weak enough as to not usurp the power of the government. The early statesmen took precautions when they insisted on a small-standing army under civilian control and purposely kept military leaders isolated from political power and policy making. Although the association between the military and society evolved (especially during the late nineteenth century), it was during World War I that a major reassessment of civil-military relations took place and the two groups began to work in tandem.

The First World War escalated the modernization of the nation's armed forces, expanded the size and power of the federal government, drew an unprecedented number of young citizen-soldiers into service, ignited a super-patriotic atmosphere on the home front that demanded unbridled conformity, and laid the seeds for an eventual military-industrial complex. The unparalleled presence of the military in American civil society during the war drew Progressive reformers, immigrant and African-American leaders, peace activists, clergymen, and radicals into intense debates over preparedness, militarism, conscriptions, and issues of civil liberties. Prevailing social philosophies of the day influenced military policy, and civilians played a key role in training, equipping, and meeting the needs of some four million American soldiers. The War Department took on a greatly expanded role in civilian society—a military role that would have shaken eighteenth century American political leadership to their core. However, early twentieth century modernity brought with it a colossal industrialized war requiring the intricate cooperation of political officials, military leaders, and civilians. This book analyzes the complex civil-military interaction during the Great War—an interaction that significantly impacted both American society and its armed forces.

Acknowledgments

I would like to thank my editors, Adam Kane from Praeger Security International, David S. and Jean T. Heidler (series editors) and Magendra Varman Nithyanandam from BeaconPMG for their assistance and patience while I was completing this book. Also, thanks to Kenneth L. Kusmer and the late Russell F. Weigley—I could not have asked for better mentors in my academic life. I appreciate the assistance from talented reference librarians and archivists, especially those from the National Archives Records Administration II and the U.S. Army Military History Institute. I am grateful to the Pennsylvania State System of Higher Education for awarding me a Faculty Professional Development Council Grant to conduct needed research and to Bloomsburg University for providing me with reassignment time to work on this project. Thanks also to my work-study student, Jennifer Perott, who worked diligently at copying primary sources, retyping original documents, and proofreading. I am indebted to my many friends for their words of encouragement and to the entire Gentile clan for giving me so much love and laughter—Sam, Jackie, Frank, Lorrie, Kristi, Julie, Jim, Denise, Jessica, Nicole, Corrina, and Jake. Thanks also to Bob, Pat, Robin, Mickey, Daisy, Quincy, and Wilson Ford. I cannot begin to express enough appreciation for my wonderful husband, Dave, who is both a perfect soul mate and a great proofreader. My daughter Miranda came into my life when she was just five years old. She brought with her the bright sunshine of a child's love, along with jelly shoes, multicolored ribbons, French braids, and lots and lots of toys. Toys gave way to boys, proms, and broken hearts. Over the years, I watched this precious gift grow into an intelligent, compassionate, and beautiful young woman. Miranda, your presence reminds me everyday that family must be my number one priority. You blessed me with the most important role of my life—motherhood. I dedicate this book to you, with all my love.

1

The Preparedness Movement: America Reevaluates Its Military

In the years just prior to the Great War, supporters of American military preparedness argued that a modern nation needed a large, organized military with the capability to expand at wartime with a federal reserve of volunteer citizen-soldiers. This would require UMT (Universal Military Training) to prepare young men as soldiers during peacetime, so as to be on the ready in times of war. The Preparedness Movement defied long-held beliefs that a strong standing army could be dangerous to the freedom of the American people. It also undermined the Organized Militia System, a system of state-controlled armies made up of citizens—a tradition that began in the early colonial years. As early as 1912, a group of preparedness reformers called for new improvements in the U.S. military, continuing the important work of Admiral Alfred Thayer Mahan's 1890 call to build up the navy and former secretary of war Elihu Root's efforts to create a more efficient and modern army (1899–1904).

By 1914, as Europe became entangled in the First World War, American military and political leaders, along with the general public, participated in a fierce debate over how to improve the Armed Forces and whether the nation should train all young able-bodied male citizens for possible war. By 1916, military and civilian leaders joined forces to stand on both sides of the preparedness debate. Advocates and opponents of UMT divided along complex lines defined by class, region, social philosophy, and political affiliation. The intense discourse over the Preparedness Movement added a new chapter in civil-military relations in America and resulted in the first peace time legislation that increased, restructured, and modernized both the land and naval forces of the U.S. military. The push for UMT helped steer America toward the 1917–1918 national draft.

AMERICA'S DEFENSELESSNESS

At the forefront of the Preparedness Movement stood former president Theodore Roosevelt (T.R.) and army chief of staff general Leonard Wood. In Roosevelt's early career, he held positions as a New York State assemblyman, New York City police commissioner, U.S. Civil Service commissioner, governor of New York, and assistant secretary of the navy. In 1898, Lieutenant Colonel Roosevelt reached "hero" status as the second in command of the "Rough Riders"—the infamous U.S. Volunteer Cavalry Regiment who scaled San Juan Hill during the Spanish-American War. As vice president of the United States, he took over the reigns of government after the assassination of President McKinley in 1901. In this capacity, President Roosevelt expanded the role of the Executive Office to lead the nation in important progressive social justice reforms, antitrust legislation, and conservation initiatives. As president, he also advocated a more aggressive foreign policy and pushed for the expansion and modernization of the U.S. military. T.R. won the Nobel Peace Prize for his role in negotiating an end to the Russo-Japanese War and mediated other international disputes. After Roosevelt left office in 1909, he continued to actively advocate for military reform and for compulsory UMT.[1]

General Leonard Wood, a Harvard-trained physician, with a long and successful military career, worked diligently for much needed army reform in an attempt to turn America's insufficient military into a first-rate force. During his earlier years in the service, he received the Congressional Medal of Honor for the campaign that led to the capture of Indian chief Geronimo and commanded the "Rough Riders" with his close friend Teddy Roosevelt. Soon after, Wood served in the post of military governor in Cuba and attempted to implement important social and economic reforms on the island. From 1903 to 1910, he held a number of key military positions including the commander of the Philippines Division and the Department of the East. He served as army chief of staff (1910–1914) under President William Howard Taft and for a short time under President Woodrow Wilson. He reported to the secretary of war and acted as a military advisor to the president. Wood, as "the Army's first effective Chief of Staff," used this key position and his significant political influence to streamline military procedures, systemize the training of soldiers, improve army divisions, and champion UMT.[2] A master of persuasion, Wood gave interviews with magazines and newspapers and took every opportunity to preach preparedness to "clubs, schools, universities, patriotic societies, aggregations of bankers, lawyers, merchants; writing articles for magazines, [and] giving interviews to the press."[3] He also published his various preparedness speeches in a book, *Our Military History: Its Facts and Fallacies,* and many national magazines reprinted excerpts from the book. After World War I, Wood ran unsuccessfully for president and served as the governor general of the Philippines from 1921 to 1927. But with all of his accomplishments, General Leonard Wood was best known as the "prophet of preparedness" for his constant struggle to reform the U.S. Army and to create a trained federal reserve of citizen-soldiers.[4]

Beginning in 1911, under the Taft Administration, Secretary of War Henry L. Stimson and Army Chief of Staff Wood joined forces to improve the effectiveness of the military and promote UMT. As a lawyer, Stimson had been a colleague of Root, before Root served as the secretary of war from 1899 to 1904. Stimson became the U.S. attorney for the New York Southern District (1906–1909), where he developed a respected reputation for successfully prosecuting antitrust cases. When Stimson (like his friend Root) became secretary of war, he continued with Root's military reform efforts working to improve the efficiency of the War Department and the military.[5]

One concern of the Stimson–Wood team was the inadequate size of the army, which was ill-equipped to fight a major war against the massive armies of Continental Europe. The two leaders were quick to point out that the nation's regular army of some 100,000 soldiers was stretched throughout the United States and in several areas of the world including China, Puerto Rico, and the Panama Canal Zone. The men considered the Organized Militia System (renamed and reshaped into the National Guard) to be inefficient and archaic. Although the army could be increased by over 110,000 guardsmen, if needed, this force would be wholly inadequate to fight a serious war. Furthermore, states' control over the National Guard could possibly limit their use. Problems with the commitment and performance of militiamen in past wars, such as the War of 1812, long haunted the military. The traditional volunteer system of citizen-soldiers increased the ranks of the army in times of crisis, but most men came untrained for combat.[6]

During the Civil War, the nation's attempt to expand the army with untrained volunteers and drafted citizens resulted in a multitude of problems. However, creating a large federal force of professional soldiers was not only expensive, but out of the question for a society that long considered a strong standing army as dangerous to the liberty of the American people. Instead, Wood and Stimson advocated modernization of the military (with an acceptable increase in the regular army), the reorganization and improvement of the Organized Militia System, and the formation of federal reserve of young male volunteer civilians trained during peacetime (by the Regular Army as to be ready for war when needed). Some military reformers looked overseas for answers to reconstruct the nation's armed forces. But adapting the continental European reservist model of a two-year military training period for citizens represented a drastic departure from America's military traditions and would no doubt meet with strong public resistance. Instead, most preparedness campaigners argued for a shorter training period for civilians that would provide the nation with "a pretrained mass army of citizen reservists, trained and commanded by regulars and coordinated by a general staff."[7]

Attempts at large-scale military reform and preparedness during the Taft years proved difficult due to resistance from status quo Old Guard Republicans (Laissez Fare Republicans) in the Senate, antimilitary Democrats in the House of Representatives, and a fiercely defiant House Military Affairs Committee. Protests also came from the well-entranced army officers who did not want to turn the Regular Army into a military training school for volunteers. Furthermore, the world was at peace, and military reform did not constitute a burning issue for the general public. After much resistance, Congress enacted the 1912 Army Appropriations Act which took a small step toward the creation of a trained reserve when it set up a seven-year enlistment plan—four years of active duty and three years as reservist (with no pay). Although this act fell far short of requiring all male citizens to receive military training (desired by UMT supporters), it set out to create a prepared backup force for the active-duty Regular Army. The act also included some unfavorable changes for the War Department, and the political struggle, along with Wood's directness and dogmatism, marked the army chief of staff as an enemy for those who resisted military preparedness.[8]

Next, Stimson assigned Captain (later brigadier-general) John McAuley Palmer (of the General Staff) to research and formulate an effective plan of action in order to convince Congress of needed changes that would further improve and prepare the U.S. military for possible war. In particular, Stimson expressed concern over the small reserve force's inadequate training. Palmer and his team produced the Army's 1912 *Report on the Organization of the Land Forces of the United States,* which adopted the British military structure. The Land Forces report, also known as the "Stimson Plan," called for some expansion of America's Regular Army and for a federal reserve force of citizen-soldiers to be trained and organized prior to being needed in a crisis. The plan required an improved Organized Militia System—the nation's second line of defense—to be "upgraded, organized into tactical divisions, and made subject to draft into the armed forces of the United States, thus freeing it for service outside the country."[9] The nation's third line of defense remained volunteers. The report did not call for compulsory UMT but instead took a "citizen-army" approach and called for a reserve of volunteers trained in peacetime. The report also called for a Council of National Defense to organize the civil-military economic mobilization in time of war. Palmer, a protégé of General John J. Pershing, and a key military reformer argued "that only if the entire military were stocked with civilians, from raw recruits to high-ranking officers, could the nation be protected against adventurism or other abuse of military power."[10]

The 1912 *Land Force* report, completed at a time of political upheaval, went nowhere due to adversaries in Congress especially Representative James Hay, chairman of the House Committee on Military Affairs. Hay, an antimilitarist, fought against a large standing professionally trained army and carefully guarded the militia system. Wood's old adversary, Major General Fred C. Ainsworth, stood firmly in opposition of the 1912 report contending that the short training time for volunteers could not possibly produce effective officers. A few years earlier when Ainsworth served as military secretary (under chief of staff), Wood and Ainsworth had fiercely disagreed about the role of the General Staff and engaged in intense disputes over the streamlining of administration procedures and other issues. At that time, President Taft pleaded with the two men to work in harmony, since "the Military Secretary in many respects is the right hand of the Chief of Staff."[11] However, the two men continued to barb and, in 1912, Ainsworth, (now an adjutant general), eventually crossed the line and Stimson threatened to court marital him for insubordination. Friends in Congress, however, convinced the secretary of war to allow Ainsworth to retire. The adjutant general's retirement only served to push the Wood–Ainsworth conflict into Congress, since Ainsworth became an unofficial advisor to Hay, and the two men became formidable opponents of preparedness and UMT in the prewar years. (Although the 1912 report on the *Organization of the Land Forces* stalled, Stimson later made some administrative improvements in the Regular Army in February 1913.)[12]

In the Fall of 1912, political tension in Congress led to a growing division between the Old Guard Republicans and the new Progressive Party led by Theodore Roosevelt (with many former Republicans in tow). The deep chasm in the Republican Party led to victory for Democratic presidential candidate Woodrow Wilson, and the Democratic Party won the majority of seats in the House and Senate. This election took place under a backdrop of an American society that was clearly not interested in military improvements, and debates over military defense did not even enter the political campaigns. Furthermore, President Wilson and the Democratic Congress did not think military preparedness was necessary. However, military reformers continued to worry that the United States was far from ready to either defend itself against a foreign enemy or engage in a major war. To make matters worse, increased border problems, stemming from the overthrow of the Mexican government by insurgents in 1913, put the U.S. military on alert.[13]

Despite his resilient struggle against military preparedness, Wilson allowed Wood to stay on as the army chief of staff, but the Democratic Party victory in 1912 saw many other changes including the replacement of Secretary of War Stimson with Lindley M. Garrison. Garrison earned his law degree from the University of Pennsylvania in 1886 and practiced law before being appointed vice chancellor of New Jersey. As the new secretary of war, Garrison fought aggressively to modernize and strengthen the nation's army and navy despite President Wilson's resistance. Garrison and Wood did not always agree on how to elicit support, and Garrison eventually told Wood to refrain from championing preparedness to the general public since it was considered bad form for a military officer to take the fight outside of military channels. This would not be the first time Garrison and Wood disagreed on the general's aggressive public approach to preparedness, nor was it the only time Garrison reprimanded Wood. But Garrison's warning generally went unheeded. During his tenure as Wilson's chief of staff and afterwards, Wood continued to take his case before the public, and he was instrumental in the formation of the Army League, a congressional lobbying group for military reform. Members in the League included big names in foreign policy and military families along with a host of prominent university presidents. The general also regularly met with federal legislators in a "semiofficial capacity" to promote his agenda. Wood's main focus on preparedness was compulsory UMT, and he continued to take the cause to reporters, well-placed members of upper class professionals, and powerful political leaders. He also asked military writers to encourage the development of the UMT system and draw attention to America's defenselessness.[14]

SUMMER MILITARY TRAINING CAMPS—1913 AND 1914

Despite the open opposition, General Wood pressed on, especially pushing for military training of all young able-bodied men and at the same time establishing a reserve of officers. As historian John Garry Clifford put it,

> [Wood] had faith in the citizen soldier. He said he could make civilians into soldiers in six months—instead of the customary two or three years. And Wood meant to put such principles into practice. He meant to breathe life into a citizen reserve.[15]

In early 1913, Lieutenant Henry T. Bull, a retired cavalry officer and Cornell University professor of military science, approached Wood with a plan that tied into the general's promotion of UMT. Bull suggested that young men attending America's colleges and universities could receive military training during the summer, if placed with Regular Army units. This would mirror a system already in place by the U.S. Navy. Wood assigned Bull to work with Captain Robert O. Van Horn and Captain Douglas MacArthur to develop specific details. However, instead of attaching college students to army units, Wood wanted the team to design plans for the establishment of officer military training camps for volunteer college men. Once Wood received the approval from Garrison, he asked university and college presidents to recruit young men to attend two experimental summer military training programs. Student response was great enough for the War Department to establish a camp in Gettysburg, Pennsylvania and one near the Presidio in Monterey, California. Wood saw college students as an untapped resource that could supplement America's small army and, once trained, the men could assist as a federal reserve officer corps in national emergencies. In a letter to an acquaintance, Wood explained that the camps would not teach "militarism" or "preach large standing armies." Instead, the experience should "revivify or perhaps recreate that sense of personal and individual responsibility for one's preparedness to discharge efficiently the duties of a soldier in case the Republic should become involved in war."[16]

Beginning in July 1913, 160 young men from sixty-one colleges received military training on the same hollowed ground where the North and the South engaged in the ferocious battle at Gettysburg. To save money, the camp used the tents and equipment set up for the fiftieth anniversary of the Union soldiers who fought in the Pennsylvania conflict. In California, a similar Students' Military Instruction Camp brought together sixty-three students from twenty-nine colleges a few miles from the Presidio in Monterey. Not wanting to ask the newly appointed Wilson Administration for additional funding, Wood required students to pay for their uniforms and food (approximately $27.50) along with all transportation costs. The cost limited enrollment primarily to students from elite families who could afford the camp expense and college tuition. For six weeks, summer trainees drilled, hiked, and cleaned rifles. They also did calisthenics, studied military theory, and learned camp sanitation, map reading, manual of arms, close order formation, range estimations, entrenchment, and patrol. Combat instruction came from hand-picked officers who also engaged their students in maneuvers to practice what they learned. During off hours, instructors encouraged their students to play sports and participate in other recreational activities. Declaring the camp experiment a success at the end of the summer, Wood told his former boss and friend, Henry Stimson, the young men "illustrated how it is that Switzerland, with only short intense periods of training, has such a good army."[17]

The continuation of the summer military training program for male college students received the backing of key administrators from Columbia, Cornell, Harvard, Stanford, and Yale Universities, and the University of California, Berkeley. The most enthusiastic advocate, President Henry Sturgis Drinker of Lehigh University in Bethlehem, Pennsylvania, created an Advisory Board of University Presidents for the National Reserve Corp. to promote future college training camps for students. Wood and Captain Horn spent the winter visiting colleges and universities to discuss the advantages of the program for both young men and the nation.[18]

In the summer of 1914, Wood and his team set up summer training camps in Ludington, Michigan; Asheville, North Carolina; Burlington, Vermont; and Monterey, California. Help from university presidents and carefully planned publicity brought nearly 1,000 students to the camps—well over the number that attended the previous summer. As with the 1913 camp, students paid for their own expenses, and not surprisingly, the trainees came mostly from the east coast elite class. Classes included both military instruction and citizenship. Final training reports complimented the students and hailed the success of the camps. Burlington camp commander, Captain

Oliver Edward, noted, "If I ever had to organize and train a regiment of volunteers for war, I would at once ask for all the men I could get...from this year's camp."[19] Wood and his handful of forward-thinking military, university and political supporters saw a bright future for training citizens in summer camps and had high hopes for the eventual establishment of a compulsory UMT system.[20]

UMT AS A "PUBLIC HEALTH PROJECT"

Most Progressive social justice reformers objected to preparedness and UMT since it promoted militarism and took attention and funding away for much needed social reform. However, many UMT supporters ironically mirrored the philosophy of the social justice movement. Progressive social welfare reformers sought to "uplift" the lower classes, build character, instill moral values (defined by the upper classes), and provide wholesome outdoor activities. After returning to the United States to serve as the army chief of staff, General Leonard Wood's call for preparedness went beyond creating a system of trained civilians, for he "believed that military discipline would develop citizens morally, physically, and politically."[21] Indeed, Wood was among a number of prominent doctors who considered UMT for all young men a "public health project" that would improve the general well-being of participants. The relationship between civilian society and the military has always been complex, and often, social philosophies found in American society made their way into the military. This was also the case with medical theories. Wood and other physicians who advocated UMT received their education during a time when medical school curriculum made a direct correlation between poor health and personal character defects. Physicians connected this "Christian Pathology" with poor public health and morality and argued that disease resulted from sin. Thus, if members of society could be morally uplifted, public health would improve, and since military training would build character in all young men, it would naturally improve the health of the general society.[22]

Many doctors, presidents of state and national medical societies, chairmen of American medical associations, and representatives from medical schools advocated UMT. This included numerous doctors, ninety-four university presidents, ten chairmen of associations, and ninety-five leaders of medical schools. Dr. Charles Burr, from the University of Pennsylvania called Americans a "soft, fat, and flabby emotional and kindhearted but mush-headed race." According to Burr,

> Unless the American boy is taught obedience, unless he learns to submit to authority, unless he learns that the highest manhood is to obey, unless he learns that work is a blessing, not a curse, this country is doomed.... Universal Military Training will do much to stiffen up, to make firm-fibered and manly the boys of America.[23]

However, a new generation of doctors eventually challenged "Christian Pathology." New ideas in medicine combined with innovative medical technology changed the philosophy and practice of healing and ultimately questioned old ideas of morality and medicine. New training for physicians changed the emphasis from social uplifting to medical training, use of new technologies, and scientific research. "Christian Pathology" doctors countered this direction, claiming newly trained physicians treated patients as machines with no soul and simply repaired "engines" instead of reforming patients' "moral habits" and applying "moral instruction and ministerial form of medicine."[24] For many older doctors, this shift made UMT of all young men even more important to public health, virtue, and character building. According to historian Michael Pearlman, Wood and other Christian pathologists tried "to turn the preparedness movement into a public health program retaining the tonic of regimen which medicine itself no longer emphasized."[25]

PREPAREDNESS DEBATES: 1914–1915

Wood left his position as chief of staff in April 1914 and assumed the command of the Army's Eastern Department, a post that held considerable power and would allow him to continue his fight with other preparedness supporters. But the plan took a sudden turn. The June 18, 1914 assassination of Archduke Franz Ferdinand, heir to the throne of the Austro-Hungarian Empire, served as the match that ignited a world war. Prewar international peace efforts could not stop global tension spiraling out of control from competition over trade and new colonies. Economic imperialism, militarism, and nationalism proved too strong, and a complex alliance system quickly plummeted much of the world into war. Modern industrial warfare turned the conflict into a prolonged bloody stalemate.

Although the United States stayed out of the war until April 1917, the world crisis forced the Preparedness Movement into an open national debate. At issue was America's traditional two-army system—a small standing army expanded by volunteers and supported by state militias. Many preparedness supporters, especially those from the urban middle and upper class, adamantly called for the replacement of the National Guard and the volunteer system with a more effective federal reserve of trained citizens. Not all military leaders agreed. For many "old pinheads," as Wood called them, the preparedness campaign "for a citizen-service threatened their sinecures [perks], their rewards, and even their way of life."[26] However, officers who supported preparedness became even louder in their call for military improvements in 1915 when the United States dispatched soldiers to the Mexican border to prevent border raids and protect American citizens.[27]

President Wilson also faced pressure to reform the land and naval forces from within his administration, including Secretary of War Garrison, new army chief of staff Hugh L. Scott, Assistant Secretary of the Navy Franklin D. Roosevelt, and Rear Admiral Bradley A. Fiske. Garrison proved to be an aggressive fighter who challenged his president at every turn, and Major General Scott strongly promoted UMT. Scott spent much of his military career on the Western Frontier before being placed in leadership roles in Cuba and the Philippines. He became the superintendent of West Point in 1906, received a special commendation for his handing of the conflict with the Navajo in 1913, served for a short time as assistant chief of staff, and became chief of staff in November 1914. Scott concluded that the only way for the nation to prepare for possible war was to create a huge citizen-reserve force, made ready under a system of compulsory military training. Franklin D. Roosevelt (fifth cousin of Theodore Roosevelt), son of a wealthy New York family, graduated from Harvard University. He attended Columbia Law School and passed the bar examination in 1907. Roosevelt began his political career in the New York State Senate before becoming assistant secretary of the navy in 1913. Admiral Fiske joined Franklin Roosevelt in the fight to improve and modernize the U.S. Navy. In the years after his participation in the Spanish-American War, Fiske advanced in rank to rear admiral in 1911 and aide of operations (later called chief of naval operations) in 1913. From his various military experiences, Fiske became an ardent supporter of military preparedness. In addition to members of Wilson's administration, former president Theodore Roosevelt, a long-time champion for a modern military, went on the attack. Among his many public addresses, T.R. gave two speeches at the Panama-Pacific Exposition in July 1915, "one vigorous in tone on military preparedness," and a "brief, personal talk" to servicemen in the enlisted men's club. The *New York Times* reported that "Colonel Roosevelt told the enlisted men that a man afraid to fight is not fit to vote [and] 'a mother who is not willing to raise her boy to be a soldier is not fit for citizenship.'"[28]

Henry Cabot Lodge, a powerful figure in the Senate, also joined the growing ranks of preparedness politicians and military leaders. Lodge was born into a prominent Boston family, graduated with a Ph.D. in political science from Harvard University in 1876, and, as a Republican from Massachusetts, served in the House of Representatives from 1887 to 1893 and the Senate from 1893 to 1924. Lodge's son-in-law, Augustus Peabody Gardner, a Republican representative from Massachusetts, also joined the cause. In 1886, Gardner graduated from Harvard and continued at the university in the study of law. Before entering politics, he became the assistant adjutant general for General James H. Wilson during the Spanish-American War. Gardner served as a Massachusetts state senator from 1900 to 1901 and a U.S. senator from 1902 to 1917. (During World War I, Gardner resigned from office to join the army, and he died at Camp Wheeler, Georgia in 1918.)[29]

After twelve years of silence concerning America's military preparedness, Gardner finally spoke out in 1914 when he presented a House resolution calling for a national security commission to examine the country's defenses. The congressman had recently visited Europe where he saw, first hand, the military might of Germany and now stood determined to bring America's fighting forces in line with other modern, industrial nations. Gardner continued to introduce congressional military bills hoping for eventual reform. Wood, Lodge, Gardner, Theodore Roosevelt, and other key allies also fired harsh rhetoric at their opponents. However, Wilson strongly disagreed. The president saw no reason to prepare the nation to protect itself but rather viewed the world crisis as a chance for America to show moral guidance to the world and arbitrate between enemies. In his December 1914 annual address, Wilson fired back at the opposition, "we shall not alter our attitude toward the question of national defense because some amongst us are nervous and excited.... Let there be no misconception. The country has been misinformed. We have not been negligent of the national defense."[30]

Preparedness supporters faced two formidable powerhouses in Congress—chairman of the House of Military Affairs Committee James Hay and his counterpart in the Senate, George E. Chamberlain. Both Representative Hay, a Democratic from Virginia, and Senator Chamberlain, a progressive Democrat from Oregon, graduated from Washington and Lee University in Virginia, practiced law, and held political positions in their states' legislature. Chamberlain became Oregon's governor, before being elected into the U.S. Congress in 1908. Hay became a U.S. representative in 1897 and served on the House Committee on Military Affairs for eighteen years.[31]

Hay often blocked efforts by secretaries of war from strengthening the U.S. military, considering such "proposals expensive, unnecessary, and militaristic."[32] The representative steadfastly opposed Secretary of War Garrison's efforts to modernize the American army and navy, claiming that the geographical position of the United States made it safe from invasion, and he expressed disdain for "militarists" who criticized the Organized Militia System. Past conflicts with the War Department escalated to the point where Hay even tried, but failed, to convince President Taft to remove Chief of Staff General Leonard Wood from his position in 1912. Unlike Hay, Chamberlain was very receptive to military reform, but he demanded an extensive and comprehensive investigation since military leaders did not agree on key issues. Chamberlain warned, "I do not think that Congress should be asked for what the War Department thinks it can get, but for what the country actually needs."[33]

PLATTSBURG TRAINING CAMP—1915

In the midst of the controversial preparedness debate, General Wood began planning the 1915 summer officer military training camps for college students. That spring, he was approached by Grenville Clark (a member of a wealthy banking and railroad family and law partner of Elihu Root). Clark, Root, and a group of lawyers and professional men (known as the Committee of One Hundred) had been working on a plan that would provide businessmen and lawyers with military training. The impetus came as a result of a powerful speech Wood gave at the Harvard Club a few months prior on military preparedness and the military obligation of citizens in a democracy. The proposal was driven further by the sinking of the *Lusitania*. Clark told the general he wanted a Business Men's Camp with "our kind of people," who felt strong enough about military preparedness to participate in military training.[34] Wood quickly jumped on the idea, and he and his officers traveled to four major cities to promote the concept of a four-week military camp for professionals. They also placed full-page ads in pro-preparedness newspapers in Boston, New York, and Philadelphia.[35]

Response was so great that in addition to his college training camps, Wood established a separate camp for older professionals in Plattsburg, New York. The camp, one hundred and fifty miles north of Albany, brought together 1,800 professionals for a four-week training experience starting in early August 1915. Finances for the camps came from the War Department, a $3,000 donation from wealthy financier Bernard Baruch, and a $30 charge from each camper for food and equipment. Most of the trainees came from the urban elite living in the northeastern part of the nation with experience in politics, business, and law. Although Wood continued to point out the nonpartisan nature of the Preparedness Movement, most of the volunteer trainees (as well as preparedness supporters) belonged to the Republican Party. The group included John Purroy Mitchel, the mayor of New York. Mitchel's presence assured national press for the Plattsburg Movement. Trainees ranged in age from thirties to fifties. Each man started his day at 5:45 a.m. with calisthenics and drill, followed by military instruction in the afternoon. Men learned camp setup, personal hygiene, the manual of arms, care and use of the army rifle, and target practice along with other important lessons.[36]

Not everyone praised the idea of the summer training camps for students and professionals. Critics condemned the idea, arguing that it took much longer than four weeks to train soldiers for war. However, Wood knew that if nothing else, the camps served as excellent propaganda for the Preparedness Movement. The general actively participated in the camps, gave lectures on national defense, and met with the trainees to discuss foreign policy issues over evening campfires. He made sure that every rookie trainee would not leave the camp without having the nation's defenselessness "hammered" home. Sometimes Wood vehemently attacked his critics and once called them "fakers who do not care to place their own precious bodies in jeopardy."[37] His plan for national exposure paid off. Not only did the press generously cover the camp activities, but the Plattsburg "graduates" wrote some two dozen articles on their experiences in various newspapers and journals. When New York mayor Mitchel completed his training, he told the press (paraphrasing Wood): "It would be a crime against the people of this country, amounting to nothing less than national suicide, to send into the field armies manned by officers and untrained volunteers."[38]

Some publicity backfired, especially the coverage of Theodore Roosevelt's visit to Plattsburg in July 1915. The colonel arrived in full "Rough Rider" regalia to give a passionate speech before the men and fervently attacked those in the nation who ignored critical defense issues. T.R. besmirched all "professional pacifists, poltroons [cowards], and college sissies who organize peace-at-any price societies."[39] The colonel's comments to the trainees included a slightly veiled criticism of President Wilson. To make matters worse, Roosevelt openly challenged the president to reporters who waited for him at the train station on his way home when he avidly argued that the country "should stand by the President [only]...so long as the President stands by the country."[40] Roosevelt's negative comments appeared in the national press the next day, including the front page of the *New York Times*. Response from the secretary of war in Washington, DC to General Wood was swift and decisive—this type of publicity should never happen again. Wood assured Secretary Garrison his order would be "rigidly adhered to."[41] Despite the setback, plans continued for the future camps.

PUBLIC DEBATE — PRO-PREPAREDNESS

Germany's renewal of indiscriminate submarine warfare, the sinking of the *Lusitania* in May 1915, and the presidential election of 1916 accelerated the Preparedness Movement. Intense public debates over defense continued for many months as congress deliberated over new military allocations and how to reshape the U.S. military. Public and political pressures were strong enough to bring a hesitant Wilson on board calling for "reasonable preparedness." But, the president's main motivation for joining the Preparedness Movement was out of fear that the Democrats would face losses at the polls if he did not get behind the campaign. His reversal greatly disappointed many Progressive reformers and pacifists who stood firm against militarism. By late 1915 and early 1916, Congress was in the throws of intense debates over several military defense bills.[42]

The public joined the debate. Spurred on by accounts of the successful Plattsburg experience, many business leaders united behind the call for compulsory military service. Fear that an open attack by an enemy would bring chaos to the economy also motivated business leaders to push for military improvements. In July, 1915, Bernard Baruch went as far as to draw a correlation between military preparedness and a "bull market." The financier concluded that a strong, modern military would protect the nation and guard American shipping that supplied war materials to Europe— subsequently bring prosperity to the United States:

The industrial business that has come to our country, not only because of war orders, but on account of the purchases of neutral nations, is sooner or later bound to be felt by the railroads. Better business for the carriers means better business generally, which means national prosperity.[43]

During a September 1915 address to bankers at a convention, New York attorney Henry D. Estabrook "stirred" the audience declaring, "No nation threatens us in so many words, but who is oblivious to hints and intimations that speak louder than words? We boast our strength to repeal attack when we know we are weaker than dishwater."[44]

The increased strength of the public preparedness debate in 1916 coincided with election campaigns. In May 1916, Preparedness and Anti-preparedness supporters faced-off in an intense discussion before the American Academy of Political Science conference held at Columbia University. The organization reprinted the various addresses in its July *Proceedings of the Academy of Political Science of New York City*. Speaking on the topic, "The Business Man and Universal Military Training," Irving T. Bush, president of the Bush Terminal Company, related military training with the need to properly prepare young men from all classes of society for life. Within a few months, The American Banker's Association adopted a resolution calling for improvements in national defense.[45]

In his speech and subsequent article, "Problems of the Common Defense," the vice president of the Academy of Political Science, Albert Shaw, argued that the long-standing tradition in America of obligatory military service was unfortunately being replaced by a professional army. Furthermore, the small size and expense of the army made it ineffective. Shaw concluded that the only solution was to create a large reserve of citizen-soldiers, "made up of the trained young manhood of the country, impelled by patriotism and civic duty."[46]

As the Preparedness Movement grew, it drew the attention of national newspapers including the *New York Times,* New York *Tribune, Chicago Tribune,* St. Louis *Star,* Toledo *Blade,* Philadelphia *Inquirer,* Cleveland *Plain Dealer,* Providence *Journal,* and Duluth *News Tribune.* Public opinion polls conducted by the press demonstrated the growing public interest in increasing the size of the American military. The Cleveland *Plain Dealer* called for UMT citing the many refusals of army surgeons to allow unfit men into the National Guard thus reducing its effectiveness, and the New York *Tribune* saw compulsory service as protection from militarism. The *Chicago Tribune* openly criticized the National Guard "as an object lesson on the inefficiency of the volunteer system" and, in another article, the *Tribune* concluded that UMT would "reduce the criminal rate, produce a higher type of manhood, and level class distinction."[47] *The New Republic* concluded that the Plattsburg leaders connect "soldiering to citizenship" and thus the camps fought against the "real danger of national disintegration."[48]

Various organizations which also took up the cause including the Navy League, Army League, MTCA (Military Training Camp Association), and NSL (National Security League). Leaders from various organizations gave speeches and produced publications and motion pictures to bring attention to the nation's defenselessness. The Navy League, established in 1913, was a well-financed lobbying group that proved to be influential in the fight for preparedness. During one League meeting, the speaker, Dr. David Jayne Hill (the former American ambassador to Germany), reminded his audience of American men, women, and children who lost their lives "without provocation," no doubt referring to casualties of German submarine warfare. Hill spoke passionately: "In the name of peace, I implore the American people promptly to make themselves strong that their words and their rights will be respected in the world. To do this, we must be prepared to act."[49] Wood joined forces with Frederick L. Huidenkoper (a Washington lawyer and amateur military historian) to create the Army League in 1913. Although, not as large or prominent as the Navy League, the Army League fought hard to lobby for military reform. In his book, *The Military Unpreparedness of the United States,* Huidenkoper called for the training of a federal reserve army of citizens. The MTCA of the United States consisted of over 16,000 members, including many graduates of the Summer Training Camps. Grenville Clark played a key role in creating MTCA which served as a "well-connected" lobbying group demanding a large regular army and UMT for civilians. The organization also produced an array of testimonies from camp graduates discussing their successful military training experiences. Eventually, MTCA worked directly with the War Department in running future volunteer military training camps.[50]

By 1916, the NSL led by New York corporate lawyer S. Stanwood Menken; former secretary of war Stimson; former ambassador to Great Britain, Joseph H. Choate; and other wealthy and prominent figures, dominated the Preparedness Movement scene. Cornelius Vanderbilt, Henry C. Frick, and Simon Guggenheim bankrolled the NSL, and membership came from leading business firms and financial institutions. NSL produced an impressive publicity campaign that called for national legislation requiring compulsory military training for all able-bodied male citizens and immigrants (who planned to remain in the United States). The League also considered UMT key to Americanizing the nations foreign-born and preventing the spread of radicalism.[51]

Chambers of Commerce throughout the United States also took up the Preparedness banner. A 1916 survey conducted by the Chambers demonstrated strong support for preparedness, and a spokesman contended that military training would not only protect the nation, but also "aid in disciplining a selfish and inefficient work force."[52] Chambers of Commerce in twenty-six states unanimously approved of compulsory military training along with a majority of chambers in sixteen states. Five states did not participate in the survey. Only one, Alabama, took an anti-preparedness stand. Other Preparedness efforts included the motion picture, *The Battle Cry of Peace,* depicted a powerless American militia unable to stop an enemy attack on New York City. Another film, *Womanhood: The Glory of a Nation* was a "supercolossal" epic of its day, depicting the destruction of the United States by an overseas invasion. Although neither pictures named the enemy, they both clearly portrayed the adversary as Germany.[53]

At the Progressive Party National Convention, the group centered their political platform on preparedness. The party argued for an increase in the regular army to 250,000 men, an expansion and modernization of the navy, and the implementation of a UMT system. The Progressive Party concluded that compulsory training would shatter the class system, end prejudice, and shape young men into disciplined and efficient citizens. The Republican Party platform also called for preparedness but did not promote compulsory military training. Many among the general pubic also got on board with the preparedness advocates. In May, 135,000 Americans participated in a twelve hour Citizen's Preparedness Parade in New York City. On June 3, 1916, ten cities hosted parades with some 350,000 marchers showing their support for military preparedness. Clearly, with the backing from members of Congress, political parties, business leaders, major presses, and many among the general public, the Preparedness Movement came into full swing. By 1916, the civilian preparedness organizations had effective leadership, significant financing, and enough positive press coverage to spread their message.[54]

PUBLIC DEBATE—ANTI-PREPAREDNESS

But not everyone agreed, and an Anti-preparedness Movement grew among pacifists, feminists, Quakers, clergyman, socialists, and farmers as well as some labor unions, Democrats and progressive Republicans. Most anti-preparedness came from the lower and lower-middle classes of rural America, and from the well-educated, upper-middle class social justice communities of the Progressive Era. Although not unified in their objections, anti-preparedness advocates stood against all forms of militarism fearing that a large army would result in the loss of civil liberties. They argued that, far from expanding democracy, UMT would turn free men into slaves of authority. Opponents from agrarian communities connected the Preparedness Movement with a detrimental departure from localism and state control toward expanding federal powers. Others warned that big businesses—seeking to make war profits and expand their global trade opportunities—stood behind the push for preparedness.

Oswalt Garrison Villard, president of the *New York Evening Post,* challenged UMT supporters when he addressed the Academy of Political Sciences

at the May 1916 forum. A civil rights activist and descendent of leading ante-
bellum abolitionist William Lloyd Garrison, Villard helped to establish the
National Association for the Advancement of Colored People and founded
the American Anti-imperial League in response to the Spanish-American
War. Before purchasing the *Post,* he wrote for several newspapers and various anti-imperialist journals. In his 1916 speech, Villard discussed the rise
of military autocracy and the "unutterable cruelties" of militarism in France,
Germany, and Russia. He reminded his audience of James Madison's warning against large standing armies used by governments to take away the freedoms of the people and the foolhardiness of thinking military training would
improve society or positively shape young men. The newspaper president
sarcastically analyzed the "amazing phenomena" of UMT calling it a
"cure-all" for all ills. He also mockingly asked if the nation trained "every
boy to be a soldier," would the United States really be safe.

> Do we wish to become industrially efficient? Then...give every American a year
> under arms, and presto! We [sic] shall outdo Germany in scientific efficiency
> and management.... Is our youth lawless and undisciplined? Universal compul-
> sory service will end that once for all. Is our democracy halting? It is the tonic of
> democratic army that we need in which all men shall pay for the privileges of
> citizenship by a year of preparation for poison gas and of learning how to
> murder other human beings.[55]

Simeon Strunsky, an American essayist and the literary editor of the *New
York Evening Post,* spoke at the same convention as Villard. Stunsky
warned that preparedness was igniting a militarist spirit among America's
economically privileged class as it became entwined with growing nationalism and a sense of duty and *noblesse oblige* to help their country. Strunsky
described preparedness as motivated by a "caste movement" and warned
that "if the militarization of the United States should be brought about by
the economically and socially superior classes exercising an influence beyond
their numerical strength, militarism would come to us as a class policy."[56]
Eventually, according to the editor, the lower classes would interpret growing militarization as oppression by the upper class and resist.

Well-known Progressive reformer Amos Pinchot (brother of Gifford
Pinchot, the first chief of the U.S. Forest Service and later governor of Pennsylvania) argued along similar lines to Strunsky. Pinchot took up an unrelenting fight against UMT. He warned Americans that if they "cut through
the patriotic pretext and flag-waving propaganda," they would see clearly
that Preparedness supporters advocated mandatory military training to keep
control of the people and to promote their own imperialist commercial
interest abroad.[57]

The AUAM (American Union Against Militarism) was the strongest of the
anti-preparedness organizations. Created in 1915 and led by Progressive
social reformers, labor lawyers, feminists, clergymen, and liberal publishers,

the organization sought to counter the growing militarist spirit. Charter members read like a "virtual *Who's Who* of advanced progressive leadership, including Jane Addams, Edward T. Devine, John Haynes Holmes, Frederic C. Howe, Florence Kelley, Paul U. Kellogg, George Kirchwey, Owen Lovejoy, and Rabbi Stephen Wise."[58] The AUAM stood firmly against a large standing army and UMT and soon boasted some 6,000 members, "50,000 sympathizers" and branches in twenty-one cities. The director, Crystal Eastman, graduated from Vassar College and New York University law school. Eastman worked tirelessly for social reform and for the Women's Suffrage Movement. She was also a member of the WPP (Woman's Peace Party). Eastman worked closely with Charles T. Hallinan who used his former experience as a reporter to publicize and distribute AUAM material and lobby for anti-preparedness. This included George W. Nasmyth's *Universal Military Service and Democracy,* a widely distributed pamphlet that condemned UMT and argued that compulsory military training would not bring about increased democracy, national unity, or patriotism as preparedness advocates contended. Prior to the First World War, William I. Hull, AUAM member and Quaker professor of history from Swarthmore College, had accurately predicted that a global arms race and militarist thinking would result in a protracted and deadly war. In 1916, Hull wrote an anti-preparedness book entitled *Preparedness: The American Versus the Military Programme* in which he warned against an "armament ring" of international financiers who used propaganda to create public war hysteria in order to make large profits from military conflicts. He also criticized the organized Preparedness Movement and the summer military training camps and challenged the need for military reform for both the land and naval forces.[59]

The WPP and the American League to Limit Armament also worked diligently to counter preparedness propaganda and oppose any increase in defense spending and arms production. WPP began in January 1915 when Progressive Reformers Jane Addams and Carrie Chapman Catt called a meeting for all women's clubs interested in peace. In addition to the WPP, Catt played a key role in the fight for women's right to vote, and Addams began the Settlement House Movement in poor immigrant neighborhoods, which provided kindergarten classes, children's clubs, gymnasiums, libraries, adult night classes, and lectures on public health, along with various and educational cultural events. Some 3,000 women attended the first WPP meeting in Washington, DC, representing a multitude of organizations including national and international women's suffrage organizations along with representatives from the National Council of Jewish Women, National Conference of Catholic Charities, Women's Trade Union League, International Congress of Farm Women, National League of Teachers, National Federation of Settlements, Woman's Christian Temperance Union, National Association of Colored Women, and the Woman's Christian Temperance Union. Members of other peace organizations also attended. WPP believed women were unique in their shared values concerning safeguarding human life. Addams spoke passionately in her call for women to stand united in their "love of justice, civilization and beauty which are all destroyed by war" and noted women were united "by hatred for barbarity, cruelty and destruction, which accompany every war."[60] The WWP received widespread criticism when, in 1916, the group charted a ship (financed by automobile industrialist Henry Ford) and sailed to Europe for an international peace conference of neutral countries in Stockholm.[61]

Henry Ford also worked tirelessly to educate Americans about the dangers of militarists promoting preparedness. In a *New York Times* article, Ford reminded Americans that "the people are the government" and encouraged them to speak out to their congressmen, senators, and the president against the constant brainwashing by preparedness alarmists. The automobile industrialists warned Americans not to let power "slip into the hands of their greatest enemies, the money lenders, the imperialists and the men who make their fortunes from the blood of armies."[62] In April 1916, Grand Master George Freifield of the Mason Grand Lodge of New York State also spoke out against preparedness asserting that 150,000 Free Masons all over the United States would do likewise. He told listeners that despite the success of preparedness advocates, "men will tire of the stock phrases and the plans for the destruction of their species" and demand change.[63]

Religious leaders also stood up to militarism. Speaking at the American Academy of Political Science gathering, Reverend Charles E. Jefferson argued that military preparedness was a danger to democracy and the world and stressed the need to put more time into moral issues and more money into humanitarian efforts. Jefferson warned that militarism would become an American tragedy, a renewal of an "old stupid experiment which has again and again soaked our planet with blood."[64] William Lyon Phelps, an ordained minister and professor of English at Yale University, provided the *New York Times* with a copy of his preparedness speech in which he noted the hypocrisy of attending church and murdering others. He reminded listeners that "Christianity condemns war" and warned that war takes away personal liberties.[65] Rabbi Dr. Stephen S. Wise campaigned throughout the Midwest against preparedness and called for the creation of an "Anti-Militarists" political party. Frederick Lynch, editor of *The Christian Work*, responded with abhorrence to NSL letters sent to clergy suggesting topics for Sunday sermons such as "The Duty of Preparedness" and "Peace through Preparedness." Lynch told readers he hoped clergymen would focus their message on the Gospels and not on militarism. The editor countered the League's letters with his own correspondence to clergy and concluded the majority of America's religious leaders would not comply with the NSL.[66]

NATIONAL DEFENSE ACT OF 1916 AND THE NAVAL ACT OF 1916

In the midst of fierce public debate, as Congress continued its fight over military reform in Washington, DC, Secretary of War Garrison instructed the General Staff to determine needed military improvements. The General Staff report, entitled *Statement of a Proper Military Policy for the United States,* called for "a 281,000-man Regular Army and a 500,000-man federal reserve. An additional 500,000 reserve force was to buttress the reserves."[67] It also sought to reduce the National Guard in status, since the General Staff considered the state system inadequate and untrustworthy and Garrison "was convinced that the existing Organized Militia was a broken reed, which could never be made into a dependable federal reserve."[68] After reviewing the report, Garrison sent a revised plan to President Wilson. It proposed a modified version of the General Staff report. This included an increase in the Regular Army of 140,000 men and a federal volunteer reserve, or "Continental Army," of 400,000 volunteers who trained for three months in summer camps over a three-year period. On December 1915, Senator Chamberlain countered with his own bill that would require all able-bodied men to participate in military "Citizen Cadet Corps" training for ninety hours a year from the age of twelve and eighteen. The young men would continue their training in the "Citizen Army" for 120 hours (with ten days of continuous training) until age twenty four. Although the *New York Times* praised the Chamberlain Bill, it proved too much of a dramatic change to receive widespread support.[69]

During House Hearings, the "Continental Army Plan" received backing from key military leaders who then testified in January 1916. Congressional advocates included Representative Frank Lester Greene, a Republican from Vermont. Greene worked for the Central Vermont Railway Company, served in the Vermont National Guard, and organized and served in an infantry company during the Spanish-American War. He became a congressman in 1912. Greene was convinced that an increase in the size of the regular army was absolutely necessary. Although he acknowledged America's "inherited dread" of large standing armies, the Vermont representative argued the "days of strong centralized monarchies" that controlled powerful armies were long gone:

> Nothing like that exists to-day [sic] nor has it ever existed in the United States. Why should men continue to terrify the multitude with the idea that any attempt to raise the United States Army must mean a militaristic domination and tyranny such as old King George once undertook here rather unsuccessfully, if memory serves aright? No such thing is possible to-day [sic] because the soldiers not only come from the people themselves, but they are paid by the people and serve the people directly and nobody else.[70]

Not all congressmen agreed with the "Continental Army" proposal. Opponents included North Carolina representative Claude Kitchen, the House Majority Leader, who stood in fierce opposition to military reform. He concluded that preparedness hysteria was motivated by "jingoes, and manufacturers of war equipment and their subtle, ramified, organized, and powerful influence."[71] Kitchen led a unified group of about thirty anti-preparedness Democrats along with other members of the "rural-dominated" Congress. According to historian Paul Koistinen, "this group opposed enlarging the military, which they held in suspicion, favored government economy, and objected to the United States taking on a world role."[72] Many congressmen also expressed outrage at the War Department's open attack on the National Guard and supported the influential National Guard Association who fought against any semblance of a Continental Army that would demote the Guard to the third line of defense or, worse yet, terminate the centuries old organization. Among the opposition to preparedness legislature was New York representative Meyer London, a socialist. London was born in Kalvaria, Russia, and became a U.S. citizen in 1896. In addition to practicing law, London, worked as an activist in the labor movements before being elected to Congress in 1915. London accused preparedness advocates of being caught up in a national panic and reprimanded politicians who only worried about receiving bad press if they did not support the cause. He also warned against large standing armies:

> Some say that the lesson of the need for preparedness is being taught by the European war. I draw an entirely different lesson from this war. The war was prepared just as surely as an explosion is prepared when enormous quantities of dynamite are accumulated. It is the very maintenance of big armies that has made the war possible—nay, inevitable. Will anyone dare gainsay [contradict] that we would all have been better off to-day [sic] if there were no armies in Europe in August, 1914?[73]

By February 1916, the House Hearings on military reform began to deteriorate when representatives pointedly asked Garrison if the volunteer "Continental Army" would be "superior" to UMT. The secretary of war answered in the negative. Further questioning revealed another major flaw in the proposal. Although Garrison believed the nation's young men would "enthusiastically" volunteer, for the Continental Army, he conceded that if the military could not attract enough volunteers, "some system of compulsion should be undertaken.'"[74] Problems with the "Continental Army Plan" mounted, and President Wilson soon found himself backed into a corner. A defeat of the plan would result in an attack on the Democrats by the Republican Party in a crucial election year. Failure would also leave the nation with an outdated and inadequate military force.

Wilson's solution came from Chairman Hay of the House Committee on Military Affairs who submitted an option to Garrison's plan and developed a compromise that would be acceptable by the many factions—Democratic versus Republicans, and urban professional elite versus the more agrarian South and West communities. The Hay Bill retained Garrison's plan for a regular army of 140,000 men. However, it not only retained the National Guard, it drastically increased the organization from 125,000 to 450,000 men and added additional federal funding and more federal control. In addition, the Hay Bill required the Guardsmen to swear their loyalty to both their state and to the nation. The defeat of Garrison's "Continental Army Plan" served as the last straw for the secretary of war, who resigned his position in February 1916.[75]

However, intense debate over Hay's proposal followed in Congress. A military crisis served to increase the stress and elevated the voices that called for a new national defense act. In early March, Pancho Villa crossed the border into New Mexico and raided the town of Columbus. Seventeen Americans died in the attack. In response, Wilson ordered Brigadier General John J. Pershing to mobilize the Punitive Expedition on the border. In the end, Congress adjusted the Hay Bill and "patched together a set of proposals drawn from the General Staff, the National Guard lobby, citizen preparedness groups, and technical-corporate elite concerned about economic mobilizations."[76]

In June 1916, the National Defense Act of 1916 passed into law. The act increased the regular army to 175,000 men (increased in increments over a five-year period) and, in time of war, allowed for a much larger army of 298,000 men. It also set out to improve the country's second line of defense—the National Guard—by incrementally increasing their numbers from 110,000 to 400,000, intensifying their training, providing federal money as the main source of funding, and allowing the federal government to order the Guard into overseas service in national emergencies. It also required all guardsmen to take dual oaths upon enlistment to both the federal government and their home state. In order to maintain a reserve of trained officers, the act called for the establishment of the ROTC (Reserve Officers' Training Corp.) on college campuses. UMT advocates expressed disappointment at the defeat of the "Continental Army" plan since the National Defense Act did not allow for compulsory military training. However, the act did provide federal funding to train 16,000 men (between the ages of 25 and 43) in summer training camps run by the War Department and the MTCA. Understanding the need to mobilize the economy in times of military conflict, the Defense Act also provided the federal government with significant emergency powers over industry and transportation. In December 1916, the new secretary of war, Newton D. Baker, brought together industrial experts to provide advice on an economic mobilization plan in case of war.[77]

The Secretary of the Navy, Josephus Daniels, the Assistant Secretary, Franklin Roosevelt, and other military reformers also pushed for improvements in U.S. Navy over the previous years. In 1916, the General Board requested a five-year program to build up and modernize the navy and bring its size and strength to an impressive fleet by 1925—second only to Great Britain. In August, Congress and Wilson approved the Naval Act of 1916 shortening the time line for building new ships to three years to guarantee a "Navy second to none." Naval modernization also led to the establishment of new navy yards, and the building of "ten battleships, sixteen cruisers, fifty destroyers, seventy-two submarines and fourteen auxiliaries." Unfortunately, it did not prepare the navy for "antisubmarine warfare."[78] Other naval improvements made during 1916 included restructuring of the Naval Aeronautic Station, creating an aviation radio laboratory, establishing an Aeronautic School, funding a Naval Flying Corps and a Naval Reserve Corps, and approving of the construction of thirty N-9 planes. New innovative navy equipment included the magnetic compass, radio direction finder, high speed seaplane, aero camera, gyroscopic instrumentation, and improvements in the hydroaeroplane. Also new was a joint Army–Navy Board "for interservice cooperation in aeronautics, later called the Aeronautical Board."[79]

THE PLATTSBURG MOVEMENT—1916 AND 1917

In April 1916, General Wood met with the new secretary of war, Newton Baker, to discuss the future of the summer officer military training camps. Earlier, Baker had denounced preparedness as artificially created war hysteria; however, General Scott was able to convince Baker of the importance of military reform. Baker approved of the continuation of the summer training program and told the *New York Times,* "I was deeply impressed with the work accomplished in the camps at Plattsburg and elsewhere last summer."[80] To enhance the national reputation of the school, Wood reprinted a November 1915 report from the Advisory Committee of University Presidents on the Summer Military Instruction Camps for Students. The report provided a "hearty endorsement" of the camps calling them "admirable" and noting the experience of students as "pleasurable and beneficial." A large contingency of university presidents and administrators signed the report representing Cornell, Harvard, Lehigh, Princeton, Vanderbilt, and Yale Universities, the Universities of Alabama, California, Illinois, New York, and Michigan along with Williams College and Stevens Institute of Technology. The superintendent of Virginia Military Institute also added his name to the document. The group agreed the camp training resulted in "a great benefit, mental and physical, to the students attending."[81]

Learning from past mistakes, Wood set out to prevent a repeat of criticism from National Guardsmen who resented the attention paid to the "millionaires" attending Plattsburg, since it overshadowed the extensive history of the Organized Militia System. In his April 1916 War Department Report,

Wood reprinted a letter from Major General John F. O'Ryan of the New York National Guard in which the high-ranking officer answered "the question...sometimes asked whether there is a conflict of interest" between the training camp men and the National Guardsmen by pointing out that a "very considerable number" of Plattsburg graduates joined the New York National Guard. Therefore, O'Ryan had "no hesitation" to urge his fellow National Guard officers to cooperate in support of future military training camps.[82]

To draw more citizens into the camps, the MTCA raised some $100,000 to cover camp expenses and provided scholarship to needy students. The organization also arranged speaking tours for General Wood to promote the camps and took out full-page advertisements in the national media. Businesses jumped on board by paying for advertisements in Plattsburg' publicity booklets. In one ad, Gimbel Brothers announced readymade or made-to-measure uniforms for the men of Plattsburg because Gimbals believed "the American gentleman likes smart clothes when he goes to war, just as much as when he strolls along the avenue." Another ad featured Fatima cigarettes with the claim that their brand was the smoke of choice in the training camps, "Ask any Plattsburg Man."[83]

The national publicity campaign was a success. Some 137 leading financial institutes in New York and Philadelphia, including banks, trust companies, insurance companies, and other corporations, announced they would permit all interested men in their employment to receive training. In addition, owners of businesses that produced glass, rubber, lumber, iron, petroleum, and chemicals located in New York, New England, Maryland, California, and Washington, DC granted permission for their male employees to attend military training camps. The *New York Times* printed the names of each company and financial institution and praised them for agreeing to send the men "with full pay and without loss of vacation."[84]

The 1916 summer Plattsburg Movement successfully recruited 16,000 participants from professionals, college students, and the first group of ROTC trainees. The War Department placed camps in various locations including Fort Oglethorpe, Tennessee; Fort Sam Houston, Texas; Fort Sheridan, Illinois; Fort Benjamin Harrison, Indiana; and of course, Plattsburg, New York. Western camp locations included California, Washington, and Utah. Despite various problems and concerns that sometimes overwhelmed camp leaders, the War Department considered the summer training a success. Other 1916 civilian training camps included a navy version of Plattsburg and a woman's training camp in Chevey Chase, Maryland (that offered classes in first aid and sanitation). Greenville Clark hoped to create a military training camp for African Americans in the summer of 1917, but this never came to fruition.[85]

The War Department also prepared extensive plans for the 1917 training camps. Section 54 of the National Defense Act authorized the secretary of war to establish fourteen Citizen Training Camps to open in May of 1917 and provided the War Department with money for expenses incurred in the camps. Colonel Chase W. Kennedy, the acting chief of the War College Division, noted, in addition to the "primary purpose of the camps as a source of reserve officers," they have another advantage in fostering amongst our best citizenship a patriotic spirit without which a nation soon loses its virility and falls into decay."[86] Plattsburg Movement planners estimated that camps could be filled with some 50,000 trainees, although the War Department limited enrollment to 35,000 due to a shortage of army officers to train the students. Trainees had to be at least twenty years and nine months (so they would be at least twenty-one after training) but no older than forty-four years of age. A report from H.P. McCain, the adjutant general, announced that the best 10,000 men would be promoted into leadership roles in case of war. The 1917 summer camps never opened since the United States entered the World War in April of that year.[87]

CONCLUSION

Prior to America's entrance into World War I, new civil-military relationships formed as groups joined together either for or against UMT and other preparedness reforms. Only after long debates and much consideration did Congress pass the National Defense Act of 1916. Since the act did not mandate compulsory military serve, Leonard Wood and other UMT advocates continued to push for legislature making it mandatory for all able-bodied men to receive military training. A congressional hearing on the subject ran from December 16, 1916 to February 1, 1917, as Senate Chamberlain's subcommittee listened to over 100 testimonies of military experts, Plattsburg graduates, National Guard officers, businessmen, medical professionals, professors, and pacifists. General Wood gave a forceful address to Congress and lined up powerful allies to give witness to the urgent need for UMT. By early 1917, President Wilson was tired of Wood's aggressiveness. No doubt this is why he weakened the general's power by dividing up the Eastern Department into three sections. Wood had three choices of command, all of which were intended to isolate him from his power base.[88]

The UMT for all able-bodied men never received the needed congressional support to become law. Ironically, Wilson's subjection of Wood came at the very time when the president could have used his support to promote a different form of compulsory military service—the national draft. "Selective service was not universal service, but it did operate on the assumption that every male citizen of military age, even if he was not selected, had a military obligation. Plattburgers regretted only that the principle was not made permanent policy."[89] The demanding work of preparedness advocates led to some success in U.S. Army and Navy improvements. Still, America generally entered the Great War unprepared.

Drafting and Training Citizen-Soldiers: New Civil-Military Relations

Although legislation approving compulsory UMT (Universal Military Training) never made it through Congress, the prolonged and intense discussions on the topic by high-ranking military officers, politicians, civic leaders, and members of the academic community made the idea of a large-scale army of citizen-soldiers familiar to the public. This no doubt helped to establish the groundwork for a national draft when the United States entered the Great War in April 1917. However, the reality of a mass conscripted citizen-soldier army significantly challenged the country, and the drafting of some four million men came with many complications. As millions of young men arrived at military training camps throughout the United States, the War Department began the overwhelming task of turning civilians into productive soldiers in a rapid and efficient manner. Ethnicity, race, religion, literacy, intelligence levels, and lack of English language skills made the training of America's diverse citizen-soldiers problematical. In addition, it did not take long for military leaders to recognize that the same social problems that plagued civilian society—alcohol, prostitution, gambling, and poor health—challenged training efforts. As such, a new civil-military relationship grew as military leaders worked closely with civilian experts—psychologists, Progressive reformers, and ethnic and racial group leaders. Civil-military cooperation not only led to the establishment of new military training policies in World War I, but it also resulted in a ground-breaking collaboration between the military and civilian society.

TOWARD CONSCRIPTION

Although officially taking a neutral stand when the Great War began in 1914, the United States clearly favored the Allied Powers in trade and war loans, and many Americans considered their nation's culture and history to be connected with Great Britain. Over the next three years, President Woodrow Wilson's foreign policy moved away from isolationism and toward international diplomacy and an "open door" policy that he hoped would prevent future conflicts, but would also protect and expand America's global economic interests. Despite this shift, Wilson continued to insist America should serve as a mediator not an ally in the European war. After the passing of the National Defense Act in 1916, preparedness advocates continued to push the president for the expansion and modernization of the armed forces and for mandatory UMT. They claimed it would "Americanize the immigrant, nurture the values of efficiency and 'service,' and overcome class antagonisms."[1]

As tension between Germany and the United States escalated, the General Staff recommended to the president that—in the event the situation worsens—the country should adopt a national draft. Wilson and his secretary of war, Newton Baker, steadfastly disagreed. Forceful opposition to a draft also came from the Democratic congressmen from the South and West—the stronghold of the party. At the same time, UMT opponents continued their battle claiming, among other things, that it "taught lessons of subordination, and slavish deference to authority."[2]

In early 1917, America's neutrality rapidly eroded when Germany resumed submarine warfare and renewed their attacks on American merchant ships trading with the Allied nations. This, combined with tension over Germany's ploy to draw Mexico into a conflict against the United States (as indicated by the Zimmermann telegram), further pushed America into the Allied camp. Wilson now reluctantly reversed his original opposition to a wartime draft, and the president privately ordered Baker, to confidentially prepare a conscription bill. Both men now accepted that, as America drew closer and closer to war, the nation would need a massive army to fight in Europe. In April, Wilson presented his war address to Congress, and, on April 6, 1917, the Senate declared that a State of War existed between the United States and Germany. Talks in Congress quickly shifted from improving America's peacetime military to implementing a national draft. Most importantly, Wilson and Baker wanted to find a way to conscript men without disrupting an industrial war economy. The answer came with the Selective Service System, a discerning system designed to bring millions of men into the military, and at the same time, retain needed workers in crucial war-related production.[3]

The day after the Senate's declaration of war, Baker presented Congress with an army bill requesting authorization to increase the regular army to 298,000 and the National Guard to 440,000. The "federalized" Guard would be put into national service. Baker's bill included plans for an immediate conscription of 500,000 men with a possible increase of 500,000 additional draftees. The plan also called for Plattsburg graduates to serve as junior officers. Concern over Baker's army bill began immediately, especially from the South and Mid-West where critics called conscription undemocratic and anti-individualistic. They noted the long history of American volunteers answering the call in a national crisis and equated a national draft with European autocracy. Others expressed apprehension over conscripting nineteen- and twenty-year olds, considered too young and unsophisticated to experience the brutality of war. Congressmen from many agrarian states protested the possibility of drafting American farmers since Wilson's plan called only for the exemption of vital industrial workers needed for production. Rural congressmen argued that farmers also played an essential role in producing food for Allied troops and soon the American soldiers. Congress approved the Selective Service Act on May 18, 1917 with some minor modifications from the original bill. It authorized the president to draft all able-bodied men between the ages of twenty-one and thirty-one into the U.S. Army. Furthermore, along with the exemption from the draft of crucial industrial workers, the president agreed to exempt selective farmers if they were deemed essential to war production.[4]

ATTEMPTS AT AVOIDING CONSCRIPTION PROBLEMS

In designing the Selective Service System, the Wilson administration carefully studied the Union draft crisis of the Civil War in order to prevent a similar plight. During that war, leadership from the North and South resorted to conscription due to a serious manpower shortage. The Northern draft was ultimately mismanaged, class-based, and ineffective. Serious draft problems stemmed from the government's decision to allow draft exemptions. This substantially weakened the original intent of the Enrollment Act of March 1863 and permitted drafted men to hire substitutes or make commutation payment of $300 (purchased exemptions). Although the Union called 206,678 for service, the draft directly affected only 46,347, since 86,724 men paid their way out of service, 44,403 men (expecting to be drafted in the future) hired substitutes, and another 73,607 drafted men found replacements.[5]

During registration process, tension quickly spiraled out of control as provost marshals searched homes seeking men eligible for the draft and arresting deserters. Draft resisters changed their identities, used names of the deceased, left town, or resorted to violence to avoid conscription. Tension over the draft often became intermixed with anger over the expansion of federal government power and with local political and labor conflicts. Draft resistance and mob violence occurred in Illinois, Indiana, Iowa, Massachusetts, Michigan, Minnesota, Ohio, New Hampshire, Vermont, and Wisconsin. But one of the most violent resistances occurred in New York City when conscription further fueled burning economic and political issues and resulted in a violent five-day draft riot.[6]

The Wilson Administration clearly wanted to avoid such problems in America's World War I draft. To help defuse the past association with the

Civil War draft, the name "selective service" was substituted for "conscription," and the government prohibited the use of substitutions and commutations. Provost Marshal General, Enoch H. Crowder, headed up the Selective Service System. To avoid the past hostility toward the national government caused by federal provost marshals going directly to homes to register men for the draft, Crowder put the responsibility for the registration of men in the hands of some 4,600 local draft boards. The boards were "comprised of local volunteers so that a man's neighbors rather than the federal government sent him into the army or deferred him."[7] Most members of the local board came from prominent native-born white families, and Crowder supplied each board with Selective Service guidelines to follow.

But the violent reaction of many to the Civil War draft still haunted Wilson and Baker, and both men worried about the prediction from a member of Congress that the streets would "run red with blood" during the first draft registration in 1917. Therefore, Baker insisted on using propaganda to "sell the draft" and connect conscription with a strong sense of patriotism.[8] To aid in this process, Baker elicited the help of state and local leaders and various patriotic organizations to create a "festive" atmosphere in the draft registration process. This well-crafted civilian-government propaganda program promoted nationalism and pushed Americans to rethink their local and state identity. Crowder agreed with the propaganda concept and argued that it was imperative to turn Americans away from traditional individualistic ideology toward a new collective nationalism and inspire "the spirit of serve" with the "spirit of America."[9]

The June 5, 1917 registration day occurred with some resistance, but without any significant confrontation. No doubt years of public discourse on UMT and the successful patriotic draft campaigns made conscription more palatable. During the "lottery" process, men received a green card with their name and a number. Blindfolded, Secretary of War Baker pulled registration numbers of men ordered to report to military training camps. By the end of the war, some twenty-four million men registered as required, and drafted men constituted 72 percent of the 3.9 million men who served in the U.S. Army during the war. Still, the American World War I draft included its own set of problems, confusion, and challenges. Although some 24,000,000 men registered with their local draft boards, the government estimated that between 2,500,000 and 3,500,000 men did not register, and some 338,000 drafted men did not report for service. Some fled the country, while others hid in isolated areas. Almost 65,000 men declared themselves conscientious objectors. Critical questions over industrial and agricultural exemptions caused much concern, as did the drafting of foreign-born and African-American men.[10]

The American Socialists Party organized against the draft. Leaders, such as Eugene Debs, argued that the war in Europe developed from decades of worldwide economic exploitation and political domination of other countries by capitalist nations. Socialists directed much of their antidraft literature toward the American working class—those who, they contended, would suffer most from the war. Socialists' posters and handouts also claimed that conscription was unconstitutional:

> In this battle the people of the United States established the principle that freedom of the individual and personal liberty are the most sacred things in life. Without them we become slaves.... The Thirteenth Amendment to the Constitution of the United States...embodies this sacred idea. The Socialist Party says that this idea is violated by the Conscription Act. When you conscript a man and compel him to go abroad to fight against his will, you violate the most sacred right of personal liberty, and substitute for it what Daniel Webster called "despotism in its worst form."[11]

DRAFTING FOREIGN-BORN SOLDIERS

Immigrants served in the U.S. military in every conflict since the War of Independence. However, political leaders did not always agree on whether foreign-born soldiers should be allowed in the ranks. After the Revolutionary War, a number of government restrictions forbade immigrants from enlisting. However, the nation repeatedly suspended these restrictions in times of military crisis due to shortages of soldiers and allowed immigrants to fight for their adopted country. But by the late nineteenth century, with the rapidly rising anti-immigrant sentiment, a number of active and retired military officers joined civilian nativists in expressing concern about the growing immigrant population. Many supported the 1894 legislation that prohibited non-English speaking immigrants from enlisting in the U.S. military. With the arrival of some twenty-three million immigrants, primarily from Southern and Eastern Europe between 1880 and 1917, the debate continued in armed force journals. Most officers continued to support an exclusively native-born military. However, once America joined the Great War, the crucial manpower needs forced seasoned military leaders to reexamine their position and convinced many new officers to support a multiethnic military.[12]

In 1917, after a series of congressional debates concerning the drafting of immigrants into the American army, the Selective Service established four classifications for foreign-born registries—Diplomatic, Declarant, Non-declarant, and Enemy Alien. "Diplomatic Aliens" received exemption from the draft. The Selective Service used the label "Declarant Aliens" to describe all immigrants from friendly nations who had filed their "first papers" (intention to become citizens) and were waiting to fulfill their five-year residence before completing the naturalization process. Congress concluded that Declarant immigrants were eligible for the draft since they received the benefits of America and, consequently, should share in the nation's burdens. "Nondeclarant Aliens" included immigrants who did not file their papers of intentions for citizenship and were, therefore, considered transitory. Nondeclarants were technically not eligible for the draft. Congress assumed that other nations would reciprocate by ensuring that America's businessmen and travelers would not be drafted into foreign armies. The Selective Service Act did not call for the drafting of "Enemy Aliens" (both declarant and nondeclarant immigrants from enemy nations) since they would be put in a position of fighting against their own countrymen.[13]

Although the Selective Service classifications appeared reasonable, disputes arose immediately over a quota system that required local boards to draft a percentage of the total population in each district. Northeast and Midwest districts with high numbers of exempted Nondeclarant and Enemy Aliens protested against the overdrafting of native-born Americans. National newspapers and journals carried stories of resentment over the "alien slacker," which helped fuel an already growing anti-immigrant sentiment. The *Chicago Daily Tribune, St. Louis Globe Democrat, Macon Telegraph, Literary Digest,* and *New York's Tribune, Sun and Globe* called for all draft-age immigrants (regardless of exception status) to serve in the U.S. military. According to the *New York Sun,* "The apparent injustices of stripping the land of [native-born] American youths to furnish a fighting force in Europe while leaving millions of aliens at home to enjoy the rewards of peaceful industry has undoubtedly got on the people's nerves." The *Chicago Tribune* concluded, "America has welcomed these strangers and given most of them a measure of prosperity they did not possess and could not hope for in their native lands.... If they are to enjoy the advantages of life in America they should be compelled to meet its responsibilities."[14]

Provost Marshal Crowder and members of Congress, led by Oregon Democrat senator George E. Chamberlain, also spoke out against overdrafting of native-born men. According to the provost marshal, "it is not too much to say that the spectacle of American boys, the finest in the community, going forth to fight for the liberty of the world while sturdy aliens— many of them born in the very countries which have been invaded by the enemy—stay at home and make money."[15] Earlier, Senator Chamberlain had called for a bill that would put dissenters on trial before a military tribunal and have them executed by a firing squad if found guilty. The bill did not pass. In August 1917, Chamberlain introduced legislation to require all foreign-born of draft age, except Enemy Aliens, eligible for conscription. If any eligible immigrant refused to serve, the bill called for immediate deportation. After some debate, the bill passed the House. However, the Senate blocked the bill after hearing the testimony of Robert E. Lansing, the secretary of state. Lansing argued that drafting Nondeclarant Aliens would not only cause diplomatic problems, it would also put Americans abroad at risk of being drafted into foreign armies. Furthermore, the secretary of state reminded Congress that deportations of European immigrant labor would cause a crisis in war production, and the exile of Mexican laborers would have a disastrous effect on the agricultural economy. Other diplomatic problems included protests from neutral nations that objected to the drafting of their citizens (Declarant and Nondeclarant) into a foreign army and Allied nations that required immigrants to serve in homeland militaries.[16]

Lansing insisted that problems related to the drafting of the foreign-born be handled through diplomatic channels, not through Congress, especially considering the 5,852 diplomatic protests received from foreign countries concerning the U.S. draft. Congress agreed to delay the discussion of the bill to allow time for the State Department to negotiate treaties. After much discussion with foreign nations, the American State Department rectified problems with reciprocal treaties of conscription and exemptions that also satisfied Congress. Any declarant from a neutral nation who accepted a military exemption status would have to give up his right to become a U.S. citizen in the future. Agreements with Allied nations allowed drafted Declarant and Nondeclarant Aliens the choice of serving in the U.S. Army or the army of their native country. The U.S. government also accelerated the naturalization process for immigrant soldiers to avoid further diplomatic problems by waiving the five-year residency requirement. Congress eventually resolved the unfair Selective Service quota in May 1918 by putting all native- and foreign-born declarant who were physically and mentally fit into Class I. The Selective Service computed the quota system based only on Class I (instead of the total population of the area), ending the dilemma of disproportionate drafting.[17]

To avoid drafting mistakes, the Selective Service required local draft boards to give immigrants a "full and fair hearing" assisted by "men of foreign race stock" who would translate. However, confusion and errors frequently occurred. Enemy aliens along with nondeclarant immigrants found themselves in uniform due to numerous mix-ups in local draft boards, especially since the burden of proving heir status lay with the immigrants. For instance, 76,545 of the 123,277 immigrants drafted in the first conscription round of June 1917, had not declared their intention of becoming U.S. citizens. Inaccuracies continued to occur in subsequent draft rounds. Yet, tens of thousands of aliens from allied, neutral, and enemy territory— drafted in oversight—expressed their desire to fight with the American army. By September 1918, 191,419 nondeclarant draftees asked to waive their right of exemption. Some 9,000 enemy aliens from the Austro-Hungarian Empire also wanted to waive their exemption status. Although "technically" the enemy, this latter group considered themselves from the "oppressed races" of the Austro-Hungarian Empire and expressed their desire to fight with the U.S. military in order to free their homeland from the Central Powers.[18]

The War Department allowed Nondeclarants who waived their exemption right to stay in the army. It gave the responsibility of retaining or discharging enemy aliens to the commanding officers who determined if soldiers from Germany or the Austrian-Hungarian Empire would be permitted to stay based on their "loyalty." A War Department "Ethnic Bulletin" concluded that the remaining "technical" enemy alien soldiers were "thoroughly loyal and enthusiastic."[19]

DRAFTING AFRICAN-AMERICAN SOLDIERS

The drafting of African-American men into the U.S. Army quickly became entwined with deep-seated racial issues, when southern leaders battled against conscription fearing retribution from militarily trained black soldiers. Despite some short-term gains toward full citizenship after the Civil War, political and economic advancement for African Americans had deteriorated rapidly by 1917. Segregation, discrimination, and violence continued to spread in the South, and the prewar Great Migration of blacks to the north seeking new industrial opportunities, increased conflict in urban areas due to labor competition and racist attitudes.

During the congressional debate over the Selective Service Act of 1917, Mississippi Democratic senator, James Vardaman, spoke out against the drafting of African Americans, claiming it would be unsafe for the white community to arm black men. Vardaman, well known for his blatant bigoted statements against Africans American, had capitalized on Southern white racist politics when elected governor of Mississippi in 1903, and senator in 1910. Speaking to a group of Mississippians in 1917, he warned that drafting black soldiers would lead to "arrogant strutting representatives of the black soldiery in every community."[20] Many other Southern politicians joined Vardaman in opposition to African-American conscription including one South Carolina representative who warned that America would not have to go to Germany to fight a war, if the military put white and black soldiers in racially integrated units.

Black leaders fought back. Most saw military conscription as a way to prove their value to the nation, promote respect from the white community, gain political and economic advancements, and acquire true freedom. Many influential African-American leaders and members of key black organizations, such as the NAACP (National Association for the Advancement of Color People), spoke out for inclusion in the Selective Service process. Caught in the middle, President Wilson and Secretary of War Baker sought to create an effective fighting force without exasperating an already difficult racial situation. Although understanding the frustration of African Americans, Wilson and Baker took a cautious approach. Subsequently, draft registration forms required all eligible men to indicate their race. This allowed the military to easily segregate African Americans from whites when called to service.[21] The situation was further exacerbated because, with the exception of "five or six" African Americans, only white men served on the local draft Selective Service boards. Baker did take some action when he replaced members of local draft boards who blatantly discriminated; but most local discrepancies went unchallenged.[22]

Despite the effort by many Southern leaders to keep blacks out of the U.S. Army, in the end, blacks were disproportionately drafted. However, they were overwhelmingly placed in labor battalions. Selective Service statistics revealed that "although blacks constituted only 9.63% of the total registration, they were 13.08% of those drafted. While 34.10% of all black registrants were ultimately induced, only 24.04% of the whites were drafted."[23] After being questioned by African-American leaders, the provost marshal Crowder tried to explain the inequality noting that it resulted from the lack of opportunity for African Americans to enlist. White volunteers far out number black since the military only permitted some 4,000 blacks to volunteer compared to 650,000 whites. Crowder also noted that black registrants received significantly fewer hardship deferments because soldiers' pay was much higher than wages received by African-American workers. The provost did not mention the critical role that racism played in the unequal draft statistics, since prominent white men who ran the local draft boards made the final decision as to who stayed home and who went to war. A. Philip Randolph, the well-known African-American labor leader, noted the irony of drafting blacks into the service: "The Negro is tubercular, syphilitic, physically inferior for purposes of degrading him; but physically fit and physically superior when it comes to sending him to the front to save the white men's hides."[24]

NEW CIVIL-MILITARY RELATIONS

New civil-military relations developed as the War Department set out to build young American men into capable soldiers. American psychologists, Progressive reformers, and ethnic group leaders worked closely with military officers, and thus helped to reshape War Department policy. In some cases, African-American leaders, saddled by prevailing racist social attitudes, were also able to effect policy.

Many civilian leaders and organizations that assisted the military with training soldiers during the Great War grew out of the Progressive Era. This era began in the late nineteenth century and brought together a variety of crusaders to do battle with the enormous problems created by the nation's rapid industrialization and modernization. The Progressive Era ushered in new academic disciplines, innovative efficiency theories, and a remarkable team of social justice reformers. Although many Progressives pushed for continued neutrality at the start of the European conflict in 1914, once America entered the war, a large number of civilians from the Progressive communities assisted the military in meeting the needs of the nation's soldiers. The military also adopted ideas from civilian scientific management experts to apply efficiency and standardization methods, and psychologists worked with the military to administer army intelligence tests. Social justice reformers worked tirelessly in army training camps throughout the United States to assist with the training of soldiers, and ethnic group leaders played a critical role in the training of foreign-born troops.

SCIENTIFIC MANAGEMENT

During the Progressive Era in the late nineteenth and early twentieth centuries, business leaders promoted the Scientific Management Movement. As with other Progressive reformers, scientific managers sought to restructure the rapidly changing urban-industrial environment. In an era when "boss politics" and political machines controlled the employment in American cities, scientific manager argued that the nation needed to turn to trained professionals. Engineers and architects could solve municipal problems in the crowded, unsanitary urban area, and standardization experts could end industrial confusion associated with a technological revolution. Scientific managers also developed regulations, streamlined systems, conducted endless timesaving studies, and developed new theories in management. But the Scientific Management Movement went well beyond cleaning up cities and reorganizing factories. As it expanded into homes, churches, schools, the government, and the military, it took on a moralistic tone, and personal efficiency became equivalent to discipline, hard work, and thrift.[25]

At the turn of the century, the U.S. Armed Forces (in the words of Peter Karsten), "underwent a virtual revolution...a revolution involving new missions, managerial and technological streamlining, professionalization and sheer growth."[26] In their efforts to reform the military, leaders studied European military models along with American scientific management theories. Articles in military journals promoted new efficiency ideas in administration and in the management of men. Elihu Root, secretary of war from 1899 to 1904, helped to transform the military from "heroic leadership" to a "managerial leadership" style. General Leonard Wood, in his role as army chief of staff from 1910 to 1914, also moved the military toward American corporate models in organization and leadership. Wood viewed scientific management principles as an "effective instrument of national policy," and encouraged many "progressive efficiency reforms" designed to professionalize and modernize the armed forces.[27] The military applied motion, time-saving, and fatigue studies to the training of soldiers, and utilized new ideas that connected psychology to efficiency and morale. Maintaining a high level of troop morale was vital, since "morale [was] as important as ammunition" in winning a conflict.[28] In 1917, the War Department assigned Morale Officers to each training camp, and the War Plans Division of the General Staff distributed a copy of Major General David C. Shank's *The Management of the American Soldiers* to each officer. The book emphasized that officers should treat their men with respect, help build character, and instill pride in a positive manner.[29]

By 1917, the War Department clearly connected troop performance with efficiency, morale, and the proper management of men. As such, they worked closely with civilian leaders to organize the soldiers, create a positive training environment, inspire a fighting spirit in young recruits, and educate soldiers toward healthy and moral behavior.

PSYCHOLOGISTS AND INTELLIGENCE TESTS

One way to efficiently organize the troops was to connect an individual soldier's intelligence level with a specific military skill. Immediately after the United States declared war, a group of forty psychologists known as the Society of Experimentalists, gathered at Harvard University to discuss how they could assist the American military. Their interest in the war effort stemmed from an unprecedented academic opportunity and from patriotism. A drafting of a massive army of young men provided the psychologists a distinct testing prospect and an unusual chance to adopt the newly developed Stanford-Binet intelligence scale. Since psychology was a relatively new discipline, statistics from the intelligence test results would provide an astonishing amount of data for future studies.[30]

Psychologists from the Society of Experimentalists met with the War Department to convince military leaders of the importance of the intelligence testing which—the scientists claimed—would match young recruits to the right military job. Secretary of War Baker understood the crucial need to rapidly train young men and assign them to jobs that best suited their particular skills. He noted,

> We have to have a selective process by which we will get the round men for the round places, the strong men for the strong tasks, and the delicate men for the delicate tasks.... Some system of selection of talents which is not affected by immaterial principles or virtues...something more scientific than the haphazard choice of men, something more systematic than preference or first impression, is necessary to be devised.[31]

Once the War Department gave its permission, Baker assigned Robert M. Yerkes and his team of psychologists to the military's Committee on the Psychological Examination of Recruits. Yerkes, a Harvard University trained psychologist, taught Comparative Psychology at Harvard, directed the Psychological Services and Research in Boston's Psychopathic Hospital, and served as the president of the American Psychological Association. During World War I, Yerkes and his assistants developed two intelligence tests using test scores from various military officers as a measurement tool. The military needed both the Army "Alpha" test for literate soldiers and the "Beta" test of illiterates after making the startling discovery that an estimated 25 percent of soldiers could not read or write. Civilian personnel managers interviewed soldiers to determine their experiences, and psychologists administered the intelligent tests. Eventually, the Psychological Examination Committee administered tests to some 1.7 million soldiers. In reality, the army intelligence test had numerous problems. It tested to a soldier's education level and economic background and included culturally biased questions. Analyzing test results took time, and results often came long after soldiers received their assignments. In addition, many military leaders harshly criticized the tests, claiming that intelligence was not the only measurement of talents. However, adopting the tests eventually helped the military move away from "Victorian emphases on character and moral virtue" and toward the more scientific approach taken by civilian scientific managers and the psychology community.[32] The civil-military relationship that developed between American psychologists and the U.S. military continued in wars to come. But America's emphasis on building character and instilling moral virtue did not end. During the war, Progressive social justice leaders took their place in army military camps to help the military socialize and morally uplift the troops.

SOCIAL JUSTICE REFORMERS

With only a short time to turn civilians into soldiers, military officers put recruits through an intense sixteen-week training program. Lessons for white native-born and foreign-born recruits included military combat, discipline, packing and tent pitching, close order drill, trench and open warfare, fire control, signaling, antigas protection, "bombing" (hand-grenade throwing), target shooting, and other key skills needed to be efficient soldiers. Wednesday and Saturday afternoons, and most evenings, were kept free for recreation or for additional drill for "backwards men." Other evenings found soldiers learning trench construction, scouting, patrolling, and night relief for troops in the trenches. Military leaders quickly discovered the same social problems that plagued civilian society—alcohol, prostitution, venereal disease, gambling, and poor health—affected American troops. Men who succumbed to these social evils would make unproductive soldiers. In order to build character and instill moral behavior in the new recruits, the War Department asked Progressive social justice reformers— well acquainted with combating vice—to assist with the training and education of American servicemen. In addition, the military educated soldiers about the "great causes" of the war, so the young men knew why they were fighting and provided patriotic lectures to keep up their esprit de corps.[33]

Beginning in the late nineteenth century, Progressive social welfare leaders saw themselves as guardians of morality and attempted to reorder society in their own middle-class image by uplifting the lower classes. Reformers engaged in campaigns against prostitution, alcohol, gambling, and social disease and struggled to educate the working class in what they deemed was "proper" moral behavior. Social welfare reformers sought to reshape the dirty, unsanitary, and crowded cities and strove to recreate the urban environment. Their twofold plan included teaching the public about the ramifications of indulging in social evils and providing positive alternatives to negative urban influences—playgrounds, sports fields, gymnasium, and public libraries.[34]

Secretary of War Baker had previously been a municipal Progressive reformer during his days as mayor of Cleveland. The War Department worked with a number of well-known Progressive reformers including Raymond Fosdick (former settlement worker and New York's commissioner of Accounts), Joseph Lee (president of the Playground and Recreational Association of America), John Mott (secretary of the Young Men's Christian Association), and others. Baker selected Fosdick to head the newly created CTCA (Commission on Training Camp Activities) and charged him with "the responsibility of cultivating and conserving the manhood and manpower of America's fighting forces" by providing a "clean and wholesome" environment.[35] Like other Progressives, Baker and Fosdick came from a new generation of reformers who sought to end the nation's problems with social engineering and attempted to reorder society in the "virtuous" image of the middle-class value system. Baker's mayoral experience in Cleveland had taught him a great lesson. After constant frustration in endeavoring to stop crime and vice through police action and jail time, he eventually reexamined the futile effort. Instead, Mayor Baker adopted a Progressive social welfare philosophy and set out to educate the public to the dangers of engaging in popular depravity. In addition, Baker worked with Cleveland social welfare organizations to offer alternative recreational activities to counter "immoral" behavior. Baker discovered "the most promising long-range strategy of urban moral control was not repression, but a more subtle and complex process of influencing behavior and molding character through a transformed, consciously planned urban environment."[36] Baker brought these lessons to his position as secretary of war.

Raymond Fosdick's outstanding reputation as a Progressive municipal reformer attracted the attention of the secretary of war. Fosdick's past experience included his position as the New York's commissioner of Accounts. Commissioner Fosdick worked assiduously to destroy the corrupt Tammany Hall political machine, stop fraudulent actions of city employees, and implement safety and sanitary regulations for New York's businesses. During World War I, Fosdick and his CTCA team made every effort to keep temptation out of the way of the young recruits and return men better than when they left home. Baker and Fosdick also invited Progressive social welfare agencies into the military camps to help with the training and socialization of soldiers. Soon, the camps included the clear presence of the Young Men's and Young Women's Christian Associations, the Salvation Army, the Playground

Association of America, the American Social Hygiene Association, American Library Association, the Knights of Columbus, and the JWB (Jewish Welfare Board). Most of these organizations traced their roots, leadership, and philosophy to the ideology of social reform and together with military officers they attempted to "morally-uplift" the soldier—"a task never before faced and deliberately undertaken by any nation."[37] In the army training camps, the Progressive social welfare reformers attempted to replace "negative" social activities with "positive" opportunities. They worked with military officers to educate troops on the immortality and dangers of prostitution, alcohol, and gambling, while providing "wholesome" alternatives to social immorality— recreation centers, sports fields, and various cultural and social facilities.

Venereal disease (VD) represented a critical problem since it left soldiers unfit for duty and threatened to cripple the efficiency of troop performance. The civil-military leadership understood the critical importance of sex education, especially considering the disturbing rate of VD cases. For instance, in October 1917, VD incidences in the American Expeditionary Forces located in St. Nazaiare, France increased dramatically from the usual rate of "forty per thousand" to "two hundred per thousand" after soldiers spent their excess free time waiting for transportation in the arms of prostitutes. American troops were not the only ones plagued with these problems. Officials noted that the Central Powers lost a significant number of men who became "incapacitated" by VD, and the British reported losing some 70,495,000 "soldier-days" per year.[38] Soldiers with VD required evacuation to a rear hospital where they remained for almost two months. This resulted in a rapid decline in military efficiency. However, controlling sexual activities was not easy since it went against the common thinking of many seasoned officers who considered sex necessary to keep up the morale of soldiers. Frederick Palmer (Baker's biographer) described this prevailing attitude held by older officers: "Men would be men. 'Sissies' were no use on the firing line. Soldiers must have women. They made poor soldiers if they did not have women."[39]

To combat VD and change the established mind-set, the military turned to the ASHA (American Social Hygiene Association). Progressive reformers established ASHA in 1913 which incorporated the Anti-Saloon League and the American Society of Sanitary and Moral Prophylaxis. In America's cities, the organization aspired to put "brothels out of business" by taking away the clientele, distributing sex education material, and promoting sports and other recreational programs. The group also pushed for legislation that would outlaw prostitution. Immediately after America entered World War I, many of ASHA's staff members either enlisted in the military or served as civilian volunteer in army training camps. The War Department assigned ASHA men to the newly created Social Hygiene Division of the Sanitary Corps (placed under the Surgeon General's Office). Bascon Johnson (a lawyer for the ASHA) was put in charge of the Sanitary Corps' Division of Law. The military commissioned Johnson as a major and made his forty assistants (mostly attorneys from ASHA) lieutenants and charged the men with the responsibility of "protecting the men in all branches of the service."[40]

ASHA began in communities surrounding military training camps. The Law Enforcement Division included the Section on Women and Girls Work and the Bureau of Vice and Liquor Control. The Division sought to educate the civilians about VD through the distribution of pamphlets and public lectures. Johnson and his team also worked with local and state health departments to campaign against vice and rallying the public to rid society of "sordid places." Fosdick and Baker worried about the possible outcome of young naive girls flirting with men in uniform. Therefore, the Law Enforcement Division and local police patrolled dance halls, moving picture shows, burlesque theaters, parks, and amusement centers as a way of both deterring prostitution and protecting young innocent girls. With the help of local authorities, officers assigned to the Women's and Girl's Work removed prostitutes working near army camps and placed them into reformatories for rehabilitation. They also encouraged local officials to get wayward women off the street by influencing courts to sentence them to "suitable institutions." The Selective Service Act helped to "clean-up" communities, since it outlawed the sale of liquor in broad zones around military camps and prohibited the sale of alcohol to soldiers in uniform. The Bureau of Vice and Liquor Control stationed their officers in towns and cities near training camps to aide in the enforcement of liquor laws and report infractions to the local, state, and federal authorities.[41]

In addition, the ASAP focused on soldiers in the nation's training camps. The War Department asked Walter C. Clarke, the second executive director of the ASHA, to head up the military's Social Hygiene Instruction Division. Clarke and his team attempted to instill new moral standards in the incoming soldiers, particularly linking soldier responsibility with sexual purity and abstinence. Hygiene workers inundated soldiers in camps with pamphlets, posters, handbills, exhibits, and films on the subjects of VD and proper moral behavior. They also spent a considerable amount of time teaching troops the nature and prevention of VD. Army films like *Damaged Goods* demonstrated the harsh reality of syphilis and *Keeping Fit to Fight* graphically depicted scenes that demonstrated the results of contracting VD.[42]

Next, thousands of civilian Progressive social reformers partnered with the military to provide "positive" recreational camp activities intended to keep soldiers away from "negative" influences. During off-duty hours, soldiers picked from baseball, volleyball, rugby, basketball, tennis, soccer, boxing, theater, reading, writing, listening to music, or playing games. The YMCA (Young Men's Christian Association) played a key role in providing off-duty activities for soldiers and assisted the Social Hygiene Division with their educational efforts. The YMCA grew out of a mid-nineteenth century evangelical reform movement with the mission to provide a safe place for anxious young men moving to the cities—a place thought to be an immoral stronghold of crime and vice. The association helped the newly arrived men to avoid "every degree of wickedness, from the slightest excesses to the foulest villainies."[43] The organization quickly spread throughout the United States, and not surprisingly it expanded greatly during the Progressive Era. During World War I, over three thousand YMCA secretaries assisted the soldiers and coordinated various activities. The YMCA built four hundred buildings that seated three thousand soldiers in U.S. Army Cantonments and National Guard camps. The YMCA supplied the "huts" with pianos, motion picture machines, phonographic, stationery, and reading materials. The organization sponsored concerts, lectures, singing events, and amateur theaters, and it showed almost ten million feet of film (both entertainment and public health). The doors were always open for socializing, recreational activities, religious services, guest speakers, and sex education classes. The YMCA also distributed its newspaper, *Trench and Camp*, to the soldiers. Although the organization technically represented Protestant denominations, all of the YMCA's recreational activities were nonsectarian.[44]

Over one hundred Playground Association representatives joined the war effort. With the assistance of area chambers of commerce, churches, clubs, and fraternal organization, the representatives design recreational activities for soldiers in nearby athletic fields, swimming pools, gymnasiums, skating rinks, tennis courts, bowling alleys, and playgrounds. The Association's WCCS (War Camp Community Service) also made sure that areas surrounding the cantonments provided well-organized social activities including receptions, dances, lawn parties, automobile rides, picnics, musicals, concerts, organ recitals, and other programs. By March 1919, some 2,700 civilian WCCS volunteers set up recreational, athletic, and social programs in 615 towns and cities. This included over 500 clubs for soldiers, sailors, and marines; many complete with kitchens, cafeterias, canteens, dormitories, and shower baths, reading rooms, pianos, victrolas, billiard and pool tables, and cigar and candy stands. Keeping in the tradition of both the Progressive Era and the new philosophy of the U.S. military, the clubs served as safe places for soldiers to stay away from crime and vice.[45]

ETHNIC GROUP LEADERS

During the First World War, foreign-born soldiers from forty-six different nations made up 18 percent of the U.S. Army. Their presence challenged the cultural, linguistic, and religious traditions of the American army and forced the military to reexamine its training procedures. The War Department turned to ethnic community leaders to assist in training, educating, and socializing the immigrant troops. As a result, military policies demonstrated a remarkable sensitivity and respect for the Old World cultures while simultaneously laying the foundations for Americanization. In addition, the military's association with immigrant organizations and ethnic group leaders allowed the military to avoid the path of "100 percent Americanism" and helped promote a dual identity for immigrants in the ranks.

As hundreds thousands of immigrants poured into army training camps, the military was alarmed to learn many of the men could not effectively speak, read, or write the English language. At Camp Gordon, Georgia, an infantry replacement camp, the situation was far more critical since the number of non-English speaking soldiers reached 75 percent of the foreign-born troops. At first, military officers inadvertently made the situation more difficult when they placed the immigrants from various countries into conglomerate multiethnic masses and assigned them "kitchen police" work and other menial tasks. This only served to greatly exacerbated communications and morale problems. Therefore, to address these critical problems, the War Department established the FSS (Foreign-Speaking Soldier Sub-Section) in January 1918 to bring "about improvements in the treatment of alien personnel within the army."[46] For much of its existence, FSS reported to the MMS (Military Morale Section) of the MID (Military Intelligence Division) under the War Department.[47]

In an emergency measure, the War Department issued a general order requiring foreign-speaking servicemen with difficulty in receiving, executing, or transmitting spoken and written orders to be transferred into special Development Battalions. Next, FSS assigned Lt. Stanislaw A. Gutowski to reorganize the battalions and create an atmosphere for easy communication and rapid learning. Gutowski, a naturalized American citizen born in Russian Poland, was fluent in Polish, Russian, and Bohemian and was acquainted with both factions of the Polish party in his native country. The lieutenant personally knew Polish leaders in America and had close ties to the Polish Press Bureau. A skilled team of foreign-born and second-generation officers with the command of the Southern, Eastern, and Northern European languages assisted in the reorganization plan.[48]

Gutowski and his assistants began their work with the Development Battalion at Camp Gordon, Georgia. After studying the situation, interviewing foreign-born soldiers, and discussing alternatives with FSS leaders, it was decided that the most efficient way to train foreign-born soldiers was to reorganize them into ethnic-specific companies. Commissioned and non-commissioned immigrant and/or second generation (bilingual) officers led each company. FSS stressed, however, that the "foreign-legion" companies were not designed to encourage "clannishness" but represented a necessary measure taken in an emergency situation. At Camp Gordon, Gutowski first created a company of Slavic soldiers (mostly Poles) and hand-selected four of the most qualified men as company officers—three of Polish "extraction," and a Russian officer. Next, he organized Italian, Greek, and Russian-Jewish companies.[49]

Secretary of War Newton D. Baker put his full support behind the immigrant soldier reorganization project and directed commanding officers at thirty-five different training camps to classify the foreign-born for possible reorganization under what became known as the "Camp Gordon Plan." Gutowski and his team traveled throughout the United States to reorganize immigrant soldiers in various army camps. Since the plan called for ethnic companies to be led by the best qualified foreign-speaking first and second-generation immigrant officers, FSS began an intensive search for bilingual and multilingual soldiers for commissioned and noncommissioned positions. The military warned native-born soldiers at the Officer's Training Schools to avoid prejudice and stereotyping of officers with "accents" by reminding them that many of these immigrants had been successful professionals in their civilian life—lawyers, doctors, businessmen, and newspaper editors.[50]

Once the immigrants were adequately trained within their ethnic company, FSS placed the soldiers in regular divisions within ethnic-specific platoons. This way, soldiers could still be in daily contact with people from their own ethnic group but be integrated with native-born soldiers at the company level where they would continue to learn English. This arrangement would provide a foundation for "Americanization" and, at the same time, kept up the immigrants' "morale much better than if put among people of entirely different customs."[51] FSS associated the platoons with an immigrant "colony" and the larger companies with the American "melting pot."[52]

Hundreds of prominent ethnic community leaders, editors, clergymen, doctors, lawyers, and businessmen assisted the military in its socializations efforts. Ethnic organizations translated thousands of copies of social hygiene pamphlets into Polish, Russian, Italian, Bohemian, Hungarian, Spanish, Yiddish, and other languages. Still, there was some confusion. When the military showed immigrant troops the English-language film version of *Keeping Fit to Fight,* the non-English speaking soldiers did not understand the antivenereal disease message provided in English and asked bilingual officers why they were shown "a smutty" film. Thereafter, FSS asked foreign-speaking military and civilian ethnic group interpreters to explain the film's message in Russian, Polish, Bohemian, Serbian, Italian, Spanish, German, and Magyar.[53]

Ethnic leaders also worked with Progressive social welfare organizations to provide "positive" recreation activities to keep immigrant soldiers away from "negative" influences. Immigrant volunteers from the Jewish Welfare Board and the Knights of Columbus played a key role since many of the foreign-born troops came from the Jewish and Catholic religions. The YWCA created a special team—entitled "Work for Foreign-born Women," that employed immigrant "international" hostesses. Edith Terry Bremer, executive director of the YWCA's immigrant program, trained Polish, Czecho-Slovak, Serbian, Italian, and Greek women as "Gray Samaritans" hostesses to aid the immigrant soldier and help "link him with his home."[54] Professor Ernest H. Wilkins, director of Education for the YMCA, also coordinated a project with ethnic leaders to supply camp huts with foreign-language newspapers, and the American Library Association provided foreign languages reading materials. This included an impressive collection at Camp Upton, New York, which housed books in Yiddish, Russian, Italian, Romanian, Spanish, and Polish.

Members of local ethnic organizations worked with the WCCS of the American Playground Association to provide the "right kind" of moral, social, and recreational activities in communities near the camps. For example, the Jewish community in Rockford, Illinois opened a "splendidly equipped" club room for soldiers of the Jewish faith and other soldiers stationed at Camp Grant, Illinois. The Jewish community at Macon, Georgia sponsored home hospitality activities for Jewish soldiers from Camp Wheeler, and 500 Greek soldiers from Camp Gordon and Camp McPherson attended a community-sponsored Christmas dinner in Atlanta, Georgia.[55]

Americanization of immigrant troops took place through English language, civics, and citizenship classes. The third assistant secretary of war, Dr. Frederick Keppel, directed the English instruction program for non-English speaking soldiers with the assistance of the Bureau of Education, the YMCA, the Jewish Welfare Board, bilingual soldiers, and civilian immigrant instructors. Foreign-born soldiers attended three hours per day of English language classes as part of their mandatory military duties. English instruction normally lasted four months, although some programs were shorter. The military encouraged American patriotism with foreign-language translations of war propaganda material (translated by ethnic group organizations), inspirational speeches by prominent native- and foreign-born leaders, and public-speaking appearances by immigrant soldiers who had been decorated for bravery by the United States and allied countries. The American Library Association sent foreign-language books on the U.S. government and history. Americanization efforts also came through music. The Camp Music Division taught foreign-born soldiers the "Star-Spangled Banner," "America," and the "Battle Hymn of the Republic" in an effort to instill patriotic spirit and American loyalty. Music directors believed that if the immigrant soldiers slowly repeated the words, they would have "fully sensed the meaning of true patriotism...making them true Americans through song."[56]

Ethnic group leaders who assisted the military were in a very unique position to educate the military about important cultural and religious customs of the immigrant troops. The War Department understood that keeping a high level of morale among the foreign-born troops was essential to creating an effective fighting force. Immigrant leaders clearly explained the connection between moral and the retention of Old World heritage. Since religion was vital to "foster[ing] a feeling of satisfaction and higher morale among both the men and their families," the military agreed to meet the specific cultural and spiritual needs of the foreign-born troops whenever possible.[57] After Polish-Catholic soldiers expressed a sincere concern about dying in battle before confessing their sins, FSS (with the help of the Knights of

Columbus) secured a number of Polish priests to conduct mass in the Polish language and hear confession. At the request of the Greek Orthodox Church, the military gave furloughs to Greek soldiers for the Feast of Saint Nicholas, an important celebration in which the members renewed their vows to the church. Together, FSS and the Jewish Welfare Board arranged religious services for Jewish soldiers and supplied matzo during Passover. The Jewish Welfare Board also convinced the War Department to furlough Jewish soldiers on important holidays including Rosh Hashanah, Yom Kippur, and Passover. Jewish organizations successfully pressured the War Department and the U.S. Congress to replace the Christian cross on the grave markings of Jewish soldiers with the Star of David. The Jewish Welfare Board supplied soldiers with over 100,000 prayer books, 80,000 bibles in Yiddish, and a Hebrew and English *Prayer Book for Jews in the Army and Navy of the United States,* compiled by a number of Jewish national organizations.[58]

FSS scheduled camp cultural festivals (at the request of ethnic group leaders) including the Italian Gala event, Italian "Fall of Rome" Celebration, and Syrian activity night. The leaders also participated in patriotic rallies for foreign-born troops, but on their own terms. At these events, immigrant leaders gave speeches that praised America's role in the war and led the singing of patriotic songs. But they followed this with talks focusing on the war efforts of foreign-born groups living in the United States and discussions on the contributions of their homelands against the Central Powers. Music selections included "Old World" favorites.[59]

Foreign-born soldiers made up almost one in five of the men who arrived in the American military training camps during World War I, and many did not know enough English to be effective soldiers. The U.S. military clearly faced a critical situation. By working closely with ethnic community leaders, the military was able to avoid harsh nativism prevalent in civilian society. Instead of forcing soldiers into a melting pot, War Department policies and new civil-military relationships created an atmosphere for the soldiers that made both American and ethnic pride acceptable.

AFRICAN-AMERICAN LEADERS

The War Department's training of African-American soldiers took a far different direction than that of white native-born and foreign-born troops. The black draftees entered the armed forces just as, in the words of Nancy Bristow, "years of violence against African Americans had climaxed in the summer of 1917 in a flurry of race riots nationwide...like an epidemic, unconcerned with regional distinctions."[60] African-American leaders worked diligently to fight against segregation, prejudice, and violence in civilian society. With America's entrance into World War I, most leaders hoped the presence of black soldiers aiding their country would help ease long-standing racial attitudes. Others hoped for key policy changes in the military that would finally challenge overt oppression. According to historian Jennifer Keene, "the suggestion that the army take an activist role in enforcing civil rights was not as far-fetched as it may have sounded at the time, although it required civilians, not military, leadership to succeed."[61] Early in the war, the Secretary of War Baker declared: "It has been my policy to discourage discrimination against persons by reasons of their race." But ultimately, he made it clear: "There is no intention on the part of the War Department to undertake at this time to settle the so-called race question."[62] Eventually, African-American leaders had some success affecting government and War Department policy; however, too often discriminatory policies prevailed.

Since congressmen from the South tried, but failed, to prevent African Americans from being drafted, Southern whites placed inordinate pressure on the War Department to create only small military units of African-American soldiers and pushed for a plan that allowed black men to serve only in nonfighting roles. Furthermore, they wanted to keep large numbers of the black troops out of Southern training camps. Although the War Department General Staff decided early on to use African-American soldiers as both troops and noncombatant laborers, specific details needed to be worked out in "unending policy discussions." The meetings "strikingly portray[ed] how racial instability preyed on the minds of army officials, especially when they realized the consequences if they faltered in containing it."[63] During this time, the War Department attempted to put out brush-fires caused by racial tension in army camps and to hold fast against pressure from both Southern segregationists and the Black press. On August 23, 1917, one of the brush-fires exploded. After months of harassment and abuse from white Texans, African-American soldiers from Camp Logan attacked white civilians in Houston. The violence ended in the death of sixteen white civilians and four black soldiers, as well as injuries to a dozen other people. The War Department reacted quickly to the riot, arresting every member of the Twenty-fourth Infantry's Third Battalion. After court-martial hearings, the military executed a total of nineteen black regulars and sent forty-three to jail for life.[64]

The Houston riot complicated an already fragile situation. African-American leaders immediately called for a meeting with Secretary of War Baker to discuss the crisis. After the conference, Baker appointed Emmett J. Scott as his "Special Assistant for Negro Affairs." Baker selected Scott because the black leader did not hold radical views on race relations. Scott had worked as a journalist in Houston, Texas before starting his own weekly newspaper, *The Houston Freeman*. In 1912, he became Booker T. Washington's personal secretary and also served as the secretary of the Tuskegee Institute. In his World War I position as Baker's special assistant, Scott spoke out against the exclusion of most African Americans from combat divisions. He also protested the disproportionate drafting of African Americans, noting "colored men, palpably unfit for military service, and others who were entitled to exemption under law, were 'railroaded' into the army while other men with no legitimate excuse for exemption were allowed to escape the requirements of the draft system."[65]

After some discussion, the War Department decided to locate African-American soldiers scattered throughout training camps in both the North and the South. It also allowed for the creation of the Ninety-second Combat Division comprised of mainly African-American soldiers. In order to keep the number of blacks in any particular cantonment at a minimum, soldiers assigned to the Ninety-second Division did not train together, but instead, were split into smaller groups and sent to several different military camps. When the military trained the black combat soldiers, they kept loaded guns away from the troop. Another Division (the ninety-third), comprised of Black National Guardsmen, "was 'given' to the French. Equipped with French arms, the 93rd Division was used extensively by the French and fought well."[66]

The War Department considered its policies concerning black troops a compromise, since it helped appease Southern fears of large groups of African-American soldiers stationed together, and also required the South to accept both the training of the soldiers in Southern camps and the organization of a black combat division. But the military did not fully reexamine its racial policies and inducted black soldiers separated from white soldiers, segregated troops, and placed the majority (almost 75 percent) of African-American soldiers in labor battalions.[67]

Earlier, the War Department gave into Southern pressure and barred all African Americans from the summer reserve officers training camps held by UMT advocates from 1913 to 1916. Senator Vardaman openly admitted that many Southerners did not want African Americans to be trained as soldiers: "Universal military service means that millions of Negroes who will come under this measure will be armed. I know of no greater menace to the South than this."[68] Despite overt resistance, Joel E. Springarn, who became the chairman of the Board of Directors for the NAACP in 1914, along with black leaders, push the government to establish a UMT officer training camp for African-American civilians. (Springarn was the son of Jewish immigrants. He was university professor until his firing in 1911 over an academic freedom debate). After considerable discussion, the War Department agreed to establish a camp for college-educated African Americans in 1916, similar to Plattsburg. However, once the United States declared war, the War Department put aside the idea.[69]

With war raging in Europe, African-American community members continued to pressure for the training of black officers. With America's entrance in the war, their efforts expanded. Beginning in early 1917, newspaper editors, ministers, college administrators, professors, and students joined with the NAACP to push Congress and the War Department for the establishment of an officer training camp for black soldiers. They petitioned the government and met with key members of the Wilson Administration. Prominent citizens also created the Committee of 100, the Committee of Ladies, and the Central Committee of Negro College Men to do battle along with the government over the issue. The executive secretary of the NAACP, Roy Nash, secured the assistance of Martin B. Madden, U.S. representative from Chicago. Madden corresponded with Baker and blatantly asked if racial discrimination lay behind the Selective Service System, and if African Americans would be given a chance to become officers. Nash also discussed the issue with the War College. NAACP board chairman, Springarn solicited the help of Professor George W. Cook, the secretary of Howard University. Cook mobilized the black academic community including administrators, faculty, and students. In April, 1917, Springarn headed up a large lobbying group from the NAACP who met with Baker.[70] Scott supported the idea, noting as

> strange and paradoxical as it may seem, America, while fighting for the democratization of the people of far-off Europe, was denying democracy to a part—an honest, loyal and patriotic part—of her citizens at home. Fourteen camps were instituted for the training of WHITE officers—none for colored officers, nor were colored men admitted to any of the fourteen camps.[71]

Eventually the African-American community achieved some success when the War Department agreed to accept black officer candidates. In October, the military commissioned 639 men as captains, and first and second lieutenants. The new officers joined the Ninety-second Division. Yet, the program was short-lived. The War Department considered the Ninety-second Division an "experiment," and concluded no further black officers were needed. The African-American community hoped that the war experience would help young men advance in civilian society. However, a large majority of African Americans inducted into the army served in labor battalions and stevedore regiments. The wartime experience for most black soldiers consisted of "digging ditches, building roads, unloading ships, loading trucks, burying the dead and performing other menial and unpleasant tasks."[72]

During their training, the War Department planned to provide wholesome activities for all troops to keep them away from negative influences. In reality, this was not always the case. The CTCA vowed not to discriminate against black troops and promised to open its programs and hostess huts to "all soldiers regardless of race and creed."[73] Still, CTCA quickly gave into pressure to segregate recreational activities in most camps, especially in the South. In an October 1917 letter from Fosdick to Baker, the CTCA director discussed about recreational activities available at Camp Jackson, South Carolina. In it, Fosdick assured the secretary of war: "The colored soldiers will be kept as far as possible in the colored sections, and the white soldiers in the white section. In other words, the race segregation system will be carefully observed."[74] In a number of camps some civilian recreational officers from the YMCA, Knights of Columbia, and Jewish Welfare Board did attempt integration. Also "at one time or another," at Camp Devens, Massachusetts; Funston, Kansas; Lee, Alabama; Meade, Maryland; Merritt, New Jersey; Travis, Texas, and Upton, New York, "white and black soldiers negotiated racial truces that enabled them to share recreational facilities; in others, the camp commander required it."[75] But these exceptions actually concerned the military, since officials were convinced that "peaceful coexistence" between the races could quickly turn into violent encounters. Even in camp that carefully segregated off-duty activities, there was an acute shortage of hostess huts and recreational equipment for black soldiers, and CTCA did not adequately supply the limited facilities available to African-American troops. African-American leaders also spoke out against military discriminatory policies concerning camp social and recreational activities in an attempt to elicit change. By the summer of 1918, CTCA began to expand its efforts to provide additional segregated facilities for black troops.[76]

Invitations from local white communities to use area sports facilities or attend family dinners were rare. With the exception of some northern cities, most white communities surrounding the camps also did not provide activities for black soldiers. However, churches and other African-American organizations located near training camps, provided books, magazines, newspapers, and sports equipment; extended dinner invitations; and held parades for black soldiers. A citizen's committee made up of African Americans from Birmingham, Alabama organized "musical concerts, lectures, athletics, and drama" for nearby troops.[77]

CONCLUSION

During the war, a new and unique civil-military relationship developed between the War Department and civilian experts, community leaders, and reformers. Drafting was made complex by America's diverse society along with prevailing ethnic and racial attitudes. Drafting, testing, training, and socializing soldiers led to new civil-military associations, as psychologists, Progressive reformers, and ethnic group leaders worked closely with the military to develop and execute new policies. Handicapped by deeply rooted racial discrimination in American society and its military, African-American leaders also endeavored to make changes for black soldiers, with some success.

3

Mobilizing Public Opinion and Suppressing Dissent: Civil-Military Cooperation and Conflict

As war raged overseas, the American home front experienced its own kind of battle—"the fight for the *minds* of men, for the 'conquest of their convictions.'"[1] During World War I, the U.S. government and military conducted an elaborate propaganda and surveillance effort. Leaders regarded a massive propaganda campaign as an effective tool in unifying a reluctant nation behind the war. In addition, civilian and military officials utilized counterintelligence measures to prevent enemy propaganda from infiltrating into the nation, spreading radicalism, and damaging America's war efforts. Civil-military intelligence efforts represented a joint endeavor as military agents worked closely with key government organizations, civilian associations, and leaders of both the native-born and foreign-born American communities. The propaganda and counterintelligence effort represented unprecedented cooperation between government agencies and the War Department, but also resulted in civil-military conflict. The combined undertaking also spurred a superpatriotic and jingoistic fervor that escalated into mass hysteria and ultimately demanded nothing less than total conformity. In this emotionally charged atmosphere, the voices of pacifists, radicals, African Americans, and the foreign-born became stifled. Civil liberties became a causality of the war.

THE PEACE MOVEMENT

The Progressive Era, a time dominated by American liberalism and a drive for humanitarian, urban, and labor improvements, greatly influenced the American peace movement. The peace movement expanded during the late nineteenth and early twentieth centuries when business and educational leaders created the American School Peace League (1908), the Carnegie Endowment for International Peace (1910), the World Peace Foundation (1910), and the Church Peace Union (1914). The new groups joined the earlier established American Peace Society (1828) to advocate international cooperation and "study, friendship, and arbitration."[2] But the effort at peace suffered under the strains of wartime conformity. With the start of World War I in 1914, issues of war and peace became much more complex— sharply dividing the peace movement.

Once America entered the conflict in 1917, many of the leaders from the peace foundations and leagues publicly supported the Allies and pointed to Germany as an evil force standing in the way of achieving world peace. In addition, many Progressive reformers joined the U.S. war effort, arguing that by assisting the government in mobilizing the home front, training soldiers, and writing war propaganda, they would be in a key position to insist on a better society at war's end. But well-known reformer Randolph Bourne warned Progressive war supporters, "If the war is too strong for you to prevent, how is it going to be weak enough for you to control and mould to your liberal purposes?"[3]

Many other Progressive Social Justice Reformers remained committed to the Peace Movement, contending the war grew out of the same injustices that dominated America for decades. They argued the war would stop advancements made in helping the poor, ending child labor, improving conditions in cities, raising wages, and establishing safety measures in factories and mines. Many now defined themselves as pacifists, reorganizing the purpose of the movement from education to political, and openly challenging government authority as they sought an end to the war.

The FOR (Fellowship of Reconciliation), made up of Christian liberal pacifists argued war was diametrically opposed to the teaching of Christ. Established in 1915 by "Quakers, social gospel clergymen, and YMCA leaders," FOR served as "the central body for religious conscientious objectors for the next half century."[4] Two other organizations heavily influenced by Progressivism took an active role in objecting to the war—the WPP (Woman's Peace Party) and the AUAM (American Union Against Militarism). The WPP began in January 1915 when Progressive Reformer's Jane Addams and Carrie Chapman Catt rallied women involved in social justice, trade unions, temperance, education, and suffrage. Members of the WPP attended the 1915 International Women's Congress for Peace and Freedom, held at The Hague and attempted to secure peace by sending emissaries to the warring nations. AUAM was established in 1915 by Progressive social justice reformers, labor lawyers, feminists, clergymen, and liberal publishers. It began as an anti-preparedness organization strongly advocating American neutrality and openly contesting any form of Universal Military Training or military expansion.[5]

The AUAM quickly grew to the largest antimilitarist group in the United States as it toiled to educate the public about the dangers of militarism and the need for peace. It published numerous writings arguing that the rights of the people were in danger:

> Constitutional rights are being seriously invaded throughout the United States under pressure of war. Men are arrested and fined for criticizing the Government or the President. Halls are refused for meetings; meetings are broken up; pamphlets and literature opposing the war are confiscated and the authors haled into court. In short, the guarantees of the Federal Constitution have been suspended at the dictate of petty officials who would compel conformity on the part of all citizens to their conception of war policies. Such a time is a challenge to all patriots to maintain the liberties guaranteed by the constitution.[6]

But the AUAM soon faced internal struggles over disagreements with its Liberties Bureau (later the American Civil Liberties Union) and Conscientious Objectors Bureau—both of which represented a more extreme branch of the organization. The two organizations divided in the Fall of 1917. Roger Baldwin, director of the Civil Liberties Bureau, stood behind his convictions as a conscientious objector. He was subsequently jailed for one year for violation of the Draft Act. According to historian Charles Chatfield, "There were liberal pacifists of various hues...and their language and experience differed significantly."[7] Despite this, the biggest threat to the Peace Movement came from government and military efforts to silence its voice.

RADICALS AND THE WAR

While many peace activists remained in the AUAM, some joined the People's Council of America for Democracy and Peace, a joint collaboration between moderate Socialists and more radical Progressive antiwar reformers. The Council aggressively criticized the draft and openly approved of the 1917 Russian Revolution. As the world military conflict continued, pacifism deepened and radicalized. This drove more reformers toward Socialism.

The American Socialists Party denounced the Great War and defined the conflict as an outgrowth of Old World imperialism and a reflection of the abuses of capitalism. They mocked President Wilson's rallying call that claimed a war against Germany would make the world "safe for democracy." In its writings, the party asked:

> Do you think [conscription] has a place in the United States? Do you want to see unlimited power handed over to Wall Street's chosen few in America? If you do not, join the Socialist Party in its campaign for the repeal of the Conscription Act.... Do not submit to intimidation. You have a right to demand the repeal of any law. Exercise you right of free speech, peaceful assemblage and

petitioning the government for a redress of grievances.... **Help us re-establish democracy in America! Remember, "eternal vigilance is the price of liberty." Down with autocracy! Long live the constitution of the United States! Long live the Republic!**[8]

The Socialist Party contended war brought "wealth and power" to the upper class but only "death and suffering" to the lower classes. It also claimed conscription took away a draftee's "freedom of conscience," since it forced a man to "kill against his will." As the Socialist Party grew and the war progressed, radicals became targets of oppression by the military, government, and general public.[9]

THE COMPLEXITY OF ETHNIC GROUP PATRIOTISM

Prior to America's entrance into World War I, German and Irish Americans joined together to convince the U.S. government to maintain its neutrality. While German Americans did not want to fight against their "brothers," Irish Americans resolved not to help Great Britain, the longtime oppressor of the Irish people. The National German–American Alliance, the Irish Ancient Order of Hibernians, editors of Irish and German newspapers, and other ethnic organizations also attempted to educate the public about British violations of international law. However, once the United States joined the world conflict, most German and Irish Americans supported the war or choose to stay silent.[10]

Over twenty million new immigrants from Southern and Eastern Europe came to the United States in the three decades before the start of the Great War. Like many other immigrant groups throughout American history, the new immigrants tended to live in ethnic enclaves where they could speak their own language, eat ethnic foods, read news of their homelands in ethnic newspapers, and find support in their community's fraternal and social organizations. Immigrants continued to retain important parts of their native traditions, but also adopted key elements of the dominant American culture.

Not all ethnic groups sought American neutrality. In fact, many of the new immigrants fled from political, economic, or religious turmoil when they emigrated from the Austrian-Hungarian Empire. This group considered themselves to be from the "oppressed races" of the realm and actively supported America's fight to defeat the Central Powers. As such, they sent relief money to their homeland to aid the suffering, purchased U.S. Liberty Bonds to help pay for the American war effort, and held patriotic parades to show their loyalty to their adopted country. Immigrant soldiers served in the U.S. Army (almost one in five were foreign-born), and thousands of immigrants not eligible for the American military joined Allied forces in foreign-born legions. Legions joined together Czech and Slovak Americans into the Czechoslovak Legion and the Polish Americans into the Polish Legion—both groups serving with French Army. The Jewish Legion (made up of many American Jews) served with the British Army in Palestine. Despite this, the general public remained suspicious of the foreign-born, openly questioned their loyalty to United States, and began a "100 percent Americanism" campaign designed to strip all immigrants of their language and culture.[11]

THE QUESTION OF AFRICAN-AMERICAN LOYALTY

Prior to the nation's entrance into World War I, the majority of African Americans supported U.S. neutrality and saw the war as an outgrowth of colonialism that subjugated the "darker people." Fully aware of the long, widespread abuses of African Americans, the U.S. government feared that blacks—some eleven million strong—would not support America's participation in the war. Most of the over nine million African Americans in the South were either former slaves or only one generation removed, and all were acutely aware that the Civil War did not bring true freedom, civil rights, or significant economic opportunities. Not surprisingly, after decades of segregation and disenfranchisement through Jim Crow Laws, voting restrictions, violence, and murder, African Americans resented the lack of federal government intervention, and many considered World War I a "White Man's War." Furthermore, few of the over one million African Americans who came north in the Great Migration (starting in 1914) found true liberty in the urban, industrialized areas. The situation in the north became even more critical when mob violence against blacks erupted in the summer of 1917, as a result of racial tension and job competition.[12]

A. Philip Randolph and a number of other black leaders spoke out against the war and predicted little would be gained by African-American participation in the American military. However, other key black leaders, such as Roscoe Conklin Simmons (Booker T. Washington's nephew) and W.E.B. DuBois, along with the majority of African-American newspaper editors, called on blacks to support their country. As historian Wray Johnson pointed out, "many blacks continued to hold out hope that participation in the war would serve as yet another demonstration of love of country and perhaps would result in reforms to the benefit of blacks as a whole."[13] Despite the loyalty of the vast majority of African Americans, racism and discrimination prevailed in the U.S. military and in civilian communities, and black leaders and organizations soon found themselves under government and military surveillance.

WAR ACTS

As early as 1914, both England and Germany initiated a major propaganda campaign in America. Both nations also attempted to conduct espionage work throughout the United States, and Germany attempted "a campaign of sabotage and subversion."[14] Allegation of German sabotage spread with every mysterious explosion, beginning with a major blast on New York's Black Tom Island in 1916, which destroyed munitions, gunpowder, dynamite, and shrapnel heading to the Allies. Concern over the nation's security led Congress to pass a number of war acts giving the government extensive power—unprecedented in the history of the United States. The Espionage Act (June 1917) mandated heavy penalties or jail time (up to $10,000 and twenty years in prison) for anyone found guilty of transmitting information about U.S. national defense to any foreign power, interfering with military recruiting, encouraging disloyalty among the U.S. armed forces, using U.S. mail for treasonous materials, and many other similar infractions. The October 1917 Trading-with-the Enemy Act forbids any form of commerce with enemy nations. In April 1918, Congress enacted the Sabotage Act, which (according to one scholar) was "designed to protect the country from an imagined network of saboteurs and spies."[15] The May 1918 amendment to the Espionage Act, known as the Sedition Act, made it unlawful to "willfully utter, print, write or publish any disloyal, profane, scurrilous, or abusive language" about the U.S. government, constitution, military, or flag. With the Alien Act (October 1918), Congress set out to restrain subversive immigrants (especially German and later Bolshevik) and authorized deportation of immigrants deemed radical. The government required all immigrants born in enemy territory to registrar at the post office, and forbid them to go near ports, war industries, and other key area. The War Department imprisoned "Enemy Aliens deemed disloyal at Fort Oglethorpe, George and Fort Douglas Utah."[16]

THE COMMITTEE ON PUBLIC INFORMATION

As soon as America joined the Great War, the War Department's General Staff asked Congress to approve of the creation of a "strict military censorship program."[17] At the same time, newspaper professionals, including well-known Progressive journalist George Creel, pressured Congress to support voluntary censorship of the American press. On April 1917, the secretaries of state, war, and navy requested President Wilson authorize "a committee to control both censorship and publicity."[18] Shortly afterward, Wilson created the CPI (Committee on Public Information)—a high-pitched government propaganda machine, designed to supervise domestic publications, infuse patriotism, and promote the war to the public. The president placed George Creel at the helm of CPI, and both the secretary of the army and navy served as advisors to the committee. Creel argued, "Now more than at any other time in history the importance of public opinion has come to be recognized. The fight for it is a part of the military program of every country, for every belligerent nation has brought psychology to the aid of science."[19]

Creel used muckraking methods to appeal to the emotions of the American people and elicit the patriotic spirit in support of the war and "drive home... great truths."[20] Beginning in the late nineteenth century, Progressive muckrakers used moving words and dramatic stories along with emotionally charged photographs to educate the public about the abuses of the working class and the need for government reform. Creel selected other prominent journalists to help with CPI propaganda—"Ida Tarbell, Ernest Poole, Will Irwin, and Ray Stannard Baker—all passionate muckrakers before the war and devotees of the progressive reforming faith."[21] Creel also brought together an impressive group of writers, advertising executives, marketing managers, historians, filmmakers, artists, photographers, and entertainers along with a small "army" of volunteers to "sell" the war to the general public. CPI supplied translated propaganda in various foreign languages for the nation's immigrant groups. CPI expanded to include the Divisions of Advertising, News, Syndicated Features, Films, Labor, Women, and Exhibits, along with the Bureau of Cartoons, and Bureau of War Photographs. CPI's Speakers Division included some 75,000 local volunteers called Four-Minute Men, who operated in 5,200 communities. The speakers gave over 750,000 short public patriotic speeches and delivered stories of German atrocities before social gatherings, civic meetings, and motion-picture features. Soldiers from the American and Allied Armies also participated in CPI speaking tours.[22]

WAR HYSTERIA

But the CPI speakers, pamphlets, posters, and other propaganda fueled an already combustible atmosphere. As the war progressed, the CPI drifted away from war education to become more of a "crude propaganda mill."[23] The reliance on tens of thousands of unsupervised volunteers led to disastrous results. Vigilantism reigned. War time anxiety, antiradicalism, and xenophobia collated with emotionally charged propaganda spun out of control to create a volatile, repressive atmosphere. Creel adamantly denied that CPI policies led to violence and hatred:

> As for the censorship on free speech, it is not imposed by Washington, but by the intolerances and bigotries of individual communities. The government is not responsible for mobs that hang innocent men, that paint houses yellow and that run up and down the country trying to crush honest discussion.[24]

America's immigrants soon found themselves targeted. CPA "organized and directed 23 societies and leagues designed to appeal to certain classes and particular foreign-language groups...carrying a specific message of unity and enthusiasm."[25] National and local nativists worked feverishly to vanquish the immigrants' Old World traditions and the foreign-born quickly fell victim to public demands for cultural conformity. Ruthless efforts at Americanization increased with wartime propaganda and resulted in oppression, forced assimilation, ruthless xenophobia, and harsh "100% Americanism." The Liberty Loan campaign capitalized on the patriotic fever and quickly connected the purchase of war bonds with a demonstration of immigrant loyalty. Volunteers dressed the city with Liberty Loan posters directed at both the native-born and foreign-born. In immigrant neighborhoods posters asked: "Are you 100% American?" "Prove It! Buy U.S. Government Bonds." Another read: "Remember Your First Thrill of American Liberty—YOUR DUTY—Buy United States Government Bonds." Liberty Loan campaigners also elicited patriotism and conformity by producing posters and pamphlets in various languages, complete with symbols of the American flag, the Statue of Liberty, and Ellis Island."[26]

Anti-German propaganda directly affected Americans of German descent, since the CPI campaign "often seemed geared to persuade the American people that every German soldier was a violent beast; that spies and saboteurs lurked behind every bush...and that Russian Bolsheviks were merely German agents."[27] Four-Minute Men speeches emphasized the dangerous "menace of Kaiserism" and feverishly appealed to "the spirit of America." CPI pressured the Bureau of Education to promote "patriotism heroism, and sacrifice" to students. High school students received "evidence" that Germany; an insidious nation based on militarism, was responsible for the current war. CPI pamphlets designed to teach elementary school children told of the horrors the Germans inflicted on the French and Belgium people, emphasized the difference between American democracy and German autocracy, and provided biographies of historical war heroes from the Allied nations. The government's Liberty Loan Campaign not only raised money for the war, it also stirred up the war spirit through posters depicting the German "Huns" as evil monsters who preyed on innocent women and children.[28]

As a result, many German Americans became selected key targets for harassment during the war. Neighbors and APL (American Protection League) members spied on German Americans and sent thousands of reports to the U.S. Department of Justice. School boards told students to use scissors to remove all references of Germany from their textbooks, and school officials canceled German language classes. Most intellectuals spoke out against the cancellation of German in school. This included Princeton president John Geir Hibben who argued that it "would be a very narrow minded policy and quite unworthy of our American Spirit," and Dr. Lyman Abbott, editor of *The Outlook,* who contended "it would be an act of unspeakable folly to cut ourselves off from the literature and science which the German people have contributed to the world.[29] But others supported such action. Harvard professor Theodore W. Richards contended that since "the diabolical methods of the German Government have so discredits Germany in the minds of decent people," teaching German is "much less important."[30]

Two well-known chemists, Dr. L.H. Baekeland and Dr. Gregory Torossian, also spoke out. Baekeland maintained that stopping the language would be of "little lost" and can be resumed when Germany proves to be "counted with civilized nations," while Torossian called the German language an "exponent of Medievalism in thought, in culture, in morals, and in deeds."[31] In many cities, public officials ordered that the playing of Bach and Beethoven in public orchestras be stopped immediately and pressured city museums to remove German art. Hamburgers, sauerkraut, and German measles became liberty sandwiches, liberty cabbage, and liberty measles. Many German Americans became victims of war hysteria, violence, and even death. In his final report, Creel refused to take blame for the ramped nativism and xenophobia, maintaining his organization expressed the attitude of "100% Americanism," as a desire to volunteer, serve, and sacrifice. He placed blame for anti-immigrant sentiment on "so-called patriotic societies" who harassed the foreign-born and "hounded" them with "laws conceived in intolerance."[32]

Creel later bragged "there was no part of the great war machinery that we did not touch, no medium of appeal that we did not employ. The printed word, the spoken word, the motion picture, the telegraph, the cable, the wireless, the poster, and the signboard—all these were used in our campaign to make our own people and all other people understand the causes that compelled America to take arms."[33]

CIVIL-MILITARY SURVEILLANCE AND COUNTERINTELLIGENCE

During World War I, no government or military organization had single authority over America's counterintelligence work. Therefore, domestic intelligence came from the Department of Justice's Bureau of Investigation, the Department of Treasury's Secret Service, the U.S. Army's MID (Military Intelligence Division), and the ONI (Office of Naval Intelligence). According to historian Theodore Kornweibel, "none of the major domestic surveillance players...began with either a strong organizational structure or clarified mission" to be able to stop German espionage and sabotage efforts in the United States.[34] Sharp conflicts also existed between the Treasury Department's Secret Service and the Justice Department's Bureau of Investigation (forerunner of the FBI). Attorney General Thomas Watt Gregory was initially reluctant to use the Justice Department to investigate "espionage, sabotage, and most subversion," claiming these matters stood outside of federal law. On the other hand, Secretary of Treasury William McAdoo pressed to put his Secret Service agents into action and "broadly interpreted the service's authority to make investigations despite recent congressional action to curtail such interpretations."[35] Soon, the two agencies became fierce rivals. Justice Bureau Intelligence agents directed by Bureau Chief A. Bruce Bielaski, soon played a major role in tracking down "slackers" who failed to register with the local selective service board, and drafted men who did not report for duty. They also monitored areas around army training camps to keep them free of prostitution and alcohol. Bureau agents were kept busy by following up on tens of thousands of complaints of treason and enemy infiltration by the general public—as neighbors turned against neighbors. Many targeted the nation's new arrivals and Americans of German decent. The Justice Bureau received assistance from some 250,000 members who made up the APL, a "band of amateur sleuths and loyalty enforcers which had managed to enter into an official relationship with [Attorney General] Gregory's Department."[36] APL "quasi-vigilantes" served as watchdogs, reporting instances of dissent or "suspicious" activities. However, the sheer size of APL and lack of effective centralized leadership led to considerable problems as members often overstepped their limited authority to terrorize private citizens. APL volunteers added to the social strain by "passing themselves off as federal detectives," complete with fake badges. Members hunted down conscientious objectors in "slacker raids," opened private mail, seized telegraphs, broke into and searched private homes, burned "pro-German" books, spied on neighbors, and attacked immigrants and radicals. Gregory praised APL calling it "a powerful patriotic organization," while a more recent authority described it as "a force for outrageous vigilantism blessed with the seal and sanction of the federal government." APL posses "bugged, burglarized, slandered, and illegally arrested other Americans."[37]

Secretary of Treasury McAdoo and the head of the Secret Service William J. Flynn "especially resented [the APL] because it further threatened the Secret Service's claim to primacy in counterintelligence matters."[38] Despite McAdoo's estimate that some 90 percent of APL's reports were worthless, and his warning that APL was dangerous to individual rights and liberties, President Wilson refused to step in to cut the Department of Justice's ties with the APL. The treasury secretary also accused the Justice Department of being incompetent and "argued that there were legions of German spies and subversives hidden in the country."[39] Gregory called the spy conspiracy "baseless" and "overblown," and Bureau Chief Bielaski protested against the encroachment of the Treasury's Secret Service into Justice Bureau of Investigation matters. Eventually, it would take the War Department to calm the waters and end the standoff between the two civilian agencies.[40]

From its inception in 1892, the Office of Naval Intelligence focused on foreign intelligence gatherings. But during World War I, ONI quadrupled the number of its men and assigned them to both foreign intelligence collection and new domestic surveillance duties. ONI agents protected war plants producing naval equipment, investigated the loyalty of factory employees, wiretapped civilians suspected of subversion, and tracked down up to

15,000 possible domestic sedition cases each week. Although ONI served a vital role in intelligence gathering, it also crossed the line. "In its enthusiasm to seek out individuals posing a possible threat to national security, ONI could be blamed for periodically engaging in 'witch hunts' or using questionable methods that would later be judged an affront to justice."[41]

The U.S. Army was "even less prepared than the Justice Department to respond to domestic security issues; yet, by war's end, it too had developed an extensive intelligence capability."[42] Although military intelligence work began prior to the Great War, the organization had only a small handful of agents who focused their efforts overseas. In April 1917, the secretary of war authorized the creation of the MIS (Military Intelligence Section) under the direction of major (soon to be colonel) Ralph H. Van Deman. The work of MIS officers focused on three areas—domestic surveillance, soldier morale, and overseas intelligence gathering. As the duties of MIS grew, the organization expanded and transformed. By June 1, 1918, Lieutenant Colonel Marlborough Churchill became the head of the renamed Military Intelligence Branch, and by August, Churchill became a brigadier general for a reorganized MID. During the tenure of both leaders, intelligence agents served in the United States and in pertinent places throughout the world. Overseas, the MID "Positive Branch" focused on the "study of the military, political, economic, and social situation abroad," while the MID "Negative Branch" located in major American cities, "sought to uncover and suppress enemy activities at home."[43] In its domestic surveillance work, the MID often worked in tandem with the Department of Justice, Treasury Department, War Trade Board, and the Alien Property Custodians.

The Military Intelligence Personnel Directory listed the names and location of MID officers stationed in the United States (captains and lieutenants) assigned to the Eastern, Western, Central, and Southeastern Divisions. MID divided each geographical area into sections with agents reporting to the chief (rank of major) in each area. MI4 agents worked in the "Counter-Espionage among [the] Civilian Population in U.S. and Foreign Countries" and performed various functions related to propaganda, law, naturalization, carrier pigeons, sabotage, labor, and espionage. MI4B in the Northeast devoted much of their surveillance work on alien enemies and radical immigrants, while agents from the Southeast concentrated their investigations of African-American radicalism and subversion. MID agents from the central states focused on German American activities, while agents stationed in the West watched over labor unions. MI4E "studied allegedly dangerous movements like the IWW, Russian Bolshevism, and the (German) Lutheran Church."[44] MID's Foreign-Speaking Soldier Sub-section included foreign-born and bilingual lieutenants who worked exclusively on the surveillance of the immigrant soldiers and ethnic enclaves. In addition to officers, MID utilized paid and volunteer civilian agents to perform counterintelligence work throughout the United States. The agents detailed their activities in countless incident reports sent to the War Department. As with the Bureau of Investigation, MID worked with the APL to investigate the background and affiliations of all MID civilian applicants.[45]

CIVIL-MILITARY DOMESTIC SURVEILLANCE

Government and military intelligence agencies initiate a major campaign to cripple efforts of peace organization, Socialists, and other radicals. President Wilson, in his June 1917 Flag Day speech "condemned the antiwar movement as treasonous and labeled its members as conscious agents or unwitting tools of German militarists."[46] The Department of Justice and MID also watched for domestic dissent and enemy propaganda in newspapers, theatre production, moving pictures, union organizations, and various pacifists, radical, foreign-born and African-American civilian associations. Civilian and military agents traced war-related rumors, studied satirical cartoons and essays, and paid close attention to pacifists, draft resisters, political agitators, labor radicals, and alleged spies.

With the growing loss of civil liberties, discrimination from the Post Master General's office, investigations by government agencies and the military, along with public harassment by amateur sleuths, "pacifists found that their meetings were broken up; their friends were harassed, run out of town, and imprisoned; their literature was withheld from mails; [and] their headquarters raided."[47] The Peace Movement also found itself directly in the path of civilian superpatriotic zealots. Under the harsh atmosphere of conformity, peace advocates became linked to slackers, traitors, socialists, and communists—"portrayed in hues from yellow to red."[48] Although MID claimed to respect conscientious objectors from the Society of Friends (Quakers), they resented "flatulent imitators" who were in actuality demonstrating "cowardice" or "anti-Americanism." MID also kept surveillance of ministers who spoke out against the war, criticized the Red Cross, or spoke of a German victory. (One MID report noted a minister who preached on the "Hellish machinery" and "bloodshed" of war.)[49]

Since the country relied on the American labor force to supply war materials, the MID and government agencies scrutinized the working class, especially focusing on radical unions and socialists organizations. After prolonged surveillance of the IWW (Industrial Workers of the World), MID concluded that "perhaps the majority" of IWW members were "innocent of treason in any form," but others clearly "devoted themselves to evil works" and engaged in "anarchism, and defame[d] the spirit and paralyze [d] the military power of the nation."[50] APL civilian agents aided intelligence officers by keeping close surveillance on labor radicals and illegally raiding IWW meeting and halls. IWW official met with violence and even death at the hands of vigilantes inspired by superpatriotic fervor. The Justice Bureau agents conducted carefully constructed mass raids that led to the arrest of many IWW leaders. The Justice Department used the Espionage act to arrest socialist newspaper editor, Victor Berger; outspoken radicals and antiwar protesters Emma Goldman and Alexander Berkman; and IWW president, "Big Bill" Haywood, Socialists Party of America leader and presidential candidate, Eugene Debs; general secretary of the Socialist Party of America Charles Schenck. Other arrest of radicals included Kate Richards O'Hare, Rose Paster Stokes, and Max Eastman.[51]

Both the government and military kept America's foreign-born communities under intense scrutiny, looking for dissent, countering pro-German propaganda, and ascertaining loyalty. According to MID, loyal immigrants were being bombarded by a "campaign of the most vicious propaganda" by the enemy.[52] The War Department was particularly concerned about German and Irish Americans, but it was also apprehensive of the millions of new immigrants from Southern and Eastern Europe. With little knowledge of the language and culture of the nation's ethnic groups, MID turned to prominent civilian immigrant leaders (after carefully confirming their loyalty) to serve as MID paid or volunteer agents to assist with surveillance of the ethnic communities to help keep out enemy influences. Civilian immigrant agents came from the well-educated, professional class and many were doctors, clergymen, businessmen, or newspaper editors. Immigrant agents also reported any signs of disloyalty in ethnic newspapers, fraternal organizations, or their fellow immigrants. In addition, the War Department promoted bilingual and foreign-born soldiers to serve as MID officers in army camps. "Inside camp" ethnic agents investigated the loyalty of immigrant soldiers, determined whether soldiers understood why they were fighting and made suggestions on how to improve the morale of foreign-born troops.[53]

The Justice Department concluded the enemy was focusing much of its propaganda toward African Americans, and the War Department contended that "emissaries of Germany traveled about with the ambition and the hope of raising negro insurrections throughout the South."[54] Even though the overwhelming majority of the black community supported the American war effort, widespread suspicion and conspiracy stories grew rapidly. Especially common were rumors of German efforts to organize African Americans against the U.S. government. Southern whites' deep-seated racism and fear of a race war along with the increasing Northern racial strain escalated the "spy scare." The Bureau of Intelligence worried that the great migration of African Americans to the North (motivated by horrific treatment in the Jim Crow South and a chance for advancement in the Northern industries) was really a German plot to ignite sedition in that part of the country. A deadly race riot in East Saint Louis, Illinois in July 1917 further worried intelligence agents. It stemmed from accusations of voter fraud and from the hiring of black workers in an all-white factory that needed additional laborers to fulfill government war contracts. A vicious attack by whites on the African-American community started the violence, stopped only by the National Guard. The violence resulted in the deaths of thirty-nine blacks and eight whites. Bureau agents quickly investigated the possibility that "German intrigue" stood behind the conflict.[55]

National protest over the St. Louis race riot from the Black community and a State Department warning that Germans spies had infiltrated Harlem, New York served as a pivotal point for the MID. By August 1917, MID added to their mission the surveillance of African Americans looking for alleged "Negro Subversion." MID agents investigated claims of German agitation, scrutinized the black press, examined the activities of the NAACP (National Association for the Advancement of Colored People), and conducted surveillance of African-American leadership. The military agency also began conferring with Justice Department Bureau Chief Bielaski and working with both his agents and the APL.[56]

To help create a "black counterintelligence system," the War Department turned to Major Walter Howard Loving, a retired African-American military conductor of the Philippine Constabulary, a group that was well known for their many national music performances.[57] Loving organized an intelligence gathering team of African-American leaders who investigated rumors of sedition involving black civilians and soldiers. He also solicited the aid of black intellectuals, ministers, and newspaper editors to inspire loyalty. In his final report, Loving blamed the war for the sharp growth of black radicalism. However, he also spoke frankly when he chastised the U.S. government for their failure to ensure civil rights and warned that returning black soldiers, especially those who experienced "the total absence of color prejudice among Frenchmen...[would]...arouse the most bitter resentment among Negroes throughout the country...The Negro has finally decided that he has endured all that he can endure."[58]

Joe Springarn, the white chairman of the Board of Trustees of the NAACP and now a major in the U.S. Army, also assisted MID by watching out for signs of disloyalty among African Americans. The War Department assigned Springarn to MID in May of 1918, with the responsibly of investigation radicalism and "negro subversion." He accepted the position convinced he could affect government policy and sway black opinion, but recognized that in order to make real change; major barrier had to be broken. This included the government's refusal to deal with black civil-rights issues during the war and Southern hostility to any advancement for African Americans. Springarn also hoped this opportunity would put him in a key position to pressure for an antilynching bill, making the act a federal crime during wartime. As with Loving, Springarn concluded racism, not "pro-Germanism," was the real cause of black "despair." Ultimately, MID's investigations "unearthed no real evidence of enemy subversion targeted at blacks."[59]

The U.S. postmaster general, Albert Sidney Burleson, an antiradical super-patriot and "the foremost official enemy of dissident," used the war acts as powerful weapons against pacifists, radicals, and immigrants—weapons that seriously wounded American civil liberties.[60] Burleson frequently overstep his authority in preventing the mailing of circulars, newspapers, and pamphlets he deemed subversive in his personal crusade for conformity. The Post Office's Bureau M-1 monitored the ethnic, radical, and black press and watched out for "pro-German, anti British, and anti-ally propaganda plus socialists' attacks on capitalism and the government." M-1 also focused on the writings of the WPP, the AUAM, and the IWW.[61]

Burleson refused second-class mailing privileges to many presses forcing small newspapers, which could not afford first-class mail, out of business. Using the Trading with the Enemy Act, he required the editors of ethnic newspapers to supply his office with English translations of all articles and editorials, adding to expenses, delaying publications, and indirectly censoring the ethnic press. Burleson found assistance from more than four hundred volunteers—including college professors who translated the foreign-language presses.[62] The postmaster general justified his actions by exaggerating the definition of sedition and distorting the Espionage Act to control what would be allowed to pass through the nation's post offices. Burleson's attack on radicals promoted socialist leader Norman Thomas to conclude the postmaster general "didn't know socialism from rheumatism."[63]

CENSORSHIP BOARD

Beginning in October 1918, representatives from the CPI, the secretaries of war and navy, the War Trade Board, and the Post Office formed the Censorship Board. The Censorship Board was "concerned primarily with censorship of mail communications from the United States to areas outside the country and control of 'the printing, publication, and distribution of matter in a foreign language.'"[64]

Censorship of the English language press fell under the auspicious of CPI, but generally continued on a voluntary basis. In a pamphlet entitled "Preliminary Statement to the Press of the United States," CPI did, however, provide the press with instructions of what information should not appear in the nation's newspapers. The War Department's chief military censor also kept the American press informed on what areas were strictly off-limits. This included all information related to airplane development and production. The U.S. military's chief of Intelligence Section of the AEF censored newsmen attached to the U.S. military, and the U.S. Navy censored all news concerning war-related naval activities.[65]

The Censorship Board sent representatives to major ports and towns along the border. Of particular concern was the spread of key military information or photographs to the enemy, and the government sought to prevent false rumors from infiltrating into the American public. Presidential Executive Orders gave the War Department authority to censor all overseas telephone and telegraph lines and allowed the U.S. Navy to censor all radio transmissions from wireless stations. The navy and war secretaries regulated use of the telegraph and telephone lines, and the director of the Naval Communication Services censored all submarine cables. MI10 agents in the "Censorship" Section also monitored newspapers, photography, periodicals, telegraphy, and foreign language publications.[66]

The many civil and military agencies involved in censorship, "led to a great deal of confusion, some inefficiency, and considerable friction."[67] Frustrated, the UPA (United Press Association) filed a formal complaint. In it, the UPA listed all the civilian and military agencies involved in censorship. As a result, the War Department designed a plan to centralize the censorship process into one joint civil-military committee; however, the war ended before the change could be made.

CIVIL-MILITARY CONFLICT

Although the military generally worked in harmony with government agencies in matters of counterintelligence work, civil-military relations sometimes resulted in conflict. A somewhat acrimonious relationship also existed between the Office of Naval Intelligence and Army Intelligence and both the military organizations tangled with government intelligence agencies. In their 1918 study of "Propaganda in its Military and Legal Aspects," the War Department's MID Executive Division acknowledged its important and "powerful" partnership with the U.S. Department of Justice in fighting against enemy propaganda. Justice Bureau agents were indispensable in directing military related material to MID. However, military leaders strongly disagreed with key judicial judgments which defined disloyalty. MID was disturbed when the Justice Department dismissed a number of antiwar writings after concluding they did not violate the Espionage and Sedition Acts. Specifically, MID contended that the Department of Justice should have "been embarrassed" by some judicial decisions that dismissed the writings of "hostile propagandists," simply because no specific military information had been given to the enemy. Furthermore, it criticized the Department of Justice's "Interpretations of War Statues," which helped judges and juries determine which propaganda was punishable under the Espionage Act. In response, MID outlined the War Department's opinion of what constituted dangerous dissent and disloyalty. This included propaganda that created "hostile spirits," making it difficult to raise money to fight the war or undermined the morale—"therefore, the fighting power"—of the American troops.

> Of equal military importance is the propaganda that disheartens the people at home. . . . Everything that weakens the determination of the people or its confidence in its army, weakens the determination of the army and its confidence in

its people. Everything that tends to slow up the military activity or the civilian activity, has an instant influence upon the success of the war. Propaganda is, in short, a form of invisible, almost inaudible gas attack, either upon the trenches or far back of the line.[68]

For its part, the Department of Justice feared "that army intelligence was trying to supplant its own investigative prerogatives."[69] The department vigorously opposed an early 1918 congressional bill that would divide the nation into large war zones surrounding factories that produced war-related material and around military training camps. The Justice Department opposed the idea and Attorney General Gregory argued "a drastic measure like military control of large parts of civil society was unnecessary and dangerous."[70] The Justice Bureau also pointed to "overzealous" MID agents who formed a "Volunteer Intelligence Corps" in the Northwest and targeted for destruction of the radical union, the IWW. MID fired back accusing the Justice Department of being too slow in reacting to domestic subversion. The Treasury Department's secret agents and the Justice Department's bureau agents continued to complete and turf wars expanded. Conflict and confusion grew so great between Bureau agents, the Treasury Department Secret Service, ONI, and MID—sometime had to be done. In response, the War Department organized weekly meetings (lead by Justice Department officials) between the civilian and military organizations to share information and coordinate intelligence efforts. In the end, despite the conflicts, the civil-military and "interdepartmental alliances...forged into America's first comprehensive political intelligence system."[71]

THE U.S. ARMY CRUSHES IWW

During the war, the demand for American lumber for wartime construction became acute. Airplane manufacturing particularly relied on Sitka spruce wood from Washington and Oregon, and the maximum production of three million feet per month was wholly inadequate to meet the demands from both the United States and Allied armies. But the lumber industry was plagued with problems. Critical labor shortages began when many of the Northwest loggers left their jobs to serve in the Forestry Engineer regiments with the AEF in Europe. Long hours, fluctuating wages, and horrific working conditions created disgruntled workers among those who remained. The U.S. War Department understood the difficulties, but concluded that such problems created a "sinkhole of discontent in which the I.W.W. delegates and agitators could spawn their anarchistic ideas and ideals, with splendid hope of an excellent breeding ground."[72] A series of IWW strikes and sabotage in protest of the widespread abuses by lumber industry owners in the spring, summer, and fall of 1917 disrupted the production of spruce lumber in the Northwest. But it was the IWW strike in the summer of 1917 which "paralyzed the entire lumber industry region," that served as the last straw for the government and the military.[73]

Debates in Washington on how to respond to IWW activities quickly ended when in September 1917 the Department of Justice conducted raids on western IWW union halls. The arrest of IWW president Bill Haywood along with 166 top IWW officials (under the Espionage Act) dramatically crippled the radical union. MID also stepped in to undermine the radical union. But lumber production shortages did not end. Facing "one of the great problems of the war," the War Department assigned Colonel Brice P. Disque (soon to be general) to find a solution. What resulted was an unprecedented move, as the U.S. Army "placed every [spruce lumbering] operation under military discipline and administration" by creating the Spruce Production Division of the Bureau of Aircraft Production.[74] The War Department searched U.S. training camps for soldiers and officers with experience as loggers and lumbermen, eventually securing some 30,000 men. By October 1917, the army deployed the soldiers in 234 lumber camps on the west coasts of Oregon and Washington.[75]

In an extraordinary move of military intervention, the U.S. military set up its own corporation. Disque served as the commanding officer of the Spruce Division and the president of the newly created United States Spruce Production Corporation. Colonel Cuthbert P. Stearns served as the general's chief of staff and Major Frank D. Erman became the vice president and general manager. The division was further divided into the five production districts under the chief of staff. Additional corporate-military officers served at the rank of major and captain in various capacities (personnel director, surgeon, inspector, quartermaster, chief engineer, military intelligence, and attorney). Officers also headed-up the Sales, Purchasing, and Traffic Departments, and the Spruce Fir Production and Logging and Railway operations. According to the U.S. military:

> This was probably the first time that soldiers of the United States Army were ever used to labor in private industry. It was a radical departure from a custom as old as the nation, but rendered absolutely essential, and was promptly approved by the Secretary of War as a necessary war measure.[76]

The 30,000 officers and rank-and-file soldiers joined some 125,000 civilian workers in the lumber industry. Soldiers in the Spruce Division received the same wages as civilian workers. This meant an increase in pay for the servicemen.[77]

Bringing soldiers into private industry did not come without resistance. Members of the badly weakened IWW resented military interference, and military leaders viewed the union men as an organized "menace" that used the threat of strike and sabotage as a weapon. According to one army report, the IWW hid equipment, removed key parts of machinery, concealed spikes in logs in order to break equipment, and sometimes resorted to blowing up facilities. Government representatives searched for a way to check any further radicalism. The U.S. Army plan was two fold. They improved the "atrocious" conditions found in the industry and created their own "union," the Loyal Legion of Loggers and Lumbermen. According to historian Robert L. Tyler, General Disque designed the legion hoping it "would achieve the mutuality between employer and worker...heal the wounds of the strike and constitute the collective agreement that trade unions depend upon in more favorable climates."[78]

The War Department placed Captain M.E. Crumpacker in charge of organizing the workers and assigned 100 officers to assist (this number grew rapidly). After six months, membership in the Loyalty Legion stood at over 80,000. By October 1918, membership reached 125,000. Each man signed a loyalty oath in which he solemnly pledged to "defend [his] country against enemies both foreign and domestic...[and] stamp out any sedition or acts of hostility against the United States Government."[79]

In order to keep workers morale up and avoid labor strikes disputes, the Spruce Divisions' Industrial Relations Section met frequently with Loyal Legion worker representatives to discuss hours, wages, and camp conditions. Field officers, representing the workers, "inspect the books of the different logging companies and mills" to insure that "labor condition, wage scales, etc. are being complied with." A Central Council and a District Council, made up of workers, officers, and management representatives engaged in "a frank and open discussion" in order to solve all labor issues.[80] This unique labor relationship resulted in the eight-hour day with time and a half for overtime, paid holidays, and improvements in both camp sanitation and living conditions which now included bath houses and reading rooms. The Spruce Division's Lyceum Section served as a "bureau of morale," organizing entertainment including moving picture shows, musical programs, and sports events to raise the spirits of the soldiers and civilian workers. The YMCA, the Knights of Columbus, the War Camp Community Service workers, the American Red Cross, and the American Library Association assisted. Lyceum officers also "preached the gospel of cooperation" whenever possible, and the army also produced and distributed some 90,000 copies of the Loyalty Legion magazine, *The Monthly Bulletin*.[81]

The army considered their first attempt in civilian labor relations a triumph. Production soured, and by April 1918, the Spruce Division produced almost 14,000 feet of lumber a month. When the demand for lumber rose, the division set a goal of 30,000 a month and greatly increased its output accordingly. By war's end, the U.S. Army claimed success in reordering the chaotic lumber industry into a productive machine and reorganizing over 120,000 workers into a much more benign lumberman's union. Disque claimed the success of the Loyal Legion read "almost like an Industrial fairy story." The general proudly concluded "strikes sedition and sabotage were wholly eliminated," and the influences of the radicalism was "reduced to a minimum where not completely nullified."[82]

CONCLUSION

During World War I, the government's Committee on Public Information's propaganda campaign, designed to inspire support for the war and prevent enemy propaganda from infiltrating American society, ultimately helped to fuel a superpatriotic atmosphere that quickly escalated into mass hysteria, clear violations of civil liberties, and the demand for "100 percent Americanism." Officials used the Espionage and Sedition Acts to silence dissenters, and trample the First Amendment. The blatant misuse of war acts led to social turmoil. As noted by historian Harry Scheiber, the Alien Act served as "the capstone of a long succession of laws which removed those legal guarantees traditionally enjoyed by Americans against the arbitrary action of hysteria or irresponsible government officials."[83]

Fearing enemy infiltration and dangerous dissent, the U.S. government and the War Department cooperated in their propaganda, censorship, and counterintelligence efforts. This civil-military cooperation was unprecedented, and although acrimonious at times, the collaboration was generally effective. But civil-military efforts also ignited the jingoist spirit, led to abuses of civil liberties and fueled public hysteria. Constitutional scholar Zechariah Chafee, Jr. summarized this time period as "the greatest executive restriction of personal liberty in the history of this country."[84] At war's end, the hysteria that made so many suspects to the American cause did not simply disappear. In fact, much of the emotion of the day was redirected into a Red Scare—an early twentieth century witch-hunt to purge the country of "dangerous" radicals, and close the door to mass immigration with the 1924 National Origins Act.

4

Over There: Science, Technology, and Modern Warfare

The Industrial Revolution in the late nineteenth and early twentieth centuries resulted in innovative technological inventions that brought both progress and tragedy to the United States. America, like Europe, sought progress in the machine age. Mass production of consumer goods; improvements in communication and mass transit; recent development in petroleum, chemical, and steel; and new corporate management theories resulted in the rapid modernization of the nation. Exciting inventions such as the telephone, gramophone, and automobile, along with electricity and motion pictures, transformed the country. The increased migration of rural Americans combined with the massive immigration of primarily Southern and Eastern Europeans resulted in the extraordinary growth of cities. However, urban areas quickly became crowded, unsanitary, and disease ridden. An often poor national market forced many into a family economy, escalating the number of women and children who joined men in working long hours for low pay, often in dangerous jobs. A significant distortion in the country's distribution of wealth put a relatively small number of industrialists and financiers in a position far above the economically disadvantaged masses.

The Industrial Revolution also changed the nature of warfare. As the first decade of the new century came to a close, the extraordinary force of machine power would astonish the world and result in a prolonged World War—a war with unprecedented destruction and a shocking loss of life. Between 1914 and 1918, the Industrial Revolution brought not progress, but death. Ultimately, almost fourteen million died and twenty-two million were wounded during the Great War. Over sixty-five million men became locked in mortal combat against deadly engines of war. Modern "machine" armaments, air power, and chemical weapons created a total war sending millions of soldiers into the muddy, lice filled, and rat infested trenches, creating a "no man's land" between the opposing armies. As the long stalemate continued, commanding officers sent soldier after soldier up against machine guns, artillery, tanks, and poison gases, resulting in mass slaughter. World navies attacked each other on seas with well-armed battleships, cruisers, and destroyers and under the ocean with submarine torpedoes.

When the United States entered the war in April 1917, the War Department faced overwhelming obstacles in their attempt to supply some four million soldiers with equipment and modern weapons. With the War Department's rush to be combat ready, the military worked directly with prominent American inventors, chemists, physicists, physicians, and psychiatrists. The result was a new and expanded civil-military relationship. Despite best efforts, it took time for the military to select the best available armaments and procure them with American companies. Many American weapon manufacturers were already committed to European war contracts, and time was needed for other industries to retool for war-related production. Delays forced the American Army to rely greatly on Allied equipment to help defeat the enemy. When U.S. troops arrived at the front lines, they quickly learned the devastating consequences of the union between the Industrial Revolution and war—especially as the number of wounded and dead mounted.

MECHANIZED WEAPONS

Prewar Europe saw widespread militarization as empires stocked new mass-produced industrial weapons—weapons with extraordinary killing power. When the Allies and Central Powers did battle in 1914, they arrived equipped with lethal machines of war. This included massive artillery— the "highly efficient, quick-firing engine of destruction"—capable of discharging high-velocity explosive, chemical, and shrapnel shells.[1] Artillery bombardment could destroy machine gun nests, break apart enemies' strongholds, cut barb wire protecting the trenches, and supply smoke screens to hide advancing troops. Both sides had millions of rounds of artillery ammo. The French fired 4.5 million rounds per month by 1916. The Germans used of eight million rounds of ammunition per month by 1918. Yet the amounts proved insufficient and home front manufacturers rushed to produce more.[2]

The heavy mortar Howitzers proved particularly frightening, with names like the Paris Gun, Big Bertha, and Long Max. The best Howitzers had the capability to hurl half ton shells into the air landing up to seventy miles away. Small metal balls inside Shrapnel shells fired from 75-mm guns scattered over the battlefield inflicted multiple wounds. Rail guns equipped with firing platforms allowed the enormous guns to recoil along a rail after firing shells weighing thousands of pounds more than thirty miles into enemy territory. In 1914, the French came to battle with over 3,800 75-mm guns,

but German artillery power proved stronger with 5,086 77-mm field guns
and 2,280 Howitzers. Trench Mortars (tube-like guns that could be shot at
an angle) dropped cylindrical bombs directly on top of the enemy trenches.
Ordnance Pounders delivered shrapnel balls some 500 yards, and the
Sixty-Pounders sent (sixty pound) shells over 10,000 yards. As the war continued, the number of artillery weapons expanded by the thousands on both
sides. The British production lagged behind, but in 1918, the British army
had the capability of firing 3,200 Howitzers and over 3,240 light guns on
the enemy. According to historian David Zabecki, by 1917, modern artillery
"became a blunt instrument for the indiscriminate hammering of entire
patches of real estate. The main function of artillery on the battle field had
become destruction and annihilation."[3]

Despite the best efforts of military and civilian Preparedness advocates,
the United States held firm to its belief in a small standing army. Once the
nation entered the war, it dramatically increased it forces using citizen-
soldiers. Drafting, training, and equipping an army took time. Therefore,
when the AEF (American Expeditionary Force) first joined the Allies in
France, they came with an insufficient amount of men and weapons. Despite
best efforts by the War Department's artillery and ordnance officers and
American manufacturers, the United States never fully overcame various
structural obstacles in the production of artillery (and other weapons).
Therefore, arrangements were made to ship steel to France manufacturers
who produced 3,000 75-mm and other large guns for the AEF, and throughout the war, United States relied primarily on French-made artillery.[4]

Grenades and flamethrowers also joined the battlefield. German planners
saw the advantage of the grenade and stockpiled some 70,000 hand grenades
and over 10,000 rifle grenades by 1914. The British soon stormed ahead by
mass producing an average of 250,000 grenades per week. Both the British
and Germans made maximum use of grenades by attacking in groups or
bombing parties. "The flamethrower, introduced by the French in the
Argonne Forest in the fall of 1914 and perfected by the Germans, offered
instant cremation."[5]

The invention of the internal combustion engine led to the design and
manufacture of thousands of tanks. Tanks, such as the German A7V, the
British Mark series, and the French Renault FT, had the capability of
traversing through difficult terrain, maneuvering over massive potholes left
by artillery shells, and climbing over barbed wire. Tanks also protected
advancing infantry. The Allies' far superior numbers of tanks gave them an
advantage; however, the large machines were slow moving, clumsy, and
particularly unreliable, since they often broke down. When working—and
armed with machine guns—tanks were very effective. On the naval front,
submarines terrorized the oceans. Mines sunk ships and eliminated submarines. Cruisers, subchasers, and destroyers fought on the seas along with
enormous battleships equipped with massive artillery guns. The U.S. Navy,

a small force by European standards, transported and protected American soldiers heading to the front. But more than half of the Doughboys arrived on British and French ships. By war's end, the U.S. Navy patrolled the seas with 373 vessels.[6]

MACHINE GUNS

The union between the Industrial Revolution and war brought about a deadly automatic direct-fire infantry weapon—the machine gun—that changed the nature of combat. During the First World War, the machine gun's devastating destruction forced soldiers into trenches stretching hundreds of miles, and attempts to go "over the top" resulted in extraordinary loss of human lives.

Although American inventors developed the first successful automatic rapid fire "machines" in the late nineteenth century, the U.S. military made minimum advancements in applying these weapons to modern warfare by 1917. During the Civil War, the Union Army generally showed limited interest in Richard Jordan Gatling's "Gatling Gun," a hand-driven, crank operated, rapid fire weapon. But Union General Benjamin Butler personally purchased twelve Gatling Guns and used them successfully toward the end of the Civil War. During the preceding Indian Wars, the U.S. Army did use Gatling Guns on the frontier. In the early 1880s, Maine-born Hiram Maxim designed the first truly automatic machine gun which fired 500 shots a minute using a water-cooling system. Although the American military did not pay a great deal of attention, other countries soon adopted the new weapon into their growing arsenal. In England, the Vickers Company manufactured the Maxim machine gun, and, after buying out the company (with Maxim as director), the weapon eventually became known as the Vickers. In 1895, American John Moses Browning introduced the gas-operated machine gun and continued to design more effective machine weapons. The U.S. Army eventually used an improved model of the Gatling Gun in the Spanish-American War, but the military "persisted in writing it off as little more than an ordinance novelty that burned ammunition and boiled like a steam engine."[7]

Research and development of new weapons suffered a major blow with post-Spanish-American War military budget cuts, which further delayed the updating of the U.S. Army's arsenal. In the early 1900s, General John T. Thompson attempted to transform and modernize the Army's Ordnance Department. He clearly connected mechanization with modern warfare. Thompson argued that the nations with superior firepower would have the advantage in future conflicts, and openly disagreed with the War Department's reluctance to embrace the machine gun. But the general had little success, and when he retired, no one took over his causes. Europe's massive militarization helped to push American weapons inventors overseas where

they could obtain research funds, find interested manufacturers, and supply
a ready market.[8]

By 1909, the U.S. military had several hundred Maxim machine guns and a
larger stock of Hotchkiss Benet-Mercie Machine Rifles (a French designed
weapon made at an American owned company in Europe). But the immense
weight of most of the machine guns restricted its use and constrained further
purchases as did congressional financial resistance to prepare the nation for
possible war. Since the tactical value of the machine gun was unclear, and
without general grade officers championing its use, the U.S. Army assigned
only four machine guns per regiment. However, by 1915 as the machine
gun clearly took center stage in the war in Europe, the U.S. secretary of war
created a joint board of officers and civilians to study the weapon and make
recommendations. Eventually, the board recommended the purchase of over
4,500 newly improved Vickers heavy-type machine guns and planned to
test the new Lewis gun—a lightweight, air-cooled weapon named after its
American inventor, Colonel I.N. Lewis—for possible adoption. However,
America entered the war before tests took place. The Marlin Machine Gun
Model 1918 invented under the leadership of the Marlin brothers (sons
of the well-known Connecticut gun inventor John M. Marlin), promised to
be an important addition to American aircraft, and 38,000 came into
production before war's end.[9]

When America joined the world conflict in April 1917, the army had only
1,100 operating machine guns—670 Benet-Mercie machine rifles, 282
Maxim Model 1904s, and 148 Colt-Browning weapons. In comparison,
Germany started with over 50,000 machine guns in 1914. When working
effectively, the modern rapid fire machine gun could outpower 80 rifles
and spewed 600 bullets per minute. By the end of the war, improvements
in the weapon allowed it to fire more than 1,200 bullets per minute. Set
against an advancing army, the machine gun fire led to nothing less than
mass slaughter. Placed together in a corps, the weapon proved even deadlier.
Although the weight of the guns prevented easy portability by manpower,
machine guns mounted on tanks and aircraft increased their diversity.[10]

Once the United States committed to the European conflict, Benedict
Crowell, the American assistant secretary of war and the director of Munitions, ordered additional machines guns. But production was hampered by
the limited number of American companies manufacturing the rapid fire
weapon—and those who did were already overwhelmed by French and
British orders. Therefore, the U.S. Army's First Division arrived in France
with an insufficient number of weapons, and the French government stepped
in to better equip the American soldiers. Throughout the war, the U.S. Army
Ordnance Department continued to test various improved machine gun
designs and placed tens of thousands of orders for new models. It took time
for American manufacturers to put the weapons into full production, compelling the United States to continue to rely on Allied weapons. At wars end,

the United States had placed over 288,000 machine gun orders. According to Crowell, the total production of machine guns and machine rifles manufactured between April 6, 1917 and November 11, 1918 by U.S. manufacturers eventually exceeded 181,600.[11]

WAR TAKES TO THE SKIES

War in Europe began only ten years after the Wright brothers' successful flight at Kitty Hawk, but technology and the use of the plane changed quickly with the rapid expansion of the industrial age. In response to the use of the airplane in battle, Orville Wright lamented, "We thought we were introducing into the world an invention that would make future wars practically impossible."[12] At the start of World War I, military leaders saw the plane as only good for observation and reconnaissance—an improvement over hot air balloons. But soon, waves and smiles between enemy pilots photographing troop positions turned ugly, and exchanges between flyboys turned to throwing bricks, ropes, and grenades. By October 1914, planes armed with machine guns moved the destructive nature of war into the sky, and air combat ruptured over the front lines. By January 1915, pilots began dropping high-explosive bombs on enemy soldiers below. Ace pilots quickly became folk heroes, but the reality of being in the air service was a short life expectancy—most of the pilots who died in battle were in their early twenties. "Only one pilot in every fifteen had a better than even chance of surviving his first decisive combat—but after five such encounters, his probability of surviving increased by a factor of *twenty*."[13]

In the United States, a lack of congressional funding and the military's failure to understand the importance of air power in war left the country far behind the race to dominate the skies. In his evaluation of U.S. military aviation at the start of the war, the commander of the AEF, General John J. Pershing, noted the "very primitive state" of the nation's aviation. The situation was so bleak that the general concluded, "Every American ought to feel mortified to hear it mentioned."[14] Once America declared war, Congress allocated money to build planes, and the military began training thousands of pilots. In May 1917, the U.S. Air Service had only fifty-five planes, but none were adequately prepared for combat. Due to industrial delays, only 12,000 airplanes—half of the requested number—were produced forcing the United States to acquire planes from the French. America began with three Air Service squadrons flying noncombat ready plane but expanded to forty-five squadrons flying war-ready aircraft. By November 1918, the United States had 11,425 officers (4,307 serving with the AEF). The U.S. Army Air Service shot down 755 enemy planes, and lost 357 U.S. planes in combat. Most of the 677 American deaths came from plane accidents in the United States and Europe. One third of all American pilots who flew over the fields of France were killed in action.[15]

CHEMICAL WARFARE

At the first Hague Peace Conference in 1899, twenty-six nations resolved to prohibit the use of asphyxiating gas in military conflicts. All the major European countries signed the agreement; however, Captain (later rear admiral) Alfred T. Mahan, head of the U.S. representatives, refused. Mahan, a prominent theorist of sea power, played a key role in the modernization of the American navy beginning in the late nineteenth century. During the Hague Conference, Mahan asserted that the death of men by asphyxiation from drowning after a submarine torpedo attack or after a gas attack was probably similar, and he even implied gas was perhaps a more humane weapon.[16]

When war began in 1914, both sides called for a quick decisive offense. Unfortunately, the powerful enemies had both the economic capability and modern weaponry for a long drawn out conflict. As the war deteriorated into deadlock, both the Allied and Central Powers violated the Hague agreement. During the summer and fall of 1914, the French Army tried intermittently and unsuccessfully to open land areas by delivering tear gas in 26-mm rifle grenades with no visible effect on the German soldiers. The French soon gave up on the ineffective grenades. But at the Kaiser Wilhelm Institute for Physical Chemistry and Electrochemistry in Berlin, scientists scurried to develop shells and cylinders to deliver deadly weapons. Germany responded in January 1915 with tear gas against the Russians and in March 1915 against the British. But the brutality of lethal gas weapons became apparent in April 1915, against the French and their colonial (Algerian) troops in Ypres, Belgium. The latter attack released 6,000 cylinders of chlorine gas (a by-product of the dye industry) which caught 20,000 troops off guard and resulted in the death of some 5,000 men. "The soldiers literally drowned in their lungs' own fluid, released in reaction to the damaging effects of chlorine."[17] A British eyewitness recorded the chaos and despair of the French troop during the German gas attack at Ypres:

> Utterly unprepared for what was to come, the [French] divisions gazed for a short while spellbound at the strange phenomenon they saw coming slowly toward them. Like some liquid the heavy-coloured [sic] vapor poured relentlessly into the trenches, filled them, and passed on. For a few seconds nothing happened; the sweet-smelling stuff merely tickled their nostrils; they failed to realize the danger. Then, with inconceivable rapidity, the gas worked, and blind panic spread. Hundreds, after a dreadful fight for air, became unconscious and died where they lay—a death of hideous torture, with the frothing bubbles gurgling in their throats and the foul liquid welling up in their lungs. With blackened faces and twisted limbs one by one they drowned—only that which drowned them came from inside and not from out.[18]

Two days later, German forces gassed Canadian troops. In May, the British troops became victim to several German gas attacks with mixed results due to wind shifts and the use of crude gas masks.

Response to the spring chemical attacks from the American media was mixed. Both the *Chicago Tribune* and the *New York Evening Sun* saw poison gas as a more civilized weapon than other forms of warfare. The *Sun* went as far as to equate gas weapons with the success of the scientific community and a victory for chemists. As historian Hugh Slotten noted, "For some Americans, in fact, their characterization of gas as a humane weapon grew out of their faith in the inevitable progress of science. Modern war would be more humane simply because it was becoming more scientific."[19] However, other newspapers expressed revulsion. The *New York Times* rebuked the Germans for unleashing the new barbaric weapon, and the *San Francisco Chronicle* pointed out the fine line between scientific advancement and a return to "savagery and barbarity of primitive society."[20]

After the German gas attacks at Ypres, the French and British made the decision to retaliate in order to keep up the morale of the troops. The Allies struck back with deadly gas artillery shells near Loos, Belgium in September 1915 by unleashing 5,500 cylinders filled with some 150 tons of chlorine, supplemented with a smoke screen. The gas caused much confusion, jammed military equipment, and penetrated gas masks—the race for new chemical weapons had begun. Eventually, scientists would develop over fifty types of chemical weapons.[21]

Germany's prewar domination of the chemical and dye industries translated into superiority in poison gas during the war. European chemists now toiled to make effective gas masks and manufacture highly toxic gases such as phosgene and hydrogen cyanide. The irritant diphenylchlorarsine made soldiers sneeze and vomit. Mustard gas "burned out the lungs if breathed and raised huge, painful blisters on exposed skin; many were blinded by it."[22] Administered in liquid form, it penetrated clothing and boots and poisoned soldiers even when wearing gas masks. The poisonous residue could theoretically last up to twenty-five years. Chemical warfare—now used by both the Allies and the Central Powers—joined the arsenals of the world powers causing unspeakable horrors.

AMERICAN CHEMISTS

As war escalated in Europe, key American military and political leaders began to argue for the expansion and modernization of the U.S. military. But the research and development of gas weapons was not part of the conversation. Since war news was filtered through the British, Americans received graphic details of Germany's brutal gas attacks. However, once the Allied retaliated in kind; the British provided only limited information on chemical warfare and eventually blacked out all related news. Lack of knowledge about gas warfare and the "perception that chemical warfare was somehow inhumane and sullied the honor of the professional soldiers" resulted in little action by the American military. A November

1915 U.S. Army War College report did not address gas warfare despite knowledge of the German poisonous gas attacks in Belgium. Nor did chemical research play a role in the June 1916 National Defense Act. In addition, despite reports arriving from American medical officers (sent to observe the French and British Army medical personnel) noting the Allies attempts to heal gas attack survivors, the surgeon general did not take action. As historian Charles E. Heller noted, "Thus on the eve of the American intervention, the army acted as if it had barely heard of chemical warfare."[23]

During the later nineteenth and early years of the twentieth centuries, the American academic community transformed as the connection between science and industry strengthened and resulted in many new inventions. Scientists conducted research for specific purposes, but the era also offered the opportunity for scientists to conduct pure research—research for its own sake. In addition, Progressive ideals that encouraged public service influenced scientists who saw themselves "duty-bound...to devote [their] energies to the good of society," and the National Academy of Science rewarded scientists for accomplishments in "socially responsible work."[24] This new public role expanded the status of chemists beyond the academic community and gave them a national voice. The American Chemical Society used this voice to lobby for a scientific agenda. This included the chemists' push to replace the dwindling supply of foreign dyes with American made organic dyes—thus promoting a new industry. The scientific community also pushed for gas warfare research.

From 1914 to 1917, the role of scientists expanded as they studied the world conflict and discussed the responsibility that came with the militarization of science. In early 1917, the American Chemical Society and the Bureau of Mines conducted a census and collected data on America's chemists. This list soon proved invaluable. The nation's chemists clearly understood the devastating effects of chemical weapons. They also knew Germany's scientific superiority had turned the war into "a struggle between the industrial chemical and chemical engineering genius of the Central Powers and that of the rest of the world."[25] Once America entered the war in April 1917, many chemists considered it patriotic to help defeat the enemy. Although the war no doubt interrupted the individual research of the scientists, many hoped their wartime accomplishments would lead to industrial growth, national reorganization, and postwar funding. While some chemists enlisted, others argued they would play a much more important role in university laboratories. According to the *Literary Digest,* when the military asked leading scientists from universities and industry for help, only one chemist refused to work in developing gas weapons.[26]

In order to become war-ready, the army first turned to the Department of Interior's Bureau of Mines for help. Prior to 1917, the Bureau, a civilian organization, conducted most of the research on poison gas in order to protect mine workers and had connections with top scientists in academia throughout the United States. The director, Van H. Manning, suggested a miner's rescue device, a self-contained breathing apparatus, could be developed into a gas mask. The bureau's facilities also included a test chamber. Next, the War Department established Washington, DC's American University as their chemical development headquarters, and placed James Conant in charge of a team of scientists. (Conant would later direct the Manhattan atomic bomb project.) By spring 1918, American troops were engaged in battle on the Western Front. As casualties mounted, the military committed one out of four field hospitals exclusively to treating soldiers suffering from gas attacks. (Ultimately, over one fourth of AEF casualties came from chemical weapons.) On the front, "the chaos became so great and the AEF gas casualties so numerous that, on 28 June 1918, President Woodrow Wilson authorized the establishment of a Chemical Warfare Service as a separate branch of the AEF."[27] At first, chemists' feared working under the military would prove inefficient. But the new civil-military relationship succeeded and the American chemists joined the chemical arms race to produce effective, paralyzing gasses. Soon, American University housed between 1,200 and 1,700 scientists in war-related laboratories located in fifty buildings. Over 700 prominent names in the field, along with less experienced chemists labored at American University and twenty other universities, including Johns Hopkins, Harvard, Yale, Princeton, Columbia, Cornell, Massachusetts Institute of Technology, and Catholic University. In addition, some 1,100 helpers assisted the chemists.[28]

Scientists working under the Chemical Warfare Service (headed by Colonel George Burrell, a former civilian chemist) labored to synthesize materials, check their potency, and test the gasses before sending them out for production. Delays in manufacturing occurred because of a lack of companies willing to produce the hazardous weapon and an insufficient number of laborers willing to work under such dangerous conditions. Many other companies could not consider taking a chemical weapon contract from the government, since they were rushing to complete other war-related contracts. This forced the War Department to build its own plants to make the needed chemicals at places like Gunpowder Neck and Edgewood, Maryland. Scientists produce chlorine, phosgene, mustard, and other powerful chemicals. By the end of the war, Edgewood Arsenal manufactured thirty tons of mustard gas daily. But much of the gases went unused due to the army's lack of artillery shells needed to deliver the chemical to the enemy. American chemicals dropped on the enemy's front lines often came in the form of French and British shells. American chemists also worked on "incendiary bombs, smoke funnels, smoke screens, smoke grenades, colored rockets, gas projectors, and flame throwers, [as well as] thermal methods of combating gas poison, gases for balloons and other materials directly or indirectly connected with gas warfare."[29]

THE DEW OF DEATH

In 1918, the United States developed its own deadly gas weapon. Julius Aloysius Nieuwland, a priest studying for his doctorate in chemistry at Catholic University in Washington, DC, inadvertently produced a toxic substance while experimenting with acetylene in 1903. In 1917, Winford Lee Lewis, the head of chemical weapons research at Catholic University's Chemical Warfare Service, learned about the experiment from the priest's former thesis director. Lewis, with the assistance of Conant, purified the chemical compound into a new poison—Lewisite (named after Lewis). Further experiments took place under the direction of Conant at American University, but despite some concerns over the possible breakdown of the chemical, the new weapon went into production. As with mustard gas, Lewisite in a liquid substance promised devastating results, since death would come quickly to anyone who inhaled or touched even a small amount (less than a teaspoon). Lewisite was an "oily, faintly yellow liquid that caused painful blistering when applied to the skin and severely damaged the eyes and respiratory system. Because of its arsenic content, a small quantity inhaled or dropped on the skin could readily cause death."[30] Tests indicated the possibility of it being less effective when dropped as a vapor cloud. The American military planned to deliver the new weapon to the enemy either in artillery shells or release by airplanes, and Lewis envisioned the new cloud-weapon like a "dew of death" would fall across the battlefield.

Beginning in July 1918, in a secret location (Willoughby, Ohio) soldiers toiled day and night to manufacture Lewisite. Production peaked in November 1918 at some ten tons a day. But the war ended before America could use the weapon in battle. After the war, the Chemical Warfare Service took the gas cylinders out to sea and unloaded them. Although Nieuwland never intended to assist in the creation of a chemical weapon, both he and Lewis concluded it was more humane to use gas in war than other weapons, since there was a chance surviving with gas masks. In a 1936 interview, Nieuwland, by then a professor of chemistry at the University of Notre Dame, maintained, "In biblical times, thousands of men met in the middle of a plain and slashed one another until only a few were left standing. Today, the primary aim is not to kill but to incapacitate. And poison gas is an ideal method of achieving that aim."[31]

GAS MASKS

Perfecting the gas mask took time. British scientist replaced the first crudely made mask composed of a cotton pad dipped in hyposulphite to counter gas attacks. The pad was easily lost in battle and quickly dried out. The second design—a helmet style mask—was not as effective on all gases and was hot and stuffy. The masks also obstructed vision. Since soldiers often did not wear their gas masks in hot weather, both the Allies and Central Powers primarily executed gas attacks during the summer for maximum causalities. Other gas mask designs followed, some taking their cue from miner masks. A more comfortable mask filtered poisonous gas through a box worn on the chest, and allowed soldiers to breathe through a mouthpiece. A rubberized cloth protected the face and eyes, and a nose clip went over the nose. Eventually, the British developed a more effective box filtering system using a treated charcoal from fruit pits and nuts.[32]

Shortly after entering the war, the U.S. War Department turned George Burrell, who at the time was working for the Bureau of Mines, to design an effective gas mask. The General Staff put pressure on Burrell and the bureau's Research Laboratory since some 25,000 masks were needed for troops immediately. Once manufactured, the War Department sent the masks to the British for inspection. But examiners rejected the masks as defective. Clearly a new and more effective gas mask was needed. In April 1918, American scientists finally designed an effective gas mask based on the British SBR model, but full production did not occur until one month before the end of the war. Therefore, for most of America's participation in the war, the War Department utilized millions of gas masks purchased from the British and French. Eventually, warning sirens alerted soldiers to don masks. But in reality, even sirens and effective gas masks were no match against the destructive powers of chemical warfare. Unlike vapor gas, mustard gas, delivered in liquid form by artillery shells and bombs, did not completely dissipate for several days. In damp weather, the gas lingered for up to a week or longer. The liquid also burned skin and blinded eyes. After a gas attack, a sighted soldier leading a long line of blinded men became a common site at medical aid stations. Since mustard gas penetrated clothing, researchers experimented with improving materials used for uniforms, and hundreds of oiled gloves and suits arrived at the front in hopes of protecting artillery soldiers who handled Allied mustard gas weapons. Mobile degassing units, overseen by medical gas officers, stood ready to assist the casualties, and tank trucks attempted to decontaminate the toxic ground. Since consumed food exposed to mustard gas would burn the soldiers' stomachs, troops were supplied with tarred paper to protect supplies.[33]

GAS DEFENSE TRAINING

When the United States sent its First Division overseas without proper gas defense education, General Pershing quickly realized that such training must take place in France. He asked the War Department to create an overseas Gas Service, based on the British Special Brigade. Within days of its authorization in August 1917, the General Staff appointed Lieutenant Colonel Amos A. Fries as the director of the Gas Services of the AEF. Fries studied British and French materials and spent time with the British Special Brigade. Without an American chemical doctrine and short of equipment, the officer of the new

AEF Gas Services struggled to succeed. Meanwhile, unprepared for gas warfare, casualties mounted among American soldiers in the AEF. Back on the home front the newly created Medical Department's Gas Defense Service began training a small handful of inexperienced officers. Lack of equipment, limited printed material, inadequate training, and rumors of ghastly deaths at the hand of Germany's chemical weapons forced the War Department to turn to the British for assistance. Starting in October 1917, the British gas experts, under the direction of Major S.J.M. Auld, trained the American Gas Defense officers, provided educational pamphlets, and convinced the War Department to remove responsibility from the Surgeon General's Medical Department to a combat branch. In January 1918, the Army Corps of Engineers took over. The War Department also followed Auld's advice and established the Army Gas School at Camp A.A. Humphrey in Virginia for gas officers, who learned how to use the gas mask, to detect gas, and to dig proper trenches. Auld also assigned the first group of enlisted American chemists to be trained as gas officers. Still, even with these improvements, most American troops did not receive gas defense training until they arrived in France.[34]

Despite eventual improvements in training, problems occurred. In February 1918 the First Division of the AEF, while occupying the Ansauville sector, began to bombard the enemy lines with cyanogen chloride and phosgene gas weapons. On February 26, the German artillery responded by launching a massive gas attack on American soldiers from the Eighteenth Infantry. Total chaos followed as soldiers scrambled to put on their masks. As panic erupted, some soldiers accidentally knocked off the masks of their comrades as they rushed to secure their own protection. Wet masks proved worthless. One officer took off his mask to warn the men they were removing their equipment too soon, and quickly succumbed to gas poisoning. The initial attack resulted in 37 percent casualties. Problems continued even after the shelling subsided and causalities mounted. General Robert Lee Bullard, the commander of the First Division, explained:

> It appears that certain noncommissioned officers permitted men under their command to remove their masks within a half hour after the last gas shells fell. It also appears that after daylight some men were permitted to work in the vicinity of the shelled area without wearing gas masks, and men who inhaled small quantities of gas were not required to rest quietly. These failures to carry out existing orders on the subject have resulted in increased causalities of this gas attack about 50%.[35]

Soldiers also fell ill the following morning after eating food contaminated by the chemical weapons.[36]

PHYSICISTS AND FLASH AND SOUND RANGING

Physicists also played a key role in World War I, and this new civil-military relationship proved quite successful. Since enemy artillery could be placed up to five miles from the front and still effectively deliver its deadly payload, pinpointing its location became imperative. In June 1917, General Pershing cabled the War Department requesting the help of American physicists. Since 1916, the National Academy of Sciences had been studying sound and flash ranging when it created the NRC (National Research Council). On the recommendation of NRC, the War Department selected Princeton University professor Augustus "Gus" Trowbridge and made him a major in the Signal Corps Reverse. The physicist's ability to speak French served as an asset when he met with the French scientists in July 1917 to learn more about the skill of tracking enemy artillery using powerful telescopes, microphones, and other sound equipment. After visiting the front lines in September 1917 with distinguished Harvard physicists, Theodore Lyman, Trowbridge and now Captain Lyman finalized decisions on how to equip and organize an AEF ranging service. The NRC assisted in the process. The council began by requesting the transfer of engineers from the American Ambulance Serve to join newly enlisted physicists. Harvard also created a ranging school to assist with training.[37]

In March 1918, the well-trained Twenty-ninth Engineers arrived at St. Mihiel along with new sound and ranging equipment. The American SRS (Sound Ranging Section) team did so well; the French were able to remove their physicists and engineers to other locations. "After just a few weeks in field, SRS No. 1 was pinpointing guns that French sections had been unable to locate even approximately, and the rangers could report the location of a new gun within three or four minutes after the first boom."[38] Once reporting the location, American artillery bombarded the enemy target. In June, Pershing ordered Captain Lyman and the SRS No. 2 and FRS (Flash Ranging Section) No. 1 to the Marne. Despite some weather problems the two teams successfully discovered the position of ninety-six enemy batteries. In July at Chateau-Thierry, FRS No. 1 suffered from shell and gas attacks and lost seven men. Still, the Flash Range team performed well, locating thirty-four enemy batteries. Power struggles and disputes over equipment between Trowbridge and the army continued throughout the war. However, the SRS and FRS teams—now in high demand—excelled in the fields of France. The teams also assisted the Military Intelligence staff with battle mapping.[39]

MILITARY PHYSICIANS AND THE INFLUENZA CRISIS

The War Department considered the new civil-military relationships between weapons inventors, chemists, and physicists a success, but the inter-action between the military and those in the medical field resulted in much tension. By the early twentieth century major medical improvements began to transform public health. New technology, germ theory, pasteurization, and improvements in sanitation soon lowered death rates, increased infant survival, and allowed physicians and scientists to make progress in their war against cholera, dysentery, typhoid, and other deadly diseases. Medical research universities and teaching hospitals produced a new generation of scientifically trained physicians. Military physicians joined civilian doctors in celebrating the new era. The vast improvements in scientific medicine created a "sense of pride" and "self-worth" among Army Medical Department officers. They saw themselves "as members of a modern industrial nation that was stepping onto the world stage. With new scientific tools to fight disease, the medical profession took steps to consolidate its authority and power in society, and medical officers likewise sought to reinforce their status."[40]

According to historian Carol R. Byerly, "civilian physicians suffered culture shock when they joined the army, losing many of their freedoms and rights and having to obey orders."[41] In addition, military medicine was proved to be very different from civilian medicine. The new recruits experienced great difficulty balancing their civilian medical training that taught them to see their "mission as humanitarian" with a radically different military mission—war. The War Department insisted that the first priority of the medical physician was to maintain the potency of the army in the nation's training camps and in the battlefields of France. While the medical officers saw each ill or wounded soldier as individual patients, the military took a collective "mass entity" approach to medicine—that "reduced soldiers to units in the war machine."[42]

In an attempt to stop the spread of disease in the nation's army training camps and subsequently to overseas troops, military physicians provided vaccinations to keep the men in uniform healthier. They also called for the creation of strict sanitation regulation. The biggest stain between the War Department and military doctors came when the latter elicited the help of the American Medical Association and congressional leadership in their fight against overcrowding in training camp and troop ships—environments prime for a pandemic. Military physicians struggle escalated into a congressional investigation, forcing the War Department on the defense, and angering high-ranking military officials. But civil-military tension quickly gave way to shock as an extraordinary epidemic shook the nation. Soon, "the influenza virus exploited conditions in military camps, battlefields, and trenches to transform from a common winter ailment dangerous only to the infirm, into a lethal disease that could sicken at least a quarter of all people it came in contact with and could kill even the very strongest."[43] The deadly flu quickly spread throughout the nation and across the seas to Europe to overwhelm both ally and enemy troops. The medical doctors' failure to convince the War Department to improve camp and ship transports helped the virus strengthen, mutate, and multiply—with no cure in sight. In a letter addressed to a fellow physician, a medical doctor assigned to Camp Deven described the devastation,

These men start with what appears to be an ordinary attack of LaGrippe of Influenza, and when brought to the Hosp. they very rapidly develop the most viscous type of Pneumonia that has ever been seen. Two hours after admission they have the Mahogany spots over the cheek bones, and a few hours later you can begin to see the Cyanosis extending from their ears and spreading all over the face, until it is hard to distinguish the coloured [sic] men from the white. It is only a matter of a few hours then until death comes, and it is simply a struggle for air until they suffocate. It is horrible. One can stand it to see one, two or twenty men die, but to see these poor devils dropping like flies sort of gets on your nerves. We have been averaging about 100 deaths per day, and still keeping it up. There is no doubt in my mind that there is a new mixed infection here, but what I don't know.[44]

Ultimately the 1918 epidemic resulted in the death of more civilians and soldiers in one year than the total of those killed in the four years of the Great War. Estimates of deaths worldwide vary from twenty million to fifty million people—making the Influenza Epidemic of 1918 the most destructive on record.[45]

"DEATH IS A MIGHTY BIG RELIEF FROM ALL THIS HELL"

Modern weapons used in World War I developed directly out of the European and American Industrial Revolution in the late nineteenth and early twentieth centuries. This led to the design and manufacture of significantly deadlier weapons than in the past. The Allies prolonged strategy of attrition combined with the new industrialized weapons resulted in mass slaughter and unspeakable suffering on the front. Modern weapons forced the soldiers into the trenches where the smell of the dead lingered in the air. In between the enemy lines lay "no man's land"—a place destroyed by heavy bombardment and riddled with unexploded shells and corpses of brave young men. Soldiers' accounts tell of men maimed and disemboweled by guns, blinded and chocked by poison gas, and terrorized by the crackling of machine guns and the thundering bombardment of artillery. French poet and novelists, Henri Barbusse wrote of being under attack: "a diabolical uproar surrounded us. We are conscious of a sustained crescendo...a hurricane of hoarse and hollowing banging of raging clamors, of piercing and beast-like screams."[46] British artist and war painter, Paul Nash, also described the front:

No glimmer of God's hand is seen anywhere...the rain drives on, the stinking mud becomes evilly yellow, the shell-holes fill up with green-white water, the roads and tracks are covered in inches of slime, the black dying trees ooze and sweat and the shells never cease. They alone plunge overhead, tearing away the rotting tree stumps...annihilating, maiming, maddening, they plunge into the grave which is this land; one huge grave, and cast upon it the poor dead. It is unspeakable, godless, and hopeless.[47]

Americans also experienced the brutal realities of industrialized war. The muddy, lice and rat-filled trenches allowed the festering of deadly diseases. Soldiers died from influenza, pneumonia, and meningitis. The stories of AEF soldiers reveal the daily routines of the day, but diaries, memoirs, and interviews also disclose the fear, exhaustion, sleeplessness, hunger, and pain experienced by young American men fighting in World War I. Soldiers dug trenches, constructed barbed wire, and participated in raids and counter-raids along the enemy line. The young men described the deafening roar of artillery, the crackling of machine gun fire, and the devastation of gas attacks. They toiled to help the wounded, and they struggled to come to terms with the dead.

Two weeks after the United States declared war on Germany; twenty-four-year-old Private Nathaniel Rouse enlisted and served with the Sixty-fifth Infantry, Forty-second Division. In his diary, Rouse recorded his war experience. During the Third Battle of the Champagne, the American Forty-second Division fought with the French Army. Describing his first experience under fire, Rouse wrote on July 15, "They started to shell us about 12:05. Oh my God, how they shelled. I hope never to have to go through it again." But the bombardment continued into the night. The following morning the young American soldier recorded his thoughts: "Oh God, what a night. They shelled us something terrible. I had my gas masque [sic] on for 4 hours straight." The German attack continued, and on July 18, 1918 Rouse wrote "I was in hell for 6 hours. We held them back. I haven't had any sleep or anything to eat for 50 hours. I don't know how I stand it."[48]

In his journal, written in January 1919 in France, while waiting to return home, Private Mathew Chopin of the 356th Infantry, Eighty-ninth Division, described the devastation at Chateau-Thierry as he marched through the village in September 1918,

> What was once a beautiful and peaceful French town now appeared a ruin of crumbling walls and shell-torn roofs.... As we marched on, scattered here and there were hundreds and hundreds of graves, each marked with a red, white and blue circle, graves of our boys who had fallen in the defense of France! I gazed at the names of the heroes and wondered if such was destined to be my fate.... They were heroes—yes, every one of them, but...their glory would only sleep the sleep of dead! I thought of their mothers, fathers, sisters and brothers—of a dear one, perhaps, still waiting their return. Here there was no sign of animal life, all was death, destruction, desolation—the deplorable price of war![49]

Chopin also wrote of being exhausted, thirsty, and hungry, when he finally reached the St. Mihiel sector by September 28. The next night the men experienced the terror of being under a German bombardment. He described the "great guns...belching forth their hail of destruction.... We had seen German shells bursting above us...soon, soon, we were to be in the midst of that chaos of terror." Chopin continued, "Every few seconds we heard the awful whizzing and moaning sound of the enemy's huge shells followed by the heavy dull explosion that shook the very ground over which we passed!...As I lay there,...my thoughts drifted back to home and mother." Days later, after a gas attack and more artillery shelling that killed eight American soldiers and injured forty others, Chopin recorded his awful experience, "I gazed on those poor, lifeless young forms, with masses of their limbs, flesh and blood scattered in every direction, it was a sight that called madly for vengeance—a crime for which we should notch thrice on our guns for that valiant blood spilled by the Huns. One by one, we carefully bore our heroes away and laid them in one big common grave."[50]

While training with the Australian Army, American sergeant Albert K. Haas (309th Infantry, Seventy-eighth Division) kept a journal of his experience. On July 21, 1918, during the intensity of a flamethrower and machine gun attack, Haas and a number of Australian soldiers dropped to the ground to avoid a barrage of bullets. The Sergeant recalls, "In doing so, one of the Australians encountered the putrid body of a dead German who had been there for some time. The stench from it was almost unbearable."[51] In October 1917, Hass described being shot while under enemy fire in the Argonne Forest. "I became conscious of dull thud and a stinging sensation that lasted but a second. A man to the left of me let out a yell of pain; one just to the right stiffened up and fell dead."[52]

Clarence Richmond, a student at the University of Tennessee at Knoxville, enlisted in the Fifth Marine Corps Regiment, Second Division in 1918 when he was twenty-three years old. Shortly after the war, Richmond recorded his experience on the front: "The rats were so bad, that when you were on watch, you could not tell whether a raiding party was coming or not on account of the noise they made, and when you tried to sleep, they ran around over the shack, and sometimes over you, till sleep was impossible. I seldom got much sleep out of my two hours off." The former student wrote: "I somehow enjoyed watching the German observation balloons even though I knew that when they were up, they were directing artillery fire or observing our movements." Recalled an artillery barrage in September 1918, Richmond described "continuous flash of light," and noted "the earth began to tremble...the noise was so great that you could hardly hear your own voice." As the young soldier crossed "No Man's Land," he saw that "the earth was utterly blown-up. The shell holes were numerous."[53]

New York private Wilfred H. Allen served with the 308th Infantry, Twenty-seventh Division in France. On September 29, 1918 Allen was ordered "over the top." In a smoke screen launched by the Germans, Allen became disoriented and lost his company. After the attack, the private jotted notes into his journal. "Crawled in shell hole. Sniper bullets hitting all around me. One went through my mess kit. Dug hole with jackknife to crawl in. Man wounded near me. Took off his pack and gave him a drink.

Put him in my hole and dug another."[54] As soon as it was safe, Allen took the wounded man to the first aid station.

James Pierson, a soldier from Canandaigua, New York who served with the Twenty-seventh Engineers, kept a diary as he battled his way through the Argonne Forest. He described the rain and cold coming down in the muddy trenches and told of a nearby river full of dead horses and dead soldiers. On September 1918, Pierson assisted in "building a narrow gage [sic] road over no man's land to put sulfurs over the dead. Found men in shell holes that have been there so long their clothes have all rotted away." On October 3rd, after an intense attack from the enemy (especially from airplane machine gun fire), over 450 wounded and dead Americans remained trapped in the woods. Pierson expressed his frustration in his journal: "Roads to the hospital are all blocked. Heavy rains and cold, had to pack grub up to the front on mules. Drove the Huns but couldn't hold them, lack of supplies." By October 5th, Pierson recorded: "We are loosing [sic] lots of men. The 313th has been blown up entirely, those dam [sic] Huns are sure there with the machine guns." On October 30th, Pierson discovered a letter that a comrade started to write to his girlfriend. However, the young soldier never completed his task for "a shell hit him dead center."[55]

In his diary, A. W. Miller, a gunner from Hdqr. Company, 108th Infantry, expressed the danger and steer anxiety he experienced in the battlefields. After surviving a heavy bombardment near the Hindenburg Line on October 1st, the young man found the "battlefield covered with dead, dying and wounded. Many a man in the throes of death would call loudly for his mother or some other loved one." That day, Miller's division lost 11,000 men. In his journal, he expressed his utter exhaustion: "It is a long time since I have slept. I am very tired, very muddy, very wet & very haggard." The next day, the soldier found the bodies of friends riddled with bullets, slashed by bayonets, and mutilated by shells. Bodies in good condition were taken to the cemetery. Others were buried on site by Miller and other of his comrades who "saw many horrible sights, arms—legs—heads—and chunks of flesh lying all over the battlefield." After an enemy gas attack near Tincourt, France, Miller wrote: "I wonder if I can live thru another rain of shells. It is very evident that I was slightly gassed as my mouth is blistered & I am vomiting green." Another heavy bombardment and gas attack on October 9th close to Braincourt, France, left the young gunner saddened over the death of four members of his company. He questioned if he would be next, then he recorded these words: "Still—death is a mighty big relief from all this hell."[56]

PSYCHIATRY AND TREATING SHELL SHOCK

Not surprisingly, the brutalization of industrialized war resulted in many psychological causalities, and many soldiers suffered from shell shock and postwar trauma. At the turn of the century, the field of psychiatry was not judged by society to be an important profession and "psychiatrists were often considered as strange as their patients, with their terminology practically incomprehensible to other medical practitioners and laymen alike."[57] However, the First World War helped to establish psychiatry as a legitimate and professional field, and many psychiatrists assisted the military in administrating intelligence tests to inductees and helped to heal soldiers overwhelmed by the realities of battle.

At first, officers wrote off cases of shell shock or as cowardice, but as battle trauma casualties mounted, the military turned to psychiatrists for assistance. European and American military psychiatrists theorized that shell shock could be the result of the disturbance of brain's physiology from head injuries, heavy bombardment of bursting shells negatively affecting the cerebral-spinal fluid, or an extreme emotional reaction to horror or fear. On the front, psychiatrists found trembling and comatose soldiers staring wide-eyed into the distance. Other traumatized men experienced acute exhaustion, sleeplessness, or panic attacks. Still others gave out blood curling screamed as they awoke from horrific recurring nightmares that replayed the images of the dead and dieing. Major William Boyce, an American surgeon with the Thirtieth Infantry, spoke of the shell shock cases he witnessed, "Some of them cursed and raved and had to be tied to their litters; some shook violently…some trembled and slunk away in apparent fear of every incoming shell, while others simply stood speechless, oblivious to all surroundings."[58]

Although World War I psychiatrists did not fully understand shell shock they did their best to help soldiers to recover from acute war trauma. American colonel Thomas Salmon studied shell shock cases in British and French hospitals before designing a program for soldiers in the AEF. Salmon's "three-tier treatment program" began at the front where shell-shocked soldiers received "rest, hot food, and emotional support."[59] Treating soldiers close to the front allowed men who recovered quickly and return to duty as soon as possible. If soldiers did not improve, they were sent to division hospitals where they would receive therapy (including hypnotism) from psychiatrists, along with food and rest. Psychiatrists provided intense treatment to the most severe cases in army hospitals. There the men struggled with vivid nightmares and flashbacks. In his memoirs, British poet and author Siegfried Sassoon recorded how hospitalized men experienced battlefield flashbacks. "Each man was back in his doomed sector of a horror-stricken Front Line, where the panic and stampede of some ghastly experienced was re-enacted among the livid faces of the dead."[60] Many soldiers experience unrelenting postwar trauma for decades after the end of the conflict, and psychiatrists in the interwar years continued to learn ways to help the veterans.

CONCLUSION

The Industrial Revolution led to the development of modern mechanized warfare. New American civil-military relations formed as American inventors, chemists, and manufacturers worked closely with the War Department to design and begin producing modern weapons—artillery, tanks, planes, machine guns, and chemical weapons. However, the nation's prewar resistance to preparedness and delays in creating a successful wartime economy forced the U.S. military to rely heavily on French and British equipment. Some four million American soldiers served in the First World War. Of the two million men that went overseas, most were not sufficiently trained for battle.

Industrial war proved deadly for all armies involved. Artillery became the "King of Battle," and caused a significant number of World War I causalities.[61] Soldiers endured hours and even days of massive bombardment. Enormous craters made troop advancement difficult, and large artillery capable of firing long distances could be pulled back from the front, making their location difficult to find and destroy. The AEF turned to American physicists to help locate enemy artillery using flash and sound ranging.

Machine guns changed the nature of warfare between individual men. No longer did a soldier select his target and fire. Instead, machine guns spewed hundred and hundreds of bullets per minute indiscriminately, killing soldier after solider as troops dared to go up against the deadly mechanized fire power. The impact of the new industrial weapons resulted in a prolonged war of unprecedented bloodshed—fought with new, modern, machines of death. Gas warfare also created extreme anxiety. Soldiers scrambled to put on gas masks as chemicals fell, causing, burns, blindness, blisters, and death. According to British major general Charles H. Foulkes, the "appearance of gas on the battlefield...changed the whole character of warfare."[62] As more and more AEF soldiers suffered from shell shock, psychologists stepped in to help.

The postwar period saw a growing backlash against chemical weapons, especially since European civilians also became victims of gas attacks miles from the front lines. General John Pershing spoke of chemical weapons in his *Final Report:* "Whether or not gas will be employed in future wars is a matter of conjecture, but the effect is so deadly to the unprepared that we can never afford to neglect the questions."[63] In postwar congressional hearings, the army chief of staff, General Peyton C. March told the U.S. Senate he opposed the use of poisonous gas because it "went beyond the bounds of warfare." March had witnessed the gassing of 195 small children some ten miles from the front. He testified: The children were "suffering from gas in their lungs, innocent little children who had nothing to do with this game at all."[64] As a result of the postwar hearings, the role of the Chemical Warfare Service was greatly reduced, despite organized resistance and lobbying from American chemists. The scientists argued for the humanity of chemical warfare, claiming soldiers had a far greater chance of surviving than by injuries from other weapons. "With some bitterness, chemists complained of the hypocrisy of those who opposed weapons such as gas, but permitted disemboweling by bayonets or disintegration by artillery shells."[65]

When the guns finally fell silent on November 11, 1918, the death toll stood at staggering numbers: Russia 1.7 million, Germany 1.6 million, France 1.3 million, and Great British 900,000. The total number of wounded in all participating armies soared into the millions. Since America joined the war much later, the number Doughboys killed or wounded was not as great as the European nations. AEF battle casualties climbed to 255,970 with the U.S. military losing 50,280 men in combat.[66]

Upon learning that the conflict had finally come to a close, American soldier James Pierson wrote in his diary, "This day will go down in History. It is a great day here. All the French soldiers are drunk. And all you can hear is Finis La Guer[r]e"—the end of war was here at last.[67]

Demobilization and Reemployment:
The War Department Steps In

The demobilization of some four million American soldiers at the end of the First World War occurred simultaneously with widespread social unrest, rising unemployment, and economic hardship characterized by frequent labor strikes and the nation's first Red Scare. Successful solutions to combat the economic crisis did not come from Progressive Reforms, the U.S. Labor Department, Congress, or the White House, but from an unlikely source— the U.S. War Department. In an effort to reestablish soldiers into civilian life and keep the young men out of the "clutches" of Bolshevism, the War Department created a massive campaign to convince American employers to "Put Fighting Blood" in their businesses. The War Department's "Emergency Employment Committee for Soldiers, Sailors and Marines of the Council of National Defense" gathered together leading economists and well-educated officers to formulate inventive reemployment strategies including specialized employment services, creative publicity campaigns, citation awards, and public works projects.

BRING THE BOYS HOME

Although demobilization was underway by January 1919 (mostly men stationed on the home front), some two million men still anxiously waited abroad for their homecoming and a return to the job market. According to a War Department report, "with labor conditions already bad and with... many men yet to be demobilized...the situation was extremely uncomfortable."[1] Demobilization was not an easy task. The Secretary of War, Newton D. Baker, emphasized that it was important to return the men "back into the normal life of the country without filling the country with unemployed men."[2] Yet, the U.S. Army chief of staff, General Peyton C. March explained the difficulty of returning millions of men into the postwar civilian society. March concluded, "There was no precedents afforded by experience of our former wars," since in past conflicts soldiers generally returned in much smaller numbers and often to an improved economy due to "economic and territorial expansion of the nation."[3] As former president and colonel Theodore Roosevelt noted at a meeting of the Brooklyn Chamber of Commerce, "after the Civil War we still had a frontier. We absorbed a great many of the restless people on the frontier. We have no frontier now."[4]

Slowing the demobilization process was not an option, especially considering that the citizen-soldiers and their families demanded an immediate return home. Cost was another key issue. Assistant Secretary of War, Benedict Crowell, estimated that the price tag for the conflict had reached "about $50,000,000 day" by November 11, 1918. Crowell added, "Everyday of indecision in adopting" and implementing demobilization "added tremendously to the burden of taxation...for generations to come."[5]

The War Department planners came up with four options: Demobilize by prewar trades or occupations, by length of service, by original point of induction, or by military units. Although returning soldiers by trade or occupation may have helped prevent a sudden rise of unemployed men, it would have required the massive regrouping of soldiers before the discharge process. It would also necessitate a clear understanding of the labor market and industrial situations not readily available. After some discussion, General March agreed the best plan was to return soldiers with their units. This was important since, as one military report put it, there was "strong sentiment among the men" who had fought together to come home together and "perhaps have a parade before the home folks."[6] However, this decision, although considered to be the best for the morale of the soldiers, would worsen an already growing economic recession.[7]

Most divisions did return to American de-embarkation centers together and were then divided into groups based on home territory. Each group was sent to one of thirty-three demobilization camps, located throughout the United States, which placed soldiers in "close proximity" to their homes. There, soldiers were deloused, bathed, and inspected before receiving back pay, a bonus of $60, and a new uniform, shoes, and a coat. Social welfare volunteers took soldiers directly to railroad stations so the men could buy tickets home (at reduced prices). "This encouraged men to return directly to their homes instead of squandering their money and lingering in large urban area."[8]

The military demobilization process had its share of critics in Congress and the press. In addition, communities suffering from the closing of munitions factories "protested" the return of soldiers that would escalate their economic crisis. Production that once flowed quickly eroded in most industrial areas, and cities that lost war contracts faced escalating unemployment. In early January 1919, the U.S. Department of Labor conducted a survey of 122 U.S. cities and reported 39 percent had an "oversupply" of workers. This number would rise rapidly in coming months.[9] To add to the crisis, in early 1919, over 100,000 men a month began arriving back in the United States. Shortly, the number rose to 10,000 a day. The Statistical Branch of the General Staff noted the number of doughboys out of work grew from 16 percent in February to 33 percent in March 1919. By April 1919, unemployment rates for returning soldiers rose to 41 percent. A War Department investigation indicated that, in parts of the country, over a million former soldiers could not find employment.

The unemployment in the nation's major cities also reached critical levels. "In some of the larger cities and manufacturing centers, hundreds of discharged men, most of them still in uniform, were walking the streets looking for work."[10] In early 1919, U.S. Labor statistics estimated that discharged men made up 25 percent of the unemployed in New York City. Labor experts expected this number to double by April 1919 with the continued demobilization of the Twenty-seventh and Seventy-seventh Divisions. Other government investigations indicated, "returning soldiers added to the labor tension" in Seattle and Portland, and soldiers could be found "among the waterfront workers [causing] continuous unrest."[11] Reports from around the nation also told of former soldiers, still in uniform, who were "peddling and panhandling" to make a living.[12]

Although a number of social welfare agencies were graciously trying to help soldiers find jobs, including the Red Cross, Y.M.C.A, the National Catholic War Council, Salvation Army, the Jewish Welfare Board, and the American Legion, they had limited success. The War Department found the agencies' reemployment efforts were often hampered by "factional jealousies and local animosities" from the groups who did not coordinate their efforts and had a limited knowledge of the workplace. The result was "wasted effort, useless expense" and "duplication."[13]

CRISIS IN THE DEPARTMENT OF LABOR

Problems in the U.S. Department of Labor made the postwar situation worse. Influenced by reformers during the Progressive Era, Congress created the Department of Labor in 1913 "to foster, promote, and develop the welfare of the wage earners of the United States, to improve their working conditions [and] to advance their opportunities for profitable employment by maintaining a national system of employment offices."[14] President Woodrow Wilson appointed William B. Wilson (no relation) as the first secretary of labor. William Wilson, a former secretary-treasurer of the United Mine Workers of America, and a former member of Congress, oversaw the establishment of the U.S. Employment Service during the war as an emergency agency.

Although Congress approved the original financing of the U.S. Employment Service, the agency was struggling by 1919. The Service's newly created Bureau for Returning Soldiers, Sailors, and Marines was in place in many cities but was also severely crippled and ultimately ineffective due to financial constraints. To make matters worse, many local Chambers of Commerce across the nation refused to work with the federal Employment Service since they associated the agency with the hiring of "labor men," and therefore, with unionization. In fact, businesses that made up the Southern Metal Trades Association appealed to Congress not to renew funding for the agency claiming, The Employment Service was clearly "dominated by agents of labor unions," and the service was "conducted in the sole interest of unionism."[15]

In March 1919, Congress refused to provide additional funding to the employment agency, further reducing its effectiveness. A few months later, Representative Thomas Lindsay Blanton (Texas Democrat) shouted down another attempted appropriation to the U.S. Employment Service, declaring it "unauthorized by law." Frustrated supporters of the agency predicted it would soon "be forced to curtail its operations even more strictly...or disband completely."[16]

The debate over the effectiveness of the U.S. Employment Office continued through the spring, summer, and fall of 1919. In June 1919, the Senate began to debate a possible Labor Department appropriation of $400,000. At the forefront of Labor Department supporters was Senator Henry Fountain Ashurst (Arizona Democrat), who argued for the continuation of the federal Employment Service and adamantly denied it "was simply a device in the hands of the American Federation of Labor."[17] The senator also pointed out that employment agencies needed to be equipped to assist some four million returning soldiers. During the July 1, 1919 discussion, Ashurst presented excerpts from hundreds of articles "from Democratic papers and Republican papers, wet papers and dry papers of all kinds" along with letters and telegraphs from soldiers, businessmen, and social welfare agencies supporting the U.S. Employment Service.[18] The *Des Moines News* called the decision to appropriate money for the continuation of the Employment Bureaus, "one of the most urgent and patriotic duties now before Congress." The *New York Journal of Commerce* noted the U.S. Employment Agency (along with state and local efforts) was "worth much more than its cost and having a patriotic as well as generous quality." The *Literary Digest* pleaded for the retention of the agency, concluding the nation was "under a moral obligation to give its discharged soldiers an opportunity to return to civil life in a manner that will not cause them to sacrifice their self-respect by becoming objects of charity." The *Washington Times* asked, "Shall we fail our fighting men?" The War Department advised Congress to rethink the cutbacks to the U.S. Employment Service, warning that without the agency "reestablishing" soldiers back into civilian life would be "injured to an extent...impossible to exaggerate."[19]

But the opposition shot back with vengeance, repeating their allegation that the U.S. Employment Service was securely in the hand of organized labor, and many directors had links to unions. They also charged the agency with corruption, blatant misspending, and "junketing trips to France." Representative Blanton led the attack and claimed that when the secretary of labor was asked for an itemized accounting of Labor Department expenses the secretary told "us to go to the devil...and having Samuel Gompers and the American Federation of labor behind him, we sit here supinely and let him do it."[20] Blanton supplied Congress with testimonies revealing a "waste of public money" and pro-unionism within the federal Employment Service. Pushing for the return of laissez-fare government, opponents argued that private employment agencies along with municipal and state agencies should handle the unemployment situation, not the federal government. Those who opposed funding the U.S. Employment Service ruled the day, and eventually its ability to assist civilians and discharged men was reduced by 80 percent.[21]

Why the U.S. Congress chose not to promptly address the rapidly growing economic crisis is up for debate. Surely, Congress was inundated trying to "unscramble much of the wartime legislature," including returning the railroads, telegraphs, and telephone systems back to private control.[22] On the first day of the session in the House, over "600 measures" materialize. Postwar stress brought forth Americanization and immigrant restriction legislation. Taxes, women's suffrage, and prohibition made the agenda. Although Congress immediately discussed the repeal of the wartime espionage act, the Senate, now caught up in the Red Scare, was busy adopting a number of resolutions calling for the investigation of "radical intellectual" and checking "the spread of bolshevism." Congress members vowed to uncover organizations thought to be "planning to overthrow the American government by violence."[23] There were also long, heated debates over the League of Nations and the country's movement toward isolationism. Debates over federal versus state responsibility also crippled Congress. Congressional discussions on how best to help with problems associated with demobilization quickly stalled in a quagmire of investigating commissions that tended to print findings in "volumes very rarely read."[24]

THE WAR DEPARTMENT STEPS IN

Clearly the nation faced a major crisis. Secretary of War, Newton Baker, "foresaw that, unless something was done and done quickly, the results of the breaking-down of the [federal] employment Service [sic] would be both far-reaching and of untold danger." Baker declared that "it was obviously up to the War Department to step into the breach," and he approved of a massive campaign to find jobs for returning doughboys.[25] To expedite the process, Baker created the Office of Assistant to the Secretary of War on March 3, 1919. (This would eventually develop into the Service and Information Branch of the War Plans Division of the General Staff.)

In the lead was Colonel Arthur D. Woods, the new assistant to the secretary of war. A graduate of Harvard College and the University of Berlin, Woods' civilian life included work as a schoolmaster, reporter, businessman, New York police commissioner, and associate director of Foreign Propaganda for the Committee on Public Information (CPI). He was commissioned in the army's Aviation Section in March 1918, and after his honorable discharge from his position as the assistant director of Military Aeronautics in January 1919, Woods took on the project of finding jobs for the returning troops.[26]

Woods saw the War Department's reemployment efforts "not as a charity, or even as a kindness, but as a duty that rests on everybody with power and opportunity to assist the Government in meeting its moral as well as its technical obligation to those who have served it so heroically."[27] Colonel Woods believed that the War Department's ethical responsibility for returning doughboys extended beyond the $60 bonus and free transportation home, especially considering the sacrifices of the American soldiers who did their patriotic duty but now returned home to a poor economy that offered little opportunity. In addition, Woods noted, "If no legal responsibility, at least a moral one, rested upon the Government, which had taken these men out of civil life."[28]

LABOR STRIFE AND THE RED SCARE

However, the postwar return of intense labor and capital hostility also worried military leaders, and the rapid onset of the Red Scare served as the key motivation for the War Department's involvement in finding jobs for its doughboys. Prior to the First World War, many Progressive Reformers and union leaders opposed unregulated capitalism that resulted in a sharp disproportion of wealth and left much of the urban and rural poor living and working in unsafe, dangerous, and disease-ridden squalor. Workers' gains in wartime brought on by labor shortages and lucrative government war contracts, temporarily improved conditions and inadvertently helped fuel the rise in labor union membership. However, the sudden end of the First World War brought about the hasty cancellation of profitable war contracts. Workers' demands to hold on to economic advances made during the conflict and the rapid rise of inflation led to widespread labor antagonism. Faced with reduction of wages and hours, mounting economic uncertainty, and increasing job competition, workers reacted. At war's end, strikes plagued postwar America. In 1919 alone, over 3,300 strikes involving some four million workers (one in every five) shook the nation as laborers joined the fight for better wages and working conditions in bitter disputes. The U.S. Labor Department reported strikes in twenty-four different states as the economy worsened.[29]

This widespread labor unrest collided with postwar social stress and the lingering superpatriotic hysteria stemming from the war that demanded total conformity and an end to radicalism. While the AFL (American Federation of Labor), the leading trade union, sought to soften the disparages of capitalism, the IWW (Industrial Workers of the World), a socialist union, stood firm against the abuses of a system that exploited the workers and left so many Americans trapped in the underclass. In reality, the American Socialist and Communist organizations fragmented over conflicting ideology and had relatively low membership. However, the harsh and prolonged reaction of the American public and government to the 1917 Bolshevik Revolution in Russia left no room for radicalism, perceived to be on a rapid rise in America. By 1919, radicalism became synonymous with unionism. The acute tension in the nation mounted as Attorney General A. Mitchell Palmer arrested thousands of suspected communists and deported some 250 foreign-born radicals in the legendary "Palmer Raids."

Assistant Secretary of War, Colonel Arthur Woods, feared that the outcome of labor strikes created an unstable work place that would prevent the assimilation of soldiers back into American society. As labor unrest spread and strikes grew more frequent, governors called out the National Guard to suppress the strikers. Although not specifically stated in their reports, the War Department was surely aware that the growing labor unrest increasingly pitted the National Guard against ex-soldiers. With the growing antagonism between capital and labor, Woods also warned against "the crucial danger of discontented soldiers" being tempted by radicals. Woods told his staff, "the soldier is unsteady...he is wayward and impatient and unsettled.... We cannot let them alone to wander about the streets and listen to the Bolsheviki."[30] Colonel Woods reminded his men that the key to locking out radicalism was to assist the returning soldiers in readjusting to civilian life, since the soldiers' sympathies would be determined by how they were treated.[31]

Former army chief of staff, Major General Leonard Wood, who fought hard to improve the military in the prewar years, joined the voices warning against the danger of radicalism. Wood told the *New York Times* that without jobs soldiers could become "more susceptible to the influences of Bolshevism."[32] After a new union made up of returning servicemen, called the Soldiers, Sailors, and Marine Council, joined the American Federation of Labor, the general asked the new unionists in Chicago to "disband their organization." They refused. The general also alerted business leaders about another group of "radical units" consisting of unemployed discharged soldiers who created problems in Chicago. As soon as the men received help finding jobs, the situation became "much healthier."[33] In an Associated Press dispatch, General Wood called discharged men "potential reds," declaring it was "absolutely essential" for the federal government to find jobs for returning soldiers in order to "combat Bolshevism." He added, "many of the men who have returned are sick, both physically and mentally, and waiting with nothing to do and finding on every hand radical orators only too willing to sow the seeds of discontentment."[34]

Early in 1919, the *Infantry Journal* also warned against the spread of communism:

> The millions in the Army must be reabsorbed into industry. Prices will fall and wages will fall with prices, but more slowly.... The problem of unemployment will again thrust up its head.... Bolshevism will be quick to make capital out of maladjustment and discontent.[35]

The solution, according to the journal, was to instill the "spirit" of Americanism and good citizenship in all soldiers, especially in the many foreign-born soldiers who served in the American army. An editorial in the *Infantry Journal* warned its readers about the dangers of unions by focusing on the police strike in Boston and the "Bolshevik attitudes of policemen." The editor asked the reader to imagine a union of "soldiers, and officers, seamen and officers.... Pretty picture, isn't it? It is then but a step to the reddest spot of Russia, the soviet, an American Lenine [sic], and a Disunited States of America."[36]

EMERGENCY EMPLOYMENT COMMITTEE

In March 1919, Colonel Arthur Woods took charge of the demobilization crisis by creating the "Emergency Employment Committee for Soldiers, Sailors and Marines of the Council of National Defense." The *New York Times* announced the new committee, "composed of some of the ablest men in Washington," and explained that its creation was necessitated by the "radical curtailment" of the U.S. Employment Service.[37] According to the *Times,* since Congress refused to allocate funds, the federal Employment Service would be "forced to order the closing of all of its branch offices except those in fifty-six important industrial centers."[38]

Woods began by sending an investigation team of military officers to inspect the economic situation throughout the United States, and the group met on April 11, 1919 to share information in a brainstorming session in Chicago, Illinois. General Leonard Wood joined the discussion with Colonel Woods' team which consisted of sixteen military career officers (majors, captains, and lieutenants). Most of the officers had worked in the business field prior to enlistment.

Next, Woods divided the nation into four districts and selected district chiefs to head each area. Major Carl Clyde Rutledge led the Eastern District. Rutledge, who worked as a welfare executive and as an assistant general manager in the oil business before the war, received degrees from Wesleyan University and the U.S. Naval Academy. He also graduated from the General Staff College in Langres, France and participated in a number of battles in Europe, including the Somme. Major J.C.R. Peadbody, chief of the Northeastern Department, was a military career officer with experience as an aide-de-camp to two generals before he served with the Fifth Division in Europe during the Great War. Peadbody joined Wood's team after being disabled in the conflict.[39]

Woods also selected Major (later lieutenant colonel) John Bateson Reynolds to head up the Central Department, made up of seventeen states. Reynolds was a Columbia University graduate with a former career in advertising and business. During the war, Reynolds worked in the Personnel Division before he became the chief of correspondence and assistant executive to chief of the Air Service. In this position, he served as a liaison between the military and Congress. The Western District director, Captain Edwin Copely Wemple, earned a degree from the University of Virginia and took graduate courses in forest engineering at the University of Michigan. He served as a timber investment specialist before starting his own lumber company. During the war, Wemple served with the Fourth Battalion, Twentieth Engineers. After being wounded in France, he returned to the states and went to work with Colonel Woods to oversee Emergency Employment activities in nine western states.[40]

In March, Woods sent Reynolds to Camp Lee, Virginia to select thirty-five officers (majors, captains, and lieutenants) to serve as field representatives from the pool of "emergency officers desiring Regular Army commissions." These officers coordinated the employment efforts in each state and reported to their area's district chiefs. A number of naval officers also served with Woods. The team soon reached 172 members divided among the Publicity Section, Public Works Section, Service and Information Section, Employment Section, and Personnel and Office Management Section. Almost all of the men selected by Woods and Reynolds were well-educated, well-trained officers. Almost all held university, college, or business school degrees, and many had earned graduate or law degrees. Many officers received their education from top universities in the nation including Columbia, Cornell, Dartmouth, Harvard, Princeton, Yale, MIT, Rensselaer, and others. While some members of Wood's Emergency team went into the service directly from college, others worked in a variety of fields prior to the war. This included advertising, business, construction, engineering, health inspection, law, management, news reporting, law enforcement, sales, social welfare, and teaching. Woods carefully selected soldiers from the AEF, since the servicemen would understand the experience of the returning doughboys and their desire to better themselves.[41]

The Emergency Employment Committee also received assistance from the Department of Labor, the Department of Agriculture, the Department of Interior, the U.S. Post Office, and social welfare leaders. Eventually, over 24,000 field representatives "stationed at reemployment centers throughout the country" came under Woods' "command." In addition, Secretary of Interior, Franklin K. Lane, volunteered 15,000 Interior employees to help Woods' team as needed.[42]

In March, the War Department estimated that some three million discharged men needed assistance securing work. To help ease economic conditions and reestablish soldiers into the workplace, the War Department team developed a number of innovative solutions. First, the military allowed officers and rank-and-file men to remain in the service (if desired) until the economic situation improved. Secretary of War Baker telegraphed commanding officers telling them to make it "clear to every soldier that where he would normally be discharged under orders for demobilization, he may remain temporarily in the military service at his own written request until such time as he can secure employment."[43] Baker made this decision not only to help the soldier but also to help the economy of the nation.

HELPING SOLDIERS ADJUST

To help veterans readjust to civilian employment, the Emergency Employment Committee's Service and Information Section distributed 3,000,000 copies—equal to six train carloads of paper—of the booklet, *Where Do We Go From Here?* The booklet, handed out on returning ships and debarkation ports, encouraged soldiers to take the first job they found, instead of waiting "indefinitely" for the right job, and provided a list of welfare organizations that offered help. The booklet also acknowledged that

> the soldier's point of view was considerably changed by his service, that he returned to civil life with different ideas about what he should do, and that many changes moreover had come over the civil surroundings he had formerly known and to which he must be adjusted afresh.[44]

Colonel Woods took the next step in solving the unemployment situation by taking the operation of Employment Service's deteriorating Bureau for Returning Soldiers, Sailors, and Marines. In an official report, Woods noted that the U.S. Employment Service was crippled by financial problems, suffered from a low "esprit de corps," and had lost the confidence of business leaders throughout the United States. The bureaus were already located in over 2,000 cities and towns but not efficiently operated due to its small staff and lack of congressional funding. Therefore, Woods sent field representatives to direct each bureau with the help of available Labor Department employees and social welfare agencies. Major William Hoffman Kobbe served as the director of Field Activities. Kobbe graduated from Yale University and worked as a forester and later in the oil business in both the Philippines and Turkey. During the war, Kobbe participated in a key gas offensive in France. After recovering from the loss of his right hand (from a defective hand grenade), Kobbe began his new job under Colonel Woods. Second Lieutenant Paige Monteagle served as Kobbe's assistant. Monteagle received a law degree from Harvard but left his legal career to attend Officers' Training School in 1915 and later served in the AEF. Dozens of field representatives (active and discharged captains and lieutenants) worked under Major Kobbe and took their place in Bureaus for Returning Soldiers throughout the United States.[45]

The War Department's Emergency Employment Committee also implemented an employment card system, rewarded businesses that rehired soldiers, retrained servicemen for skilled industrial jobs, and created an intense patriotic propaganda campaign to educate the public about the demobilization crisis. Perhaps the War Department's most ambitious program was its attempt to promote public works projects. The War Department also established employment service offices in demobilization camps.

In order to match specific soldiers with specific jobs, the War Department asked men aboard ships returning from Europe and in Demobilization Centers to fill out employment cards noting their previous experience. Detailed instructions accompanied the cards, and officers helped the servicemen as needed. Woods advised that "each soldier on a transport should be talked to, preferably in private, and made to understand that in the United States there is a great government enterprise at work solely toward assisting him to connect with the job for which he is best fit."[46]

Since many men were returning after a two-year absence and were now unfamiliar with the nation's economic changes, the War Department suggested the discharged men go directly to the Bureau for Returning Soldiers, Sailors, and Marines near their home (where the cards were sent) to meet with field representatives. The bureaus helped untrained, technically trained, and destitute ex-soldiers by matching each soldier's job cards with available employment opportunities. In addition to bureau field representatives, personnel officers also assisted in finding jobs for soldiers.[47]

The War Department also distributed millions of copies of *That Job— Your Rights,* which provided soldiers with information on the bureau and details about allotments, insurances, and bonuses. The booklet advised soldiers to be on their best behavior and show up for work. It also asked the men not to quit without notice since employers would stop cooperating with the bureau if the discharged men gave the War Department agency a bad reputation. An inspiring message told servicemen to look good for the job interviews, "spruce up—look like a winner," look the interviewer "straight in the eye, Don't flinch...do your best for your employer.... 'Go over the top' as you did in France."[48]

Discharged military officers received special attention in finding jobs from Captain Edwin L. Holloway, the director of Placement of Technical Men. Holloway was a personnel manager in a Pittsburgh lumber company before serving in the Twenty-seventh Division of the AEF and as a liaison officer between Wood's office and the chief of staff. After Holloway's resignation from the Emergency Employment Committee, Woods' executive assistant, Edward S. Gardner, a Yale-trained engineer and former member of the First Marine Aviation Force, took over the task. Gardner and his staff continued the job of finding skilled positions for ex-officers, even "hunting up" jobs by visiting companies throughout the United States.[49]

"PUT FIGHTING BLOOD IN YOUR BUSINESS"

Woods' staff also sent out 2,000 letters a week to companies throughout the nation educating them about the bureau and personally contacted executives of big businesses. Letters from the War Department went to post office workers instructing them to direct all unemployed soldiers to the bureau, and Woods sent letters to mayors of "principal cities" to ask for help in finding jobs for discharged servicemen. When learning of a civil service job opening, Woods representatives directed the unemployed men to the Civil Service Department since the agency gave preference to veterans.[50]

Knowing Chambers of Commerce throughout the country held a negative view of the U.S. Employment Service, Colonel Woods attempted to bring them on board by sending personal letters to chambers throughout the country asking them to work with the Bureau for Returning Soldiers, Sailors, and Marines. The letter noted the power of the chambers, called the effort to find jobs for soldiers a "privilege," and asked for the national organizations assistance. After some discussion, the president of the U.S. Chamber of Commerce, Harry Wheeler, agreed to set up a special committee for "soldier and sailor employment" to help in the economic crisis and established a "bureau for expediting and clearing this work."[51] Wheeler also instructed local chambers to work with the War Department or to create their own committee to find job openings. Woods reported success after receiving positive responses from several hundred chambers and the promise of assistance from over 150 more. To help in the process, Woods assigned Major Harry Taylor as his "special representative" to act as liaison between the War Department and the U.S. Chamber of Commerce. Taylor once studied law at Columbia University, served as a policeman, and became an army scout during the war.[52]

The Emergency Employment Committee clearly understood that publicity was their "most important weapon" in achieving their goals. With firsthand experience from his days working with the CPI, Colonel Woods knew the value of a creative and passionate propaganda campaign. Therefore, Woods and his team stepped up their efforts by utilizing the same high-pitched, superpatriotic propaganda machine used by the CPI during the Great War. Colonel Reginald L. Foster, a graduate of Yale and a former journalist, served as Woods' director of Publicity. Foster's publicity subsection was staffed with a number of military officers including First Lieutenant Bryon Philip Spry, who once served as the publicity manager for Paramount Pictures. Woods and Foster believed "if the entire country could read about jobs for soldiers, it would think about jobs for soldiers."[53]

The Publicity Section used automobile stickers, movie picture-slides, and posters, along with Liberty Loan workers, "Four-minute men," and school children to help spread a strong message that ex-servicemen should be rehired as soon as possible. Over 13,000 newspapers were identified and bombarded with daily press releases and photographs educating the public about the scope of the War Department's new role. Field representatives also visited editors of national papers to ask for their cooperation. Articles appeared in the *Women's Home Companion, McClure's, Leslie's, The Old Colony Magazine,* and *Life.* Soldiers' journals such as *Treat 'Em Rough, As you Were, National Service,* and the *American Legion Magazine* also helped out by publicizing the cause. This included articles entitled "The Returning Soldier and a Job," "The Employer's Opportunity," "Jobs for Cripples," "Teaching Discharged Soldiers Mining," and "The Land and the Soldier." A War Department report announced, "Practically every magazine of standing in the United States gave generous space."[54]

Woods' team also focused on newspapers, magazines, Sunday supplements, and front-page stories. Articles and "Ad Columns" in major newspapers notified returning soldiers that the War Department was there to help them. Newspapers in New York City, including the *New York World, The New York Times,* and the *Evening Globe,* offered to assist. Woods attempted to "sell" the ex-soldiers as an "excellent buy" since the returning men were "animated by an elevated spirit of citizenship," trained by army discipline, and in top physical condition. In a front-page article of the *Times,* the colonel appealed to American industries to do their share by hiring the returning soldier—"a full sized, red blooded, two fisted man, a real America." Woods supplied nine reasons to hire ex-servicemen including the men's loyalty, mental and physical endurance, and commitment to give 100 percent. According to the colonel, the army helped develop the soldier's "skill to the highest efficiency" and taught the men to obey orders "to the best of his ability without grumbling." Newspaper articles told the stories of gallant deeds of soldiers going "over the top" and tied their return to the need to help find jobs for the young heroes. Woods also gave public speeches to emphasize that a job for ex-soldiers meant "industrial peace to our country."[55]

The War Department, the Department of Labor, and the Department of Agriculture used posters to convince employers to hire ex-soldiers and distributed them with the help of social welfare agencies and the Chambers of Commerce. The Red Cross donated the money needed for the War Department to produce 550,000 copies of a magnificently designed poster "Put Fighting Blood in Your Business." The colorful, dramatic image showed American soldiers charging the battlefield. The artist located a shield listing the names of important battles in the upper left corner. The poster also read, "Here's His Record! Does He Get a Job?" Included among the more than 17,500 lantern slides developed by the War Department was a slide show entitled "Put Fighting Blood in Your Business."[56]

A similar message came in another colorful poster financed by the American Red Cross and designed by a well-known artist, Dan Smith. It showed a soldier carrying his honorable discharge paper into the Bureau for

Returning Soldiers and Sailors. The message was clear, "Jobs for Fighters: If You Need a Job. If You Need a Man." The American Library Association, Chambers of Commerce, Methodist Episcopal Church, U.S. Post Offices, Department of Interior, War Camp Community Service, U.S. Railroad Administration, U.S. Department of Agriculture, and the Jewish Welfare Board all assisted in distributing the poster. This poster also noted the new connection between the U.S. Employment Service and the War Department's Council of National Defense. Another government poster showed a man standing at attention as he was applying for a job. The boss noted, "I can tell you've been a soldier by the way you stand—Report for work tomorrow morning." A different poster showed an ex-soldier and a civilian walking down the street. Unlike the civilians, the soldier stood tall in his clean, pressed clothing. The caption read, "The Soldier in 'Cits.' Pick him out." Posters also reminded soldiers to "spruce" themselves up when interviewing for a job.[57]

The advertising campaign proved to be a success and soon letters poured into the government from servicemen seeking assistance. In one week alone, the War Department received 1,209 letters from soldiers, including a letter from a soldier writing to "Square-Deal Woods." The moniker also appeared in national newspapers. Woods appreciated the "Square Deal" label and said, "It would be hard to image a better evidence of appreciation."[58]

Churches also offered help with the War Department's new mission. The Methodist Episcopal Church designated May 4, 1919 as "Employment Sunday" and asked churches throughout the nation to join in the effort to find jobs for soldiers. President Wilson endorsed the project by adding his "voice" to the appeal. The General War Times Commission with a membership of some 150,000 churches, pledged to help along with the National Catholic War Council and the Knights of Columbus. In sermons and statements to the press, religious leaders urged the public to support the soldiers employment effort. New York monsignor M.J. Lavelle declared that "no more important work" existed before the public than finding jobs for returning servicemen, and Bishop David H. Greer called it "a patriotic duty."[59]

CITATIONS

However, articles, posters, slides, speeches, and sermons, no matter how compelling or imaginative, were not enough. To get industries on board, the War Department team designed an award program directed at "patriotic" employers. Any business who took back their former workers seeking reemployment after being discharged from the military received a "War and Navy Department Citation." Signed by Newton D. Baker and Arthur Woods, the certificate praised the employer who "assured the War and Navy Department that he will gladly re-employ everybody who formerly worked for him and left to serve in the army or navy during the Great War."[60] The citations, designed like shields, could be displayed in store and office windows or on service flags. Employers received one shield for each soldier they took back at war's end. Similar to the "patriotic" symbols used during the war, this shield showed the public that this employer was doing his duty. Each "citation" company or retail merchant also received newspaper publicity—a special thank you from the War Department.[61]

To advertise the citation awards, the War Department sent out thousands of letters to leading magazines, trade journals, manufacturers' associations, companies, retail merchants, and mayors of cities with populations over 5,000. Over 12,600 letters went to newspapers alone. A lantern slide show, shown at local picture houses, also drove home the patriotic reemployment message. Over 18,000 Boy Scout troops helped to advertise the awards by personally delivering citation application forms. The Emergency Employment Committee also asked over 1,200 Chambers of Commerce to publicize the government's citation awards in their magazines. To celebrate the success of the program, the Fifth Avenue Association of New York City sponsored a day for all stores and offices to "simultaneously display" their citation awards on July 14, 1919. The War Department followed suit when Secretary Baker announced a "Citation Week" beginning September 1, 1919. By the end of the year, War Department distributed some 70,000 citations.[62]

The citation award system was not intended to displace civilian workers and replace them with discharged men. However, according to a report filed by Major Peadbody, chief of the Northeastern District, in at least one section, employers were asked to replace "slackers, aliens, or conscientious objectors" with the "original" soldier-employee.[63]

RELOCATING SOLDIERS

Relocating soldiers to available jobs in rural America was another option to solve the employment crisis. In fact, during a congressional hearing, New York farmers pleaded for the continuation of the U.S. Employment Service because of the "alarming labor shortage in farming districts."[64] After cutbacks in the federal employment agency, the War Department's Emergency Employment Committee surveyed the farm situation in New York, Pennsylvania, New Jersey, Delaware, and Connecticut along with Midwest states and confirmed a critical need for labor. However, although farming opportunities were much more readily available than industrial jobs, the Emergency Committee soon discovered returning soldiers "exhibited generally no keen desire to go to farming."[65]

With the help of a well-crafted publicity campaign, the War Department was able to "stimulate interest in so wholesome" an occupation with the help of 800,000 copies of the booklet "Forward to the Farm, Why Not?" The booklet which provided a discussion of modern agricultural method along with farming photographs was distributed to Demobilization Centers, the remaining U.S. Employment Service offices, and the Bureau for Returning Soldiers, Sailors, and Marines. Woods' team also came to the aid of Department of Agriculture with the recruitment of some 50,000 men for the Kansas wheat harvest in danger of being lost. In addition, the Emergency Employment Committee sent telegrams to the American Federation of Labor, the U.S. Chamber of Commerce, and various welfare agencies reporting the Kansas agricultural openings. Despite the fact that discharged men had to pay for their railroad tickets, the response from ex-soldiers was so great that within a month the Kansas crisis past.[66]

INDUSTRIAL RETRAINING

Even with the success of the War Department's Emergency Employment Committee, new attitudes of the returning soldiers complicated the reemployment efforts. Military discipline, physical conditioning, and war experiences left many with a desire for improvements in their civilian lives. Perhaps even more importantly, the war experience left ex-soldiers with the belief that they now deserved career advancement and increased wages. According to a War Department report on the psychology of the servicemen, this new attitude was "due not to selfishness, lack of patriotism, or ignorance, but rather to the fact that immense experiences had supervened" and had changed "the disposition, the ambitions and the habits" of the men.[67] At a dinner meeting with the New York Furniture Exchange Association, Colonel Woods told the story of a decorated former elevator man who did not want to return to his former position to run "an elevator up a shaft only to bring it down again.... He felt the war had equipped him for better things."[68] Money was another issue. As soldiers returned home, it became clear that while risking their lives for $30 a month, war industry workers had benefited with substantial economic gains. Labor Department reports confirmed that with higher wages and overtime pay, the incomes of many families "had doubled, tripled, and even quadrupled" during the war.[69] Ex-soldiers now wanted to make up for financial losses and be paid higher wages to counter the rising cost of living.

Understanding the desire for advancement, the War Department began to oversee an "on the job" industrial retraining program to help turn unskilled soldiers into skilled workers since "lack of skill...was as much an economic disability as the loss of a hand or of eyesight."[70] During the war, the Department of Labor's U.S. Training Service had headed up a program to train civilians for much needed industrial war work. But at wars end, it could not maintain the program due to financial constraints. In July 1919, when the Department of War took over the retraining program it convinced participating companies to continue the on-the-job training and the "vestibule schools" (training schools that duplicated shop conditions for trainees before putting them on the shop floor). Francis O. Perkins (who would later became the first woman secretary of labor in 1933) assisted the War Department in organizing the programs. Industrial retraining classes for ex-soldiers took place in over 300 plants throughout the country that allowed the men to earn a living while learning a new skill. Many other companies expressed interest in hosting a training program. Woods argued that stimulating interest in retraining programs was an economic necessity in an industrial nation. It benefited both the soldier and the company since turnover decreased and production increased with "the efficiency and loyalty of workers."[71]

PUBLIC WORKS PROJECTS

Perhaps the most challenging postwar effort was the War Department's attempt to create new construction jobs and promoting public works projects to "stimulate" employment. The Emergency Employment Committee publicized a "Spruce-up Campaign," designed to encourage "individual householders, merchants, and manufacturers" to make repairs or improvements.[72] Sprucing-up in turn created jobs. The *Saturday Evening Post, Collier's, Review of Review, Independent, Scientific American, World's Work, Women's Home Companion, National City, U.S. Bulletin, Industry, McClure's Metropolitan, Leslie's, Life, American,* and hundreds of other magazines, trade, and military journals published articles about the "Spruce-up Campaign." The Labor Department assisted by flooding the country with inspirational and patriotic posters calling for remodeling and new construction. Posters targeted homeowners and businesses to do their part to help the economy. Colonel Woods and his staff gave speeches to advertise the campaign, and Woods became the honorary chairman of a New York Jewish Building Fund to help inspire construction. In October 1919, John D. Rockefeller, Jr. and Sr. donated $75,000 to the fund.[73]

Invigorating the economy through public works projects was also a way of creating jobs for discharged soldiers. According to a 1919 General Staff report, "it was felt that the Government, particularly through the War Department, could consistently endeavor to stimulate public works and to preach the gospel of building."[74] Captain Alfred Hoyt Granger served as the chief of the War Department Public Works Section. Granger studied architecture at the Massachusetts Institute of Technology and studied for two years at the Ateller Pascal Ecole des Beaux Arts, Paris before starting a career in architecture. Grander received a commission as captain, eventually being assigned to the chief of engineers. He also completed a book on the history of military construction during the war and prepared plans for the Soldiers' Home in Washington, DC. The Publics Work Section included Major Francis Smith Marlow who served as the director. Marlow, a former Cornell graduate and architectural engineer, once worked for the Department of Labor.

Woods also created the Emergency Employment Committee's Federal Aid & Works Section with Otto T. Mallery in charge. Mallery received degrees from Princeton, the University of Pennsylvania, and Columbia in economics and sociology and had previously served as a congressional advisor "on legislation to prevent industrial depression."[75] Mallery became well known during the war as a member of the AALL (American Association for Labor Legislation). Founded in 1906, the AALL pushed for workmen's compensation legislature and sought ways to combat unemployment. In 1917, Mallery wrote an act that provided funding for statisticians to help the Department of Labor "to observe the employment situation." He authored the article "A National Policy—Public Works to Stabilize Employment" for the American Academy of Political and Social Science in January 1919. (Mallery eventually became a member of Herbert Hoover's Economic Advisory Committee in 1921. He remained a well-known authority in government economics.)[76]

With a dedicated team of twenty-one staff members, Granger, Marlow, and Mallery worked diligently to

> handle many troubled projects needing Federal aid of one kind or another particularly in getting plans approved by the Chief of Engineers' Office of the Army for local river and harbor improvements, getting plans approved by the Department of Agriculture for Federal aid roads, and most important of all, expediting the release of large quantities of material from the War Department to the Department of Agriculture and its delivery to the State Highway Commission for highway construction work.[77]

With an appropriation of over three billion dollars pending congressional approval, Marlow divided his "small field force" into districts set up to stimulate public works and get public works contracts signed. Marlow received assistance from men trained in economics, engineering, and construction. Major Charles Welsh, a civil engineer, served as the chief of the Highway Sub-section of the War Department Public Works Section. The section also included Captain James Armstrong (who studied economics at the University of Chicago and Stanford University); Captain John Parker Hill (who studied at Princeton University and had experience working on military construction); Major Edward A. Keys (who received his engineering training at Lehigh University and worked as a civil engineer before the war); Captain Henry Hudson Kimball (an economic entomologist); and Captain Harry Sabiston (former supervisor of construction). Also assisting was Second Lieutenant John A. Straley (a discharged pilot, trained as an engineer at the College of the City of New York); Robert L'Hommendieu Tate (a former army engineer who earned a degree from Cornell University); and Leonard H. Whitney (rank unknown, graduate of Cornell University in Civil Engineering).[78]

Marlow's officers secured architectural draftsmen and engineers along with other men needed to finish public works projects. The officers also helped expedite paperwork for river and harbor improvements and for road and state highway construction. To keep public works projects on track, Marlow's men (with the assistance of the Labor Department) arbitrated with building trade unions in Youngstown, Ohio; Jersey City, New Jersey; and Syracuse, New York and helped with the completion of various local and state public works projects that became stalled. The military officers worked with community leaders in various districts to help raise funds, get contracts signed, and solve problems associated with public works projects as they arose. Marlow's team provided "double service" by stimulating public works thus creating jobs for discharged soldiers.[79]

With the return of laissez-faire philosophy, the federal government eventually pulled the plug on the planned railroad reconstruction programs that would have helped "absorb" returning soldiers, and Congress refused to approve a U.S. Emergency Public Works Board or appropriate the $1,000,000 needed to run the projects. However, the government eventually authorized $1,400,000,000 in public works money, made $1,100,000,000 available, and, by April 1919, issued $575,000,000 worth of contracts. The War Department's Public Works Branch claimed success after helping to contract $260,000,000 (of $575,000,000) public works projects after their officers' "direct visits."[80]

In August 1919, Woods discontinued the War Department's Public Works Branch since "it served its purpose" by overcoming an economic crisis. Even with its short existence, the War Department's public works efforts should not be dismissed. In Woods' final report, the assistant secretary concluded it

> was able, not only to overcome the unfavorable factors which had threatened to obstruct the execution of public works throughout the country, but also to speed up many new public projects together with accompanying private projects, an provide means of employment both directly and indirectly through the building trades manufacturers for a very large number of unemployed included discharged soldiers.[81]

Colonel Woods strongly advocated the future use of public works during periods of "industrial depression" or unemployment crisis.[82]

SOLVING PROBLEMS

Even with the success of its innovative employment strategies and well-crafted advertising efforts, the War Department faced problems with labor unrest, panhandling, language problems, and racial tensions, and disabled veterans needed special attention. Labor unrest and strikes sometimes hampered the War Department's employment efforts. This was especially true in the Western District where prewar and wartime strikes were more prevalent. The situation in the West was critical due to the large migration of unemployed ex-servicemen, the decline in shipbuilding, and the "danger" from the socialist union, the Industrial Workers of the World. The Central District also reported problems. Captain Scott, a field representative in Cleveland, Ohio, telegraphed the War Department about radicals from the Soldiers, Sailors, and Marines Union who were soliciting subscriptions for their *National Weekly News.* Scott also sent a copy of other "Bolshevik" newspapers to Colonel Wood's office including *Rebel Worker: Organ of Revolutionary Unionism* and *The Melting Pot: An Exponent of International Communism.* The central chief, Major Reynolds, reported that strikes in the steel and coal industries "were an ever-present problem." Reynolds and his field representatives attempted to dodge the problem by relocating and finding jobs for ex-servicemen in areas not plagued by strikes. Although the War Department understood the urgency of finding jobs, they realized that frequent labor unrest throughout the nation complicated the employment situation. Therefore, field representatives were instructed to tell applicants to use their judgment when applying for jobs in plants that were on strike.[83]

Radicalism continued to concern the War Department. According to the director of the Western District, Major Wemple, radical organizations "were putting forth a supreme effort to convert" ex-soldiers by greeting soldiers at train stations and providing them with free meals, money, and clothing. Wemple reported that his field officers worked with the U.S. Intelligence Bureau and the American Legion to breakup the "powerful" soldiers and sailors union, "pro-Bolshevik ex-soldier organizations," and other radical groups. After an investigation of growing radicalism in Spokane, Washington, the War Department arranged for "Four-Minute Men" speakers to counter radical propaganda in movie picture houses, theaters, churches, and on street corners.[84]

In August 1919, Secretary of War Baker asked Colonel Woods to deal with soldiers who were begging or peddling on the streets of America. To stop returning soldiers from peddling, field representatives asked local authorities "to refuse licenses" to men in uniform and encouraged the passing of local and state laws outlawing peddling in uniform since it exploited military service. The Emergency Employment Committee also contacted the local posts of the American Legion to assist with the panhandling problem. The legion sent veterans out to have a "heart to heart talk" with the "work slacker." In addition, Woods sent letters to police chiefs throughout the nation requesting the police redirect any peddling ex-servicemen to the closest Bureau of Returning Soldiers. If the situation continued, Colonel Woods asked police to place the ex-servicemen on probation with the American Legion instead of placing them in jail. He asked the police chiefs to watch out for fraud, including the "cooties" that employ discharged soldiers to panhandle in uniform in order to "play upon the public sympathy which the uniform arouses" and estimated that 80 percent of the men who were panhandling and peddling on the streets never served in the military, and he asked newspapers to expose "peddlers in uniform" who were "imposters."[85]

IMMIGRANT SOLDIERS

The War Department also produced employment materials in foreign languages for soldiers who spoke little English. The massive migration from Southern and Eastern Europe in the late nineteenth and early twentieth centuries brought millions of immigrants to the United States. During the war, the American military was stunned to find that over 18 percent of the soldiers in their ranks were foreign-born who spoke little or no English, but they soon became proficient in training and educating immigrant soldiers. To assist with finding jobs for discharged immigrant soldiers, the Emergency Employment Committee supplied job information to ethnic newspapers throughout the United States including Italian, "Jewish," Bohemian, "Czecho-Slav," and German language papers. Woods' team also produced the *Jobs for Soldiers* booklets, press releases, and other employment information in many different languages and sent letters to mayors throughout the United States telling them "we must not forget, also, the large number of foreign-speaking men who have served our colors with the greatest loyalty and often with extraordinary courage and enthusiasm."[86]

AFRICAN-AMERICAN SOLDIERS

Postwar racial tension made finding jobs for black soldiers more difficult. Prior to the First World War, the Great Migration from the South brought over one million African Americans North, drawn to new industrial opportunities and escaping the horrors of Jim Crow Laws, voting restrictions, and open violence by white supremacists. Employment for African Americans expanded greatly during the war. As servicemen returned from overseas, Jesse O. Thomas, the state supervisor of Negro Economics in the Department of Labor, encouraged the rehiring of black soldiers. Thomas reminded religious leaders that the reemployment "campaign [was] intended to reach, affect, and benefit every race or nationality in our common country."[87]

The employment situation became more complex when many black soldiers, originally from the South, headed to the North on their return from Europe. With jobs remaining in short supply in the industrial areas of the Midwest, the War Department's Central District Field Representatives worked with black social welfare agencies to help find jobs for African-American soldiers who "refused to return to their old homes in the South" at the end of the war.[88] However, as the economic crisis worsened and racial tension accelerated, the employment representatives began to encourage southern blacks ex-servicemen to return home. District Chief Reynolds argued that this was needed "so as not to arouse any race hatred."[89]

Although Central District's report did not specifically mention increasing racial tensions that developed into the tragic Chicago race riots that shook the city during the summer of 1919, this may have played a part in the decision. The War Department also looked in the South for employment opportunities and asked Southern commercial organizations to pay for the transportation costs of all African-American soldiers they hired.[90]

DISABLED SOLDIERS

Disabled soldiers offered another challenge. Although an act of Congress put the care of disabled men in the hands of the Federal Board for Vocational Education, the War Department continued to assist whenever possible to "lighten the burden" of the wounded soldier.[91] During their work, it became clear to Colonel Woods that the Federal Board was not meeting the needs of disabled soldiers. In response, Woods and his men were in constant touch with the Board and "as tactfully as [they] could, brought to their attention miscarriages of policy and lapses in administration."[92]

Woods also assigned Edward Leo Holl, the assistant to the Director of Placement for Technical men, to find jobs for disabled servicemen. Holl, who graduated from the University of Pennsylvania, had experience as an employment manager. He was assisted by other field representatives in the four districts, along with volunteers from social welfare organizations. One field representative, Major Rutledge (chief of the Eastern District), had previous experience as a social welfare executive in the public sector. Rutledge used his knowledge and connections to expedite Vocational Training and Compensation claims and worked closely with welfare agencies to meet the particular needs of injured ex-soldiers. Frederick Orville Perkins (who had substantial experiences in the business world as both a vice president and a company director) studied the problems of rehabilitating the disabled and explored the potential of industrial training. In June 1919, Woods announced courses for disabled men who would be paid during training and sent out bulletins providing important information about various federal, civic, and fraternal agencies that provided help to disabled veterans. To help reach "crippled men" panhandling on the streets in their uniforms, Woods asked civilians to inform the disabled men "of provision made for them by the government."[93]

After the Federal Board for Vocational Education stopped hospital visits on July 1, 1919 (due to financial constraints), the War Department's Emergency Employment Committee representatives filled the void and went to hospitals. There they made sure that wounded and disabled men knew where to go for employment help when they recovered. Woods team arranged to have "captains of industry," especially those "who overcame disabilities in life," visit the injured servicemen. Colonel Woods also wrote letters to commanding officers of military hospitals announcing plans to send successful business leaders to inspire wounded soldiers and lift their spirits. He wrote to military hospital commanders and asked them to provide stenographic records of the talks since the War Department hoped to produce a book along with "sketches" of the speakers' careers (never published). All proceeds would go toward helping disabled men. John Hays Hammond, founder of the Hammond Radio Research Corporation and inventor of radio controlled boats and a controlled torpedo system, and Charles M. Schwab, president of Bethlehem Steel Company, spoke with soldiers at Walter Reed General Hospital in Washington, DC. Steel magnate Elbert H. Gary and former U.S. attorney general, George W. Wickersham, spoke with disabled men at the U.S. Army General Hospital.[94]

CONCLUSION

With the Armistice of November 11, 1918, the United States looked forward to a new and brighter future. But rising unemployment, relentless labor conflicts, and a Red Scare coincided with the return of some four million soldiers, sailors, and marines. Cutbacks from a laissez-fare government and charges of pro-unionism all but paralyzed the Department of Labor's U.S. Employment Service. Fearful that radicalism would poison returning soldiers and motivated by a sense of moral obligation to help young men who served their country, the War Department responded to the growing employment problem.

The War Department's Emergency Employment Committee for Soldiers, Sailors, and Marines of the Council of National Defense helped find jobs through industrial retraining classes, "spruce-up" campaigns, public works efforts, citation awards, and an effective employment card service. To combat the overall economic crisis, the War Department sent military officers to head up the U.S. Employment Service's Bureau for Returning Soldiers, Sailors, and Marines. The new assistant to the Secretary of War, Colonel Arthur Woods, gathered together the best and the brightest military officers who had pertinent prewar experience and relied on economic experts for assistance. From his war experience with the CPI, the government's wartime propaganda machine, Woods understood the need for an effective publicity campaign to convince employers of their "patriotic duty" to hire Uncle Sam's fighting men.

In September 1919, Colonel Arthur Woods stepped down from his duties but not before recommending that the vital work conducted by his "office be discontinued only as the need for it disappears."[95] Major General William George Haan became the new head of the Emergency Employment Committee. Haan was a graduate of the U.S. Military Academy (1889) and served in the artillery as a Second Lieutenant in various posts before fighting in the Philippine-American War. During the Great War, Haan commanded the Thirty-second Division in France where he received the Distinguished

Service Medal. After leading the VII Corps in the occupation of Germany, General Haan returned to Washington, DC. to serve in the War Department General Staff. Lt. Colonel Mathew Smith of the War Plans Division assisted Haan with the Emergency Employment Committee. Haan and Smith continued policies established by Colonel Woods and also increased assistance to disabled ex-servicemen.

In December 1919, as the economy began to improve, the War Department phased out the Emergency Employment Committee. According to reports submitted by military officers from the Bureau for Returning Soldiers, Sailors, and Marines, 1,322,494 discharged men registered for assistance, and the Emergency Employment Committee found jobs for 949,901 by the end of 1919.[96]

After leaving the War Department in 1919, Colonel Woods continued to put his talents toward trying to solve problems associated with a deteriorating economy. On October 4, 1921, President Warren Harding announced the appointment of Colonel Woods as head of the Economic Advisory Committee. In 1931, as chairman of Herbert Hoover's Unemployment Committee, Colonel Woods unsuccessfully argued against the president's rejection of the Wagner Bill and pushed for other government economic reforms. General W. G. Haan continued his military service until his retirement in 1922. In a final report, Captain C. B. Hammond, chief of the Service and Information Section under General Woods, summarized the War Department's employment work as, "of the utmost value and importance not only to the discharged servicemen of the Great War but as well to the country at large, and in which it has been a matter of the greatest satisfaction and inspiration to have assisted."[97]

Documents

1. THE PREPAREDNESS MOVEMENT: AMERICA REEVALUATES ITS MILITARY

"Roosevelt Urges Nation to Prepare: Pacifists, He Tells Exposition Audience"

Wants a Larger Army
Asserts Readiness to Fight Is Peace Insurance—
Derides "Elocution as a Substitute for Action."

San Francisco, July 21.—Colonel Theodore Roosevelt delivered two addresses today at the Panama-Pacific Exposition, one vigorous in tone on military preparedness, the other a brief, personal talk to "the men on the line," soldiers, sailors, and marines, at the enlisted men's club.

Colonel Roosevelt told the enlisted men that a man afraid to fight is not fit to vote. "A mother who is not willing to raise her boy to be a soldier," he said, "is not fit for citizenship."

In the main speech of the day the Colonel was warmly applauded when in an explanatory way he said:

"I'm not for war, I want peace, but don't want peace for Uncle Sam because outsiders don't think him worth kicking...."

Preparedness as Peace Insurance.

"I advocate preparedness against war as the best type of peace insurance. Preparedness for war may be not only the best, but the only corrective for the spirit of militarism."

Source: New York Times, July 22, 1915, 1.

"National Defense and the Market"

Bernard M. Baruch, one of the most successful members of the New York Stock Exchange, has left New York for a six weeks' trip through the West, and his absence yesterday was construed by some of the bears on the market as evidence that he saw no immediate likelihood of an active market. Mr. Baruch was quoted yesterday as saying that the only thing which prevented a bull market was the country's unpreparedness. "The most important thing before us financially, commercially and economically," said Mr. Baruch, "is the immediate organization of an adequate military and naval defense, not only for what this country possesses, but for the protection of the ideals it represents and stands for. The industrial business that has come to our country, not only because of war orders, but on account of the purchases of neutral nations, is sooner or later bound to be felt by the railroads. Better business for the carriers means better business generally, which means national prosperity. Security values are being affected, and will be affected for some time to come by the demand for capital to continue the war and repair the war's damage; but if the uncertainty concerning our ability to defend our possessions and wealth were removed by the organization of an adequate defense I believe this country would embark on one of the greatest eras of prosperity ever experienced."

Source: New York Times, July 8, 1915, 15.

"The Pulpit and War: A Protest against Preaching a Doctrine of National Preparedness"

To the Editor of the New York Times:

I see from a report in The Times, that the National Security League has sent letters to the clergy of the city of New York, requesting them to preach on "national defense" next Sunday, suggesting such topics as "The Duty of Preparedness" and "Peace through Preparedness."

The world is passing through the greatest crisis of its history. Civilization is turned upside down. Religion is overshadowed. Humanity is groping for light. My mail brings me most distressing letters from leaders in Europe who are utterly discouraged and dismayed.

All Europe is looking to America to lead the world out of the pit and speak the word of lasting peace. Is the biggest word the American pulpit has for a groping listening world, on this Independence Day. "The Duty of Preparedness?" If there ever was a time when great nations as well as great men should be thinking of what they can do for the rest of the world, rather than of taking care of themselves, it is now. Let us hope the pulpits of New York will have some more prophetic message for the world next Sunday than self-protection—a word that does not occur in the Gospels.

It may interest the clergy of New York to know that I recently sent a letter to ten thousand of the most eminent ministers of the United States, asking them whether they sympathized with the movement to greatly increase armament, as the National Security League and Navy League are urging, or with President Wilson's recent utterance that any agitation of "America's unpreparedness for war" is unfortunate at just this time, and that twenty-nine out of every thirty answers were in sympathy with President Wilson's point of view. It is quite evident that the great majority of the clergy of this country are not being stampeded into militarism and are thinking of bigger things in these great hours than preparedness for war.

Frederick Lynch,
Editor the Christian Work.

Source: New York Times, July 2, 1915, 10.

The Plattsburg Manual: A Handbook for Military Training

This [hand]book is intended to serve as a foundation upon which the military beginner may build so that he may in time be able to study the technical service manuals intelligently. It has been written as an elementary textbook for those who desire to become Reserve Officers, for schools and colleges, and for those who may be called to the colors.

The authors have commanded companies at Plattsburg, New York, and, noting the need of such a text, compiled their observations while there.

The average man undergoing military training wants to know as much as possible about the art and science of war. He wants to acquire a good knowledge of the principles involved. He is interested in the technique of movements. He is willing to work for these things, but he often becomes lost in confusion when he attempts to study the technical service manuals. He does not know how to select the most important and omit the less important. The authors have selected from the standard texts some of the vitally important subjects and principles and have presented them to the civilian in a simple and plain way....

A Disciplined Soldier

You will be expected to become quickly amenable both mentally and physically to discipline. A clear conception on your part of what drills are disciplinary in character and what discipline really is, will help you to become a disciplined soldier. Drills executed at attention are disciplinary exercises and are designed to teach precise and soldierly movements and to inculcate that prompt and subconscious obedience which is essential to proper military control. Hence, all corrections should be given and received in an impersonal manner. Never forget that you lose your identity as an individual when you step into ranks; you then become merely a unit of a mass. As soon as you obey properly, promptly, and, at times, unconsciously the commands of your officers, as soon as you can cheerfully give up pleasures and personal privileges that conflict with the new order of life to which you have submitted, you will then have become a disciplined man.

Source: O. O. Ellis and E. B. Garey, The Century Co., New York [undated, but probably published in 1915].

Congressional Records

Mr. Greene of Vermont....

I do not hesitate to declare myself as convinced beyond all manner of doubt that our present preparations for national defense are sorely inadequate. I believe they are sorely inadequate not only in contemplation of the possibilities of the present day but even for the ordinary routine peace establishment....

The bill does not go as far as I would like in the matter of numerical strength of the Army as a whole, and in the matter of providing for the best efficiency of some branches of the military service....

Republics Unprepared for War.

It seems to me that the world has grown old enough by this time, and our democratic-republican experiment in government has become strong enough by this time, so that we might prudently venture a little readjustment of the practical application of this lesson of history. Why should we pay the terrible price of unpreparedness for war when a little foresight, a little common sense, may help us minimize the cost and the sacrifice, if not often avoid it altogether because our preparation actually prevented war? Why should we be content to dwell in a fool's paradise of fancied security from all attack just to make the philosophy of history good by blundering through to ultimate victory with a frightful sacrifice of lives and treasure when we are attacked? Why not do with the Nation as we do with ourselves individually —take out a little life insurance?

Dread of Large Standing Armies.

The English-speaking people are born to an inherited dread of great standing armies, it is true, and there was a time when English-speaking men, and men of all tongues for that matter, had a good right to dread them. But those were the days of strong centralized monarchies, practically absolute monarchies, when the soldiers belonged to the King, were paid by the King, and served the King alone. Nothing like that exists to-day [sic] nor has it ever existed in the United States. Why should men continue to terrify the multitude with the idea that any attempt to raise the United States Army must mean a militaristic domination and tyranny such as old King George once undertook here rather unsuccessfully, if memory serves aright? No such thing is possible to-day because the soldiers not only come from the people themselves, but they are paid by the people and serve the people directly and nobody else. And always and forever the people can have just as many of them or just as few of them as they please by simply keeping their hands on the purse strings....

"This is the Last of War."

After every war of modern times there have not been lacking men to prophesy that was the last of war. After every war of unusual duration, that left nations apparently exhausted by the terrible struggle, left them to mourn enormous losses among the finest and the best of the manhood in their lands, left them to care for multitudes of widows and orphans, left them to help support a mournful roll of hideously crippled veterans, left them to rebuild waste places, regain commerce, struggle beneath a burden of debt, and wrestle with desolation, hunger, disease, and poverty—after every such great historic catastrophe many men have said that such a nation can not for many a generation, at least, become a belligerent power again and participate in another such struggle as that which recently well-nigh wrecked it forever.

And yet every lesson of history from the earliest time proves exactly the contrary. One has only to study for a little while the history of Europe from the days of the Napoleonic wars, a little over a century ago, down to the present time to find that nation after nation went through just such an experience only to emerge in the end with a reinvigorated vitality, a new national consciousness and pride, a reawakened national purpose, and the inspiration to a redoubled and better organized energy that raised it to a plane of economic wealth and social greatness it had never reached before.

I will admit that simply because these benefits do come out of war despite its frightful horrors and unspeakable miseries is no reason why nations should invite war or even run the risk needlessly to become involved in war. War is a calamity to any people that must bear it, no matter how beneficial to posterity its results may ultimately prove to be. But I do suggest that when we know that any civilization that is destined to live at all and is founded upon race ideals that are determined to persist is not ruined by war, when we know that war does not have the effect of putting these great nations out of the forces on this globe to be reckoned with even to the death, it is folly for us in America to sit idly by with contentment in our fool's paradise and say, "When this war in Europe is over all the powers will be so exhausted that they can make no more war, and we shall be safe."

Source: U.S. Congress, V. 53, Part 3–5, March 17, 2006. 64th Congress, 1st Session, Feb. 4, 1916–March 30, 1916, 4330–4337.

Congressional Records

Mr. London.

In a previous address I dwelt at length on the fallacy and iniquity of the preparedness propaganda. The bill now before us provides for an unusually large increase of the Military Establishment. It carries with it an additional burden of taxes....

I suppose we all agree that the most charitable thing that can be said about the Army and Navy is that they are necessary evils. We do not want to increase the evil unless we must. In proposing an extraordinary addition to the Army we must first determine whether the increase is essential for the defense of a national policy....

The primary question, then, which we have to decide is, what is our national policy? Have we a national policy?

The fact that the Committee on Military Affairs brought in a unanimous report providing for an addition to the Army merely shows that both the Republicans and Democrats have surrendered to the clamor of the press. It means that the elected representatives of the people have suspended their judgment. Have abandoned the right to think for themselves, and have permitted two or three dozen individuals in the editorial rooms of the newspapers to fix the policy of the country....

Instead of a national policy, we have a national panic, and the national panic is particularly strong among Members of Congress. They seem to be scared out of their wits. With bulging eyes they scan the columns of the newspapers to find what the newspapers have to say about them....

With a definite national policy we can prepare adequate means to sustain it. No one will contend that the increased Army is intended for purposes of attack upon other nations. It is, then, to be used for defense. If for defense, then against whom? Is it not in order to ascertain from where and from whom danger threatens the United States?...

Some say that the lesson of the need for preparedness is being taught by the European war. I draw an entirely different lesson from this war.

The war was prepared just as surely as an explosion is prepared when enormous quantities of dynamite are accumulated. It is the very maintenance of big armies that has made the war possible—nay, inevitable. Will anyone dare gainsay that we would all have been better off today if there were no armies in Europe in August, 1914?...

It will require all the strength of strong men to resist the invasion, not of a foreign enemy, not of a great military force, but of militaristic ideas. As long as the war continues there will be men among us for whom no army will be big enough, who will always want more preparedness, more of an army, more of a navy—and the more they will get the more will they demand....

We are told that war is inevitable; that it can not be foreseen; that it comes with suddenness, and that it is a part of human nature. There was surely nothing sudden about the present war. Was not Europe preparing for a quarter of a century for this very war?

War is no more inevitable than the plague is inevitable. War is no more a part of human nature than the burning of witches is a typically human act. Men succumbed to the plague because they were ignorant. Men burned witches because they were ignorant. When men came to understand the cause of the plague, the plague became impossible. When men will understand the cause of war, war will be made impossible....

The United States has no one to fear. It is invulnerable against attack. It is not in the increase of the Military Establishment that we shall place our hope for a greater and nobler America. Unless we are determined to become a world power in the sense of competing with other nations, by force of arms, for the possession of markets and for the extension of our colonial empire we need no increase of the Army and Navy. We are now a world power, a world power for good. The average American fails to understand to what extent this Republic has been a source of inspiration to all lovers of liberty all over the world. Let this Republic remain free from the contamination of militarist ideals.

Although I believe that the Committee on Military Affairs could have done a great deal worse, I feel constrained to announce that I will vote against any increase of the Military Establishment, as such an increase would mean that Congress has yielded to the false "preparedness" campaign.

Source: U.S. Congress, V. 53, Part 3–5, March 17, 2006. 64th Congress, 1st Session, Feb. 4, 1916–March 30, 1916, 4353–4355.

2. DRAFTING & TRAINING CITIZEN-SOLDIERS: NEW CIVIL-MILITARY RELATIONS

"Roosevelt Would Ostracize Slacker"

Says Conscientious Objector Should Be Sent to Firing Line to Dig Trenches. NO STIGMA IN THE DRAFT

Mayor Welcomes American Medical Association in Patriotic Meeting in the Hippodrome.

Colonel Theodore Roosevelt delivered a scathing indictment of slackers, with especial attention to the "conscientious objector," in an address last night at a patriotic mass meeting in the Hippodrome of 6,000 delegates to the American Medical Association Convention. The Colonel stamped under foot any idea that there might be an iota of stigma attached to being drafted, and called the men who would be drafted more fortunate than their brothers who were not. He said that the boy who was drafted was just as honorable as the boy at Plattsburg or the boy who joined the National Guard. Slackers he called "miserable creatures who should be hunted out of the society of self-respecting men and women...."

"The conscientious objector," he said, "curtains his cowardice behind the statement that he objects to placing himself in a position where he might take part in killing some one. I'd guard his conscience. I'd send him to the front, but I wouldn't give him a gun. I'd put him to digging kitchen sinks and trenches so that good men could rest until the time came for them to kill some one. Then I'd watch his conscience to see what it would do. There may be albino crows, but I'll judge the crows I meet by those I've seen."

Source: New York Times, June 8, 1917, p. 5.

Long Live the Constitution of the United States Socialist Party, Pennsylvania

The 13th Amendment, Section 1, of the Constitution of the United States says: "Neither slavery nor involuntary servitude, except as a punishment for crime whereof the party shall have been duly convicted, shall exist within the United States, or any place subject to their jurisdiction."

The Constitution of the United States is one of the greatest bulwarks of political liberty. It was born after a long, stubborn battle between king-rule and democracy. (We see little or no difference between arbitrary power under the name king and under a few misnamed "representatives.") In this battle the people of the United States established the principle that freedom of the individual and personal liberty are the most sacred things in life. Without them we become slaves....

The Thirteenth Amendment to the Constitution of the United States... embodies this sacred idea. The Socialist Party says that this idea is violated by the Conscription Act. When you conscript a man and compel him to go abroad to fight against his will, you violate the most sacred right of personal liberty, and substitute for it what Daniel Webster called "despotism in its worst form."

A conscript is little better than a convict. He is deprived of his liberty and of his right to think and act as a free man. A conscripted citizen is forced to surrender his right as a citizen and become a subject. He is forced into involuntary servitude. He is deprived of the protection given him by the Constitution of the United States. He is deprived of all freedom of conscience in being forced to kill against his will.

Are you one who is opposed to war, and were you misled by the venal capitalist newspapers, or intimidated or deceived by gang politicians and registrars into believing that you would not be allowed to register your objection to conscription? Do you know that many citizens of Philadelphia insisted on their right to answer the famous question twelve, and went on record with their honest opinion of opposition to war, notwithstanding the deceitful efforts of our rulers and the newspaper press to prevent them from doing so? Shall it be said that the citizens of Philadelphia, the cradle of American liberty, are so lost to a sense of right and justice that they will let such monstrous wrongs against humanity go unchallenged?

In a democratic country each man must have the right to say whether he is willing to join the army. Only in countries where uncontrolled power rules can despot force his subjects to fight. Such a man or men have no place in a democratic republic. This is tyrannical power in its worst form. It gives control over the life and death of the individual to a few men. There is no man good enough to be given such power.

Source: Records of the United States Attorney, National Archives, Mid Atlantic Region, Philadelphia, RG 118.

Raymond B. Fosdick Commission on Training Camp Activities

The Commission's aim is to surround the men in service with an environment which is not only clean and wholesome but positively inspiring—the kind of environment which a democracy owes to those who fight on its behalf.

Source: Records of the War Department, General and Special Staffs, War College and War Plans Division, Subordinate Offices Education and Recreation Branch, Record Group 165, National Archives, Washington, D.C., June, 1918.

Capt. Edward R. Padgett

From out of the melting pot of America's admixture of races is being poured a new American, a soldier man who, warring the khaki and covered with the dust of the parade ground, is stepping forth into the ranks, file upon file of him, to make the world safe for democracy.... He is the "non English speaking solders," who along with his American-born brothers, has been selected through the draft to drive the overseas barbarians back into their lair.

There are thousands and thousands of foreign-speaking soldiers in our army camps, and thousands more will arrive with the coming draft. We know now what to do with them now, how to weed out the tares from the wheat, how to reach the best in the heart of the alien soldiers and develop it, how to loosen his tongue and to teach him the principles of American Citizens. And we know, too that he will respond to such treatments. We know that this so-called "Camp Gordon Plan" is the one which will add thousand and thousands of virile, efficient soldiers to our armies on the battle lines....

Soldier after soldiers is turned out fit and eager to fight for liberty under the Stars and Stripes, mindful of the traditions of his race and the land of his nativity and conscious of the principles for which he is fighting.

Source: The Infantry Journal, October, 1918.

Scott's Official History of the American Negro in the World War, 1919

Efforts of Dr. Springarn [Plattsburg Preparedness Training Camp, 1915]

Dr. Joel E. Spingarn consulted Gen. Leonard Wood, who was at this time in charge of the Eastern Department, Governor's Island, New York, about the establishment of a "Plattsburg" for colored men. General Wood gave assurance that the same aid and assistance could be given a camp for colored men that were given the camp for white men, provided 200 men of college grade could be secured. Dr. Spingarn set out upon a vigorous campaign, sending letters and circulars in every direction and personally visiting Howard University and kindred institutions. Success crowned his indefatigable industry, but not without great opposition.

Dr. Spingarn's efforts, by many of the important newspapers and leaders of the race, were referred to as being designed to bring about the establishment of a "Jim Crow Camp" for training colored officers. The agitation grew quite violent at times, particularly because of the fact that Dr. Spingarn was Chairman of the Executive Committee of the National Association for the Advancement of Colored People, an organization generally regarded as standing uncompromisingly for the rights of the Negro people. In his efforts to secure the establishment of this camp Dr. Spingarn had the cooperation of his aide, Dr. W. E. B. DuBois, Editor of *The Crisis*, also regarded as an uncompromising champion of the Negro, and of Col. Charles Young, United States Army, and such virile speakers and leaders as William Pickens and others. The agitation among the Negro group and the recognized friends of the Negro grew so warm that for a while divided counsels threatened the establishment of a camp. Whether through a fortunate or unfortunate turn of circumstances, while this agitation was at its height, Congress declared that a state of war existed between the United States and the Imperial German Government. Immediately, civilian training camps were abolished and fourteen Government camps were established for the training of officers.

Strange and paradoxical as it may seem, America, while fighting for the democratization of the peoples of far-off Europe, was denying democracy to a part—an honest, loyal and patriotic part—of her citizens at home. Fourteen camps were instituted for the training of *WHITE* officers—none for colored officers, nor were colored men admitted to any of the fourteen camps....

"THE COLORED PEOPLE OF THE COUNTRY MAKING STRENUOUS EFFORTS TO SECURE TRAINING CAMP FOR COLORED OFFICERS." [1917]

Headquarters and Recruiting Station at Howard University.

"According to the best authorities about 83,000 Negroes will be drafted for the New Federal Army. The Negroes welcome this opportunity of serving their country, and sharing their full responsibilities in this time of national peril. They feel, however, that Negro troops thus raised should be officered by men of their own race and are making strenuous efforts to secure a training camp in which such officers can be prepared. The War Department has stated that it is impracticable to admit Negroes to the fourteen camps for officers to be opened on May 14, 1917. And it has also stated that no officers are to be commissioned unless they receive training in one of these camps. This means that unless some provision is made whereby colored men may be trained for officers these 83,000 Negro troops will be officered exclusively by white officers; and that Negroes qualified both mentally and physically to serve as officers will be forced under the conscription law to serve as privates. The colored man is willing and ready to carry out the duties imposed upon him as an American citizen, and feels that he should be given the same opportunities in the performance of these duties as are given to other American citizens. The Negroes from every section are requesting that the Government provide means whereby colored officers may be trained. The appeal is just, reasonable, and practicable. The proposition is squarely up to the Government. This is no time for sectional differences and race prejudice and the highest patriotism demands that every American citizen be given the opportunity to serve his country in the capacity for which he is best fitted."

"Over one thousand colored men have sent their names to their headquarters at Howard University, and hundreds of others are arriving by mail and telegrams."

"Why should not colored troops be officered by colored men? Their records show them to be competent and efficient, and to deny any class of citizens the opportunity of rendering its best service belies the very theory of our democracy, and the basic principle for which the present war is waged. Our American statesmen should frown upon any procedure that does not offer an equal opportunity for all at all times, but more especially at a time when our country is faced by a foreign foe."

Source: Emmett J. Scott, AM., LL.D., Special Adjutant to Secretary of War.

Black Bayonet Fighters

The new dispatches, which, of course, come from French sources, but garbled as they are, bear the following eloquent testimony to the words of the sainted emancipator:

London, Aug. 7.—American Colored brigaded with the army of General Gourad, east of Rheims, are doing such remarkable work in action with their bayonets that they are now said to excel all other men on the fighting front in their use of these weapons. It is said they are particularly fond of this style of fighting, and have broken all bayonet records on the western front. So pleased are French commanders with the work of these men from the United States that all Colored regiments arriving from America will receive hearty welcomes to the fighting lines.

When these troops of the allies drive those of the Huns back to Berlin, it will not be the American Marines—brave as their exploits have been, and heavy as has been their heroic death toll, and from whose ranks such black bayonet fighters as these the French glorify are excluded, it will not be the American aviators from whose death-defying battalions such martyrs as Quentin Roosevelt have given their last full measure of devotion, and from whose ranks, also, such soldiers as these French call "comrade" are barred by American color-phobia, but it will be by these black boys, denied an equal chance, who bayonet their bloody way into Wilhelmstrasse.

When the war is won, and the veterans of the Stars and Stripes have had their last bivouac "over there"; when they have marched past the President in final review down Pennsylvania avenue; when they have returned such of them as are left, to their humble homes, to greet such of their families and friends as are left, to take up again their humble places as hewers of wood and drawers of water in American industry, they will submit to lynching, disfranchisement, jim-crow cars and segregation NO LONGER, as their just portion of victory.

They are going to demand—these brave black bayonet fighters—they are going to accept nothing less than an equal place in this Republic.

They are going to be equals; as declares the Declaration of Independence, in their inalienable right to life, liberty and the pursuit of happiness.

In the right to eat the bread, without leave of anybody, which their own hands earn; they are henceforth going to be equals of every living man, and see to it, as President Wilson pronounced that the laws are kept "inviolate."

Source: *Cleveland Advocate*, Vol. 5, Issue 15, p. 8, The Ohio Historical Society: The African-American Experience in Ohio 1850–1920, August 17, 1918 (linked to Library of Congress, American Memory).

3. MOBILIZING PUBLIC OPINION AND SUPPRESSING DISSENT: CIVIL-MILITARY COOPERATION AND CONFLICT

American War Measures

Committee on Public Information.—This committee, established by executive order on April 14, 1917, consists of the Secretaries of State, War, and Navy and Mr. George Creel, chairman, who is charged with the executive direction of its work. It was created to perform the combined functions of censorship and publicity; and has been organized into seventeen divisions: executive, civic and educational co-operation, official bulletin, speaking, four-minute men, news, syndicate features, films, pictures, newspapers, business management, labour [sic] publications, New York branch, women's war work, reference, art, and advertising. It publishes a daily official bulletin; and has issued 18,000,000 copies of fifteen different pamphlets in seven languages-including an annotated edition of the President's *War Message and Facts behind It, How the War came to America,* a national service handbook, a war cyclopedia, *German War Practices,* and a series of shorter pamphlets. It conducts speaking campaigns, maintains news service in European and American countries, and prepares and exhibits motion picture exhibits in the United States and foreign countries. It supervises the voluntary censorship of the newspaper and periodical press, and establishes rules and regulations for the cable censorship of press dispatches. Under the provisions of the Trading with the Enemy Act, a censorship board was appointed in October, consisting of representatives of the Secretaries of War and the Navy, the Postmaster-General, the war trade board, and the chairman of the committee on public information. It controls communication by mail, cable, radio, or vessel between the United States and foreign countries.

Source: John A. Fairlie, Esq., Ph.D., Professor of Political Science, University of Illinois, *Journal of Comparative Legislation and International Law,* 18 (1918): 98.

Public Opinion in War Time
By George Creel,
Chairman, Committee on Public Information, Washington, D.C.

Now more than at any other time in history the importance of public opinion has come to be recognized. The fight for it is a part of the military program of every country, for every belligerent nation has brought psychology to the aid of science....

Any discussion of public opinion must necessarily be prefaced by some slight attempt at definition. Just what do we mean by it? A great many people think that public opinion is a state of mind, formed and changed by the events of the day or by the events of the hour; that it is sort of a combination of kaleidoscope and weathercock. I disagree with this theory entirely. I do not believe that public opinion has its rise in the emotions, or that it is tipped from one extreme to the other by every passing rumor, by every gust of passion, or by every storm of anger. I feel that public opinion has its source in the minds of people, that it has its base in reason, and that it expresses slow-formed convictions rather than any temporary excitement or any passing passion of the moment. I may be wrong, but since mine is the responsibility, mine is the decision, and it is upon that decision that every policy of the committee has been based. We have never preached any message of hate. We have never made any appeal to the emotions, but we have always by every means in our power tried to drive home to the people the causes behind this war, the great fundamental necessities that compelled a peace-loving nation to take up arms to protect free institutions and preserve our liberties.

We had to establish new approaches in a great many respects to drive home these truths. We believed in the justice of our cause. We believed passionately in the purity of our motives. We believed in the nobility and the disinterestedness of our aims, and we felt that in order to win unity, in order to gain the verdict of mankind, all we had to do was to give facts in the interest of full understanding. It may be said that there was no great necessity for this—that this war was going on for three years before America entered it—but I cannot but feel that on April 6, 1917, there was very little intelligent understanding of fundamentals, for those three years had been years of controversy and years of passion-two things that are absolutely opposed to intelligent public opinion. You had your pro-Allies, you had your pro-Germans, you had your people who thought war was a horrible thing and who shrank from it without grasping the great significances invaded; and so on the day we entered war we had a frazzled emotionalism, with people whose sensibilities had grown numb by very violence. We had to approach people to try to drive home to them some great truths....

As for the censorship on free speech, it is not imposed by Washington, but by the intolerances and bigotries of individual communities.

The government is not responsible for mobs that hang innocent men, that paint houses yellow and that run up and down the country trying to crush honest discussion. . . .

Source: *Annuals of American Political and Social Science*, 78 (July 1918): 185–186,192.

Sedition Act
May 16 1918

Sec. 3. Whoever, when the United States is at war, shall willfully make or convey false reports or false statements with intent to interfere with the operation or success of the military or naval forces of the United States, or to promote the success of its enemies, or shall willfully make or convey false reports or false statements, or say or do anything except by way of bona fide and not disloyal advice to an investor or investors, with intent to obstruct the sale by the United States of bonds or other securities of the United States or the making of loans by or to the United States, and whoever when the United States is at war, shall willfully cause or attempt to cause, or incite or attempt to incite, insubordination, disloyalty, mutiny, or refusal of duty, in the military or naval forces of the United States, or shall willfully obstruct or attempt to obstruct the recruiting or enlistment services of the United States, and whoever, when the United States is at war, shall willfully utter, print, write or publish any disloyal, profane, scurrilous, or abusive language about the form of government of the United States or the Constitution of the United States, or the military or naval forces of the United States, or the flag of the United States, or the uniform of the Army or Navy of the United States into contempt, scorn, contumely, or disrepute, or shall willfully utter, print, write, or publish any language intended to incite, provoke, or encourage resistance to the United States, or to promote the cause of its enemies, or shall willfully display the flag of any foreign enemy, or shall willfully by utterance, writing, printing, publication, or language spoken, urge, incite, or advocate any curtailment of production in this country of any thing or things, product or products, necessary or essential to the prosecution of the war in which the United States may be engaged, with intent by such curtailment to cripple or hinder the United States in the prosecution of war, and whoever shall willfully advocate, teach, defend, or suggest the doing of any of the acts or things in this section enumerated, and whoever shall by word or act support or favor the cause of any country with which the United States is at war or by word or act oppose the cause of the United States therein, shall be punished by a fine of not more than $10,000 or the imprisonment for not more than twenty years, or both: Provided, That any employee or official of the United States Government who commits any disloyal act or utters any unpatriotic or disloyal language, or who, in an abusive and violent manner criticizes the Army or Navy or the flag of the United States shall be at once dismissed from the service....

Sec. 4. When the United States is at war, the Postmaster General may, upon evidence satisfactory to him that any person or concern is using the mails in violation of any of the provisions of this Act, instruct the postmaster at any post office at which mail is received addressed to such person or concern to return to the postmaster at the office at which they were originally mailed all letters or other matter so addressed, with the words 'Mail to this address undeliverable under Espionage Act' plainly written or stamped upon the outside thereof, and all such letters or other matter so returned to such postmasters shall be by them returned to the senders thereof under such regulations as the Postmaster General may prescribe.

Source: United States, Statues at Large, Washington, D.C., 1918, Vol. XL, pp 553 ff, Amendment to Section 3 of the Espionage Act of June 15, 1917.

War Department
Headquarters Spruce Production Division
Bureau of Aircraft Production
Yeon Bldg., Portland Ore.

September 12, 1918

BULLETIN NO. 80

1. It shall be the duty of all field officers of the Loyal Legion organization to make regular periodical visits to every logging camp and mill in their district.

2. Upon each visit such officers will inspect the books of the different logging companies and mills with a view to determine whether the provisions of the bulletins covering labor conditions, wage scales, etc. are being complied with. Reports of violations will be made to this office with a statement as to the action taken by the company after the matter has been brought to their attention, which will be done at the time by the officers making the inspection.

3. All field officers should immediately impress upon the employee members of the Loyal Legion of Loggers and Lumbermen that the successful operation of their organization during the war period will depend largely upon their co-operation. All employees should be given to understand that they have a means, through the organization of the Loyal Legion of Loggers and Lumbermen, to adjust all differences that may come up.

It is the intention of the Central Council that the membership of each local shall meet frequently to discuss their own affairs, entirely without the atmosphere of influence of the employers, and all matters discussed by employees should be handled freely, without prejudice or malice, but affording a frank and open discussion among the men themselves.

All matters requiring adjustment should be handled by the local council, who should carry them to the employers, and, failing to adjust them through this means, they should be reported to the district officers, whose duty it will be to refer such matters to the District Council.

BRUICE P. DISQUE,
Colonel, Air Services, U.S.A., Commanding

BPD/B

alg.

Source: *Spruce Production Corporation,* Bulletins, November 1917–November 1918, RG18, Box 1, National Archives and Record Administration II.

Shall German Be Dropped from our Schools?

There has been of late, as we all know, a great deal of talk and not a little ill-considered action in connection with the present and future status of German as a subject of study in our high schools and colleges. Many articles...written to show the folly of the proposed dropping of so important a subject [were written by language teachers.] It therefore seemed better to put before you something in the nature of a symposium of opinions of men of prominence who are in other lines of work than our own but who, from their experience and connections, are in position to judge of the value of German as a tool in the cultural and scientific and business activities of the present and of the coming generations of students....

The following are distinctly opposed to the study of German in our schools:...

2. Prof. [Theodore W.] Richards, director of the Wolcott Gibbs Memorial Laboratory at Harvard, thinks that the diabolical methods of the German Government have so discredited Germany in the minds of decent people that she cannot regain her former prestige and that therefore the teaching of the language is much less important than formerly.

3. Prof. Franklin H. Giddings of Columbia University writes in part as follows:..."I think it should be not merely discouraged but forbidden. It is difficult to avoid the conclusion that the entire German nation has lost all moral sense...."

4. Dr. L.H. Baekeland, of Belgium and Yonkers, a widely known chemist, says that it would be "little loss to our country if we stopped the study of German until Germany has again shown herself worthy to be counted with civilized nations.... It would have been much better for the world at large if the majority of the German literature had never existed."

5. Dr. Gregory Torossian, a well-known chemist of Cleveland, thinks that the value of German has been overrated, that the war has shown the absolute bankruptcy of the German intellect and morals, that the position of Germany after the war will be that of Scandinavia, and that the German language will cease to play any role in the world's affairs. We can ill afford, he thinks, to waste time on the study of a language which is the exponent of Medievalism in thought, in culture, in morals and in deeds. These are the only absolute opponents to the study from whom I have received replies....

All the other letters received are distinctly of a different tone and are unreservedly in favor of continuing the study of the German language and literature. You will note that this last group of replies is by far the largest.

12. President [John Geir] Hibben of Princeton writes: "I am thoroughly in agreement with you that the war with Germany should not lead us to discontinue or discourage the study of the German language in our schools. That would be a very narrow minded policy and quite unworthy of our American spirit...."

18. Dr. Lyman Abbott, of *The Outlook,* thinks that while there may be localities where it is not best to teach the German language in the public schools, it would be an act of unspeakable folly to cut ourselves off from the literature and science which the German people have contributed to the world. To do this would, he says, be to institute a blockade of our own coasts to the importation of inestimable wealth.

Source: The Modern Language Journal, Volume II, No. 5 (February, 1918)

4. OVER THERE: SCIENCE, TECHNOLOGY AND MODERN WARFARE

The Division of Gas Warfare of the War Department

By direction of President Wilson all the activities of the government concerned with manufacturing poison gas for war and experimenting in the work of devising new methods were transferred to the control of the War Department on July I....

President Wilson has signed an order transferring the chemical section of the Bureau of Mines of the Department of the Interior to the War Department in accordance with the President's decision that measures for the use of gas as a weapon of offense and defense should be coordinated under the War Department. Experiments on war gas and masks have been divided among several branches of the government, including the Ordnance and Medical Departments of the army.

The most extensive work has been conducted by the Bureau of Mines, which established a special chemical laboratory at the American University on the outskirts of Washington. About 1,700 American Chemists have given the government the benefit of their advice, experience, and services in this work and important results are predicted....

In a letter dated June 26 to Dr. Van H. Manning, chief of the Bureau of Mines, notifying him of the coordination of war gas experimental work in the War Department, President Wilson wrote as follows:...

The Secretary of War has assured me of his own recognition of the splendid work you have been able to do, and I am taking the liberty of inclosing a letter which I have received from him in order that you may see how fully the War Department recognizes the value of the services.... I want, however, to express to you my own appreciation of the fine and helpful piece of work which you have done, and to say that this sort of teamwork by the bureaus outside of the direct war-making agency is one of the cheering and gratifying evidences of the way our official forces are inspired by the presence of a great national task.

Source: Science, 48 (July 5, 1918): 6–7.

Scientific Notes and News

PROFESSOR THEODORE LYMAN, of the department of physics at Harvard University, has received from the War Department a commission as captain in the aviation department of the United States Signal Corps, and has been ordered to report for active service in France. Profesor [sic] Lyman has been since 1910 director of the Jefferson Physical Laboratory at Harvard.

Source: Science, 46 (September 7, 1917): 233.

New York Private Wilfred H. Allen 308th Infantry, 27th Division in France.

Sept 28—Si Walsh and Jordan killed by shell fire. Several wounded. Simson accidentally shot himself in leg. Joe Yund and I helped carry him out to dressing station. Stayed out all day and went back in after dark. Corp White , Grier, Clark and Stoner all from my squad were hurt during day. White and Clark were killed. Lewis and Gayno shell-shocked.

Sept 29—(Over the top) at 5.50 A.M. Several men were gassed before we went over. Advanced to top of ridge. Capt. Smith killed. 1st Lt. McKory and 2nd Lt. Kerr killed later. No officers left. Piece of shrapnel hit helmet and went through canister of my gas mask. Crawled to Rudiner and got extra mask. Lost company in smoke screen. When smoke screen lifted could look down in valley in Jerry's trenches. Crawled in shell hole. Sniper bullets hitting all around me. One went through my mess kit. Dug hole with jack-knife to crawl in. Man wounded near me. Took off his pack and gave him a drink. put him in my hole and dug another. At dusk, McCae and I took him to first aid station. Shot a Huns but don't think I hit them. Was put in sunken road as lookout, expecting counter-attack.

Sept 30—We went back to old front line trenches. Stayed there all night.

Source: Great War Society, Letters, Diaries, and Biographies, Doughboy Center: Story of the American Expeditionary Forces, Web site: http://www.worldwar1.com/dbc/biograph.htm.

Sgt. Albert K. Haas, Company E, 309th Infantry, 78th Division

Sunday, July 21, 1918: My First Time in No-Mans-Land

Just after dark [while training with Australians], I was invited to go for a walk. Not knowing where or why, I consented to without question. But when I was told to put my rifle in working order and to take a few hand grenades with me, my enthusiasm was not quite so keen. But I said nothing about my feelings to anyone. I had never seen a loaded hand grenade and we knew nothing about its operation except what I had learned from our lectures. I did know one thing and that was if the pin was pulled out of the grenade, it was time to throw it away as I had no further use for it.

I followed my two companions up and out it the trench into "No Man's Land", the area between the two front lines. At one time this area had been a prosperous farm. It was covered with wheat, now nearly ripe. While we moved along as quietly as possible, it seemed to me that the sound would be audible for miles. We proceeded until we reached a line of barbed wire in front of the Australian trenches and passed along the line until an opening was found, thru which we passed. Several times we were forced to remain perfectly still while a flare burned overhead. These flares transformed the night into day and while they burned for a comparatively short period of time, it seemed as though they would burn forever. When I heard the first machine gun bullets crack I wanted to get down on the ground, but followed the actions of the other two and remained standing. I soon learned that you could be reasonably certain that you could not be hit by a bullet that sounds that way. Once we had to get down and had to do it very quickly too! In doing so, one of the Australians encountered the putrid body of a dead German who had been there for some time. The stench from it was almost unbearable. The [Aussie] proceeded to hold a monologue in which he gave vent to his feelings with a series of oaths that would have made Satan himself blush. Without further excitement, we proceeded until we reached the enemy line of barbed wire. Passing along and examining it showed that there had been no gaps cut in the wire, which indicated that no action of any consequence was planned over the next few hours. We returned to our starting position again and sat down in the shelter of a small dug-out to rest and await further developments.

Thursday, October 17, 1918: I Get Shot

[With the Battalion attacking near St. Juvin in the Argonne Forest] we crossed through the fire at the top of the hill and back to where the [commanding] officer now lay. He had moved forward a few yards. I dropped into a small, shallow hole just in front of him. The hole was too small for me and I had to double up. We were so close that it was possible to carry on a conversation. He directed my attention to a certain point where he said he thought a machine gun nest was located. I looked, but not for a very long time. A series of whistles sent my head below the edge of the hole. Then, for a moment, I thought someone was throwing bottles at me and had hit me, for I became conscious of dull thud and a stinging sensation that lasted but a second. A man to the left of me let out a yell of pain; one just to the right stiffened up and fell dead. I then became aware of a burning sensation, but because of my position was unable to take an inventory.

Source: Great War Society, Letters, Diaries, and Biographies, Doughboy Center: Story of the American Expeditionary Forces, Web site: http://www.worldwar1.com/dbc/biograph.htm

––––––––––

A Letter to a Fellow Physician Describing Conditions During the Influenza Epidemic at Camp Devens

Camp Devens, Mass.
Surgical Ward No 16
29 September 1918
(Base Hospital)

My dear Burt—

It is more than likely that you would be interested in the news of this place, for there is a possibility that you will be assigned here for duty, so having a minute between rounds I will try to tell you a little about the situation here as I have seen it in the last week. As you know I have not seen much Pneumonia in the last few years in Detroit, so when I came here I was somewhat behind in the niceties of the Army way of intricate Diagnosis....

Camp Devens is near Boston, and has about 50,000 men, or did have before this epidemic broke loose. It also has the Base Hospital for the Div.

of the N. East. This epidemic started about four weeks ago, and has developed so rapidly that the camp is demoralized and all ordinary work is held up till it has passed. All assemblages of soldiers taboo.

These men start with what appears to be an ordinary attack of LaGrippe or Influenza, and when brought to the Hosp. they very rapidly develop the most viscous type of Pneumonia that has ever been seen. Two hours after admission they have the Mahogany spots over the cheek bones, and a few hours later you can begin to see the Cyanosis extending from their ears and spreading all over the face, until it is hard to distinguish the coloured [sic] men from the white. It is only a matter of a few hours then until death comes, and it is simply a struggle for air until they suffocate. It is horrible. One can stand it to see one, two or twenty men die, but to see these poor devils dropping like flies sort of gets on your nerves. We have been averaging about 100 deaths per day, and still keeping it up. There is no doubt in my mind that there is a new mixed infection here, but what I don't know....

The normal number of resident Drs. here is about 25 and that has been increased to over 250, all of whom (of course excepting me) have temporary orders—"Return to your proper Station on completion of work". Mine says "Permanent Duty", but I have been in the Army just long enough to learn that it doesn't always mean what it says. So I don't know what will happen to me at the end of this.

We have lost an outrageous number of Nurses and Drs., and the little town of Ayer is a sight. It takes Special trains to carry away the dead. For several days there were no coffins and the bodies piled up something fierce, we used to go down to the morgue (which is just back of my ward) and look at the boys laid out in long rows. It beats any sight they ever had in France after a battle. An extra long barracks has been vacated for the use of the Morgue, and it would make any man sit up and take notice to walk down the long lines of dead soldiers all dressed and laid out in double rows. We have no relief here, you get up in the morning at 5.30 and work steady till about 9.30 P.M., sleep, then go at it again. Some of the men of course have been here all the time, and they are TIRED....

My Boss was in just now and gave me a lot more work to do so I will have to close this.

Good By old Pal,
"God be with you till we meet again"
Keep the Bouells open.
(Sgd) Roy.

Source: The Influenza Pandemic of 1918, Web site: http://virus.stanford.edu/uda/.

5. DEMOBILIZATION AND REEMPLOYMENT:
THE WAR DEPARTMENT STEPS IN

Your Job Back Home,
A Book For Men Leaving the Service, 1919
Back to the Job at Home

When the pilot climbs aboard ship in America's debarkation harbors, or when orders come for mustering out at camp, the Job Back Home is about the most interesting and vitally important subject that presents itself to the man in uniform.

Even if he knows just what he wants to do, that job may not be waiting for him. Some of the home work is being handled by other men or women. Are they all going to step out and welcome back the men in khaki or blue? There are bound to be countless new adjustments for men to make before industry, agriculture, and commerce are back on regular schedule.

Daily drill in camp will give way to the whir of machinery, the whistles of steamship and locomotive, and the round of chores on the farm. There won't be the parades and the uniforms, nor the Captain's call to "Tenshun," nor the voices of comrades who a few months ago were helping make the world safe for Democracy. The great piece of war work is done and the Nation's own great work has begun again. That is the contented labor of a hundred millions of free people at their regular daily tasks. To maintain that labor and to preserve that contentment means that every man must find his place at once, do his best at it, and try to improve his own condition by improving himself.

As one man back from France well said it: "After I got into the army I threw off the old mental and physical lassitude that had come near making me a vegetable fit only for the boiling pot. Then something was born in me and something died, and I fought as a man can when he is in the best of physical condition and isn't afraid of anything in consequence."

"Now the war is over, and I must leave the army. But I want to keep on fighting. I think it is my duty to help my country in these days just as much as it was in the days of fighting. I am willing to do anything that will give me fighting—fighting against the difficulties of business or professional life."

That's it, up and down the line. Every man wants a week or two for visiting with his friends, and then- to work again, with new hopes, new ambitions, and a new faith in himself.

HELPING UNCLE SAM MEANS ALL THE TIME

The world has seen enough of autocracies that control the lives and fortunes of the people. It has seen enough, too, of the plots and plans by which people hope to rise by tearing down everything else. Uncle Sam's new army of democracy is a hundred million men working together, thinking together, planning together for the things that will make America a better place to live in. To be a soldier in the new army is as glorious as to have been fighting in the uniform, and the spirit of conquest need not be lacking.

Source: Library War Service of the American Library Association, Washington, 1919.

Establishing the War Department's Emergency Employment Committee for Soldiers, Sailors and Marines of the Council of National Defense

Reestablishment in Civil Life

But getting the armed forces demobilized was only part of the problem.

If no legal responsibility, at least a moral one, rested upon the Government, which had taken these men out of civil life, to render them all reasonable assistance in getting back into civil employment.

The best way of helping the home-coming men to reestablish themselves was to see to it that they went back to their old jobs or to better ones. While, at this time, there appears to have been no definite scheme for assisting the returned fighting men, the fact remains that there was in existence the United States Employment Service and it was only logical and right that its machinery should have been taken advantage of. Therefore, in cooperation with the existing national welfare organizations, Government agencies interested in demobilization, and local community organizations of all kinds, the United States Employment Service established Bureaus for Returned Soldiers, Sailors and Marines in practically every state in the Union...

Early in March 1919, the Emergency Employment Committee for Soldiers, Sailors and Marines of the Council of National Defense, with Colonel Arthur Woods, representing the Secretaries of both War and Navy as chairman, was formed in order to help meet the crisis brought about through the knowledge that the U.S. Employment Service would not have sufficient funds to continue its work.

One of the most important results of this meeting was that the interests of discharged sailors and marines were taken up as of equal concern with the interests of discharged soldiers. In all this work, consequently, either in the field or at headquarters, the interests of service men as a whole were considered without reference to their coming from the Army, Navy, or Marine Corps.

In order to attend more effectively to the inquiries from discharged sailors, and marines an officer of the Navy was detailed to the War Department for duty in connection therewith. (13)

Establishment of Office of Assistant to the Secretary of War

Even before the deficiency appropriation of the Service was cut (July 11, 1919) the Secretary of War foresaw that, unless something was done, and done quickly, the results of the breaking-down of the employment Service would be both far-reaching and of untold danger. It was obviously up to the War Department to step into the breach.

There was, therefore, created, on March 3, 1919, the office of Assistant to the Secretary of War (later taken over by the War Plans Division of the General Staff under the name of "Service and Information Branch"). Colonel Arthur Woods, Assistant Director, Air Service, was appointed Assistant to the Secretary of War to handle the problem.

Under Colonel Woods, and later under Major General Haan, together with Lieut. Colonel Mathew Smith (who succeeded Colonel Woods on Sept. 20, 1919) this organization proved of immense benefit to the returned fighting men. (14)

When this office was started in March 1919, it was estimated that of the men who had been mobilized, about 3,000,000 would require assistance in getting placed in civil life. (15) Labor conditions were already bad by reason of the stoppage or curtailment of war industry...

It was of course the desire, both of the great mass of people and of the men who were in the service, that demobilization proceeds as rapidly as possible. Industrial and international conditions weighed very little beside this desire. Accordingly, no program for relieving unemployment by slowing up demobilization was feasible.

Whatever was to be done by the War Department in the way of smoothing over the soldier's return to private life must be done by accommodating civil conditions to the exigencies of industrial life.

In the face of the fact that the soldiers were being returned to civil life, and *must* be returned to civil life, the question was what means could be devised for making that return economically satisfactory.

The return must be something more than glad home-coming, hand-shaking and story-telling. There must be jobs for the men. (16)

With the industrial situation as it was, it was not surprising that the agencies making efforts to help the discharged soldiers were unable to overcome their difficulties entirely.

The War Department's first problem was how the work of placing the ex-service men was to be accomplished.

With the crisis in the Employment Service, the continuance of its offices, already equipped to attend to the actual placing of men, was the most important portion of the problem at this time. If they could be continued it meant an immense saving to the Government as a whole, and made possible a devotion of the War Department's energies to the general problems confronting the country. (17)

Source: Colonel W.E. Haseltine, "Demobilization, Reparation and Rehabilitation of Army Personnel 1918–1919," Prepared in the Historical Section, Army War College.

Wood Sees Danger in Idle Soldiers: General Says Lack of Work Makes Discharged Men Susceptible to Radical Views

Dr. George W. Kirchway, Director of the United States Employment Service in this city, yesterday made public a statement by Major Gen. Leonard Wood, Commander of the Central Department, who declared that failure to find jobs for discharged service men would tend to make them more susceptible to the influences of Bolshevism and other radical and pernicious propaganda. He said he had learned from experience in Chicago that soldiers who had been unable to find work were drawn into radical groups.

A statement also was given out yesterday by the National Association of Manufacturers expressing opposition to the "continuation in permanent form" of the United States Employment Service. The statement urges every manufacturer to aid in the work of State or local employment agencies "and that sympathetic and efficient co-operation be given to the demobilization service" of the War Department, but declared that the Federal Service was objectionable. The first objection to the proposed Nolan bill was that of principle, the statement said, and the second was that "its adoption insures the perpetuation of the present, incompetent, extravagant and reprehensible directive administration of th [sic] Employment Service."

General Wood said that he believed that the work of the Federal Service should be conducted with vigor. Speaking of the soldiers who and sailors who had expressed dissatisfaction because they were unable to find work upon being mustered out of the service General Wood said:

When they come back to this country and find the "stay at home" occupying their positions, or in many cases better ones, it is natural that they should be discontented. Many of the men who have returned are sick, both physically and mentally, and waiting with nothing to do and finding on every hand radical orators only too willing to sow the seed of discontent, their minds are open to such propaganda.

It will be a mistake for any agency now contributing to the great work of getting jobs for these men to slacken its efforts in the slightest degree. I consider it absolutely essential for the Federal Government to continue its efforts to place discharged military men and civilian war workers in profitable peacetime jobs, and for this purpose funds should be immediately made available to continue the United States Employment Service, which has proved a potent factor in helping to solve this problem from a national standpoint.

Here, in Chicago, for example, we have had to contend with a number of radical units, most of which were made up of discharged soldiers out of jobs. We found the principal antidote for the soldier's state of mind created by idleness was employment, and, acting upon the theory that "mischief is always found for idle hands to do," we immediately through our bureau for soldiers, sailors, and marines secured profitable employment for as many of these chaps as we could find, with the result that the situation is much healthier today....

The statement of the National Association of Manufacturers pointed out that the purpose of the Nolan bill, now before Congress, was to continue the Employment Service as a permanent bureau of the Department of Labor. The objection against the principle of the proposed system is that payment of equal sums by the Federal Government and the States for the maintenance of State bureaus is made contingent upon the compliance by State bureaus with the rules and regulations of the Federal agency.

"The perpetuation of the present administration of the Employment Service is unwise," the statement says, because the service has been incompetently directed, is admittedly extravagant, and has improperly undertaken to vindicate and perpetuate its administration by the use of its personal and public funds to create a semblance of popular opinion intended to influence legislation favorable to itself.

"The present administration of the service on relation to strikes is in violation of a policy declared by the Deputy Labor Administrator for the conduct of the service and is invidiously discriminating. If carried into uniform regulations in the form proposed in the bill it would be unfair and seriously injurious to industry. The present administration has invidiously discriminated in handling applicants, and has tolerated serious misconduct by its representatives."

Source: New York Times, June 15, 1919, 13.

Colonel Woods's Nine Points: Assistant to Secretary of War Presents His Reasons for Giving Jobs to Soldiers

The present lull in our industries was caused by the readjustment presaging the period of reconstruction which our country is now facing. Our industries, once shaped back to a peace basis, will be called upon to produce in greater quantities than they ever have. Every machine in the land will have to be run to its full capacity to help restore the world to a peace basis. Our industrial army will have to be greater than our army was, to help secure the peace which we wrested from a war-mad enemy.

Roughly speaking, there are about 20,000,000 wage-earners in the United States, and out of this number 4,000,000, one-fifth, were taken out and mobilized for the different branches of our army. This army is now being demobilized at the rate of 10,000 a day and they must be reabsorbed by our different industries.

1. Because he is an ex-soldier. He was loyal to us in war times. We should be loyal to him during the peace times he has won for us.

2. Because he is physically a better man. Life in the army has hardened his muscles and given them endurance.

3. Because he is a 100 percent man he will give you a 100 percent service. Efficiency will be the greatest asset in our coming industrial life. Every man and every machine will have to work at 100 percent capacity. Two hundred million days a year are lost to our industries through sickness alone. The returning soldiers are the cream of the health of our nation.

4. Because many of the skilled men that entered our army were put to work, each at his particular trade, and have developed their skill to the highest efficiency.

5. Because the ex-service man has learned to obey. And because to obey orders has become second nature with him he will perform his work to the best of his ability without grumbling.

6. Because he is mentally a better man. No man could have gone through what our doughboys went through without becoming a better man. Remember that they have faced death. The long marches have taken out the shiftlessness of youth. Every ex-service man is a steady man.

7. Because you must help the ex-service man restore himself financially. He must not be allowed to feel that you are not doing unto him as he did unto you. Practically each one of them has to start life anew, financially.

8. Because work for our ex-soldiers means industrial peace to our country.

9. Because every ex-service man is a man, a full sized, red blooded, two fisted man, a real American.

Source: New York Times, June 27, 1919, IV, 1.

Notes

CHAPTER 1

1. Key publications that discuss preparedness include: John Patrick Finnegan, *Against the Specter of a Dragon: The Campaign for American Military Preparedness, 1914–1917* (Westport, CT: Greenwood Press, 1974); John Whiteclay Chambers II, *Draftees or Volunteers: A Documentary History of the Debate over Military Conscription in the United States, 1787–1973* (New York: Garland Publishing, 1975); John Whiteclay Chambers II, *To Raise an Army: The Draft Comes to Modern America* (New York: Free Press, 1987); John Garry Clifford, *The Citizen Soldier: The Plattsburg Training Camp Movement, 1913–1920* (Lexington: The University Press of Kentucky, 1972); Donald M. Kington, *Forgotten Summer: The Story of the Citizens' Military Training Camps, 1921–1940* (San Francisco: Two Decades Publishing, 1995); Michael Pearlman, *To Make Democracy Safe for America: Patricians and Preparedness in the Progressive Era* (Urbana: University of Illinois Press, 1984); Michael Pearlman, "Leonard Wood, William Muldoon and the Medical Profession: Public Health and Universal Military Training," *New England Quarterly,* 52 (1979); George C. Herring Jr., "James Hay and the Preparedness Controversy, 1915–1916," *Journal of Southern History,* 30 (November 1964); Chase C. Mooney and Martha E. Layman, "Some Phases of the Compulsory Military Training Movement, 1914–1920," *Mississippi Valley Historical Review,* 38 (March 1952): 641; Paul A.C. Koistinen, *Mobilizing for Modern War: The Political Economy of American Warfare, 1865–1919* (Lawrence: University Press of Kansas, 1997); J. Garry Clifford and Samuel R. Spencer Jr., *The First Peacetime Draft* (Lawrence: University Press of Kansas, 1986); and Peter Shapiro, ed., *A History of National Service in America* (College Park: Center for Political Leadership and Participation, University of Maryland, 1994), online book: http://www.academy.umd.edu/publications/NationalService/index.htm.

2. James E. Hewes Jr., *From Root to McNamara: Army Organization and Administration* (Washington, DC: Center of Military History, U.S. Army, 1975), 14. Online book: http://www.army.mil/cmh/books/root/index.htm#contents.

3. Quoted in Mary T. Reynolds, "The General Staff as a Propaganda Agency, 1908–1914," *Public Opinion Quarterly,* 3 (July 1939): 395, 394–98.

4. Chambers, *To Raise an Army,* 74; Pearlman, *To Make Democracy Safe for America,* 35; Wood biography from http://www.army.mil/cmh-pg/books/cg&csa/Wood-L.htm; Finnegan, *Against the Specter of a Dragon,* 11–12; Clifford, *Citizen Soldier,* 1–29; Reynolds, "General Staff as a Propaganda Agency," 404. For more specific details on the life of Leonard Wood see, Jack McCallum, *Leonard Wood: Rough Rider, Surgeon, Architect of American Imperialism* (New York: New York University Press, 2006).

5. Finnegan, *Against the Specter of a Dragon,* 11–12; Pearlman, *To Make Democracy Safe for America,* 62–63.

6. Finnegan, *Against the Specter of a Dragon,* 5–6; Chambers, *To Raise an Army,* 74–75.

7. Chambers, *To Raise an Army,* 74; Finnegan, *Against the Specter of a Dragon,* 6, 11–15.

8. Finnegan, *Against the Specter of a Dragon,* 15–16.

9. Ibid., 18, 19–21; Allan R. Millett and Peter Maslowski, *For the Common Defense: A Military History of the United States of America* (New York: The Free Press, 1984), 339.

10. Shapiro, *History of National Service in America,* 6; John B. Wilson, *Maneuver and Firepower: The Evolution of Division and Separate Brigades* (Washington, DC: Center of Military History, U.S. Army, 1998), 31–33, Online book: http://www.army.mil/CMH-pg/books/Lineage/M-F/index.htm; Finnegan, *Against the Specter of a Dragon,* 18–21.

11. Quoted in Hewes, *From Root to McNamara,* 13.

12. Hewes, *From Root to McNamara,* 15–18; Finnegan, *Against the Specter of a Dragon,* 15–16.

13. Finnegan, *Against the Specter of a Dragon,* 17; Wilson, *Maneuver and Firepower,* 34–36; Hewes, *From Root to McNamara,* 15.

14. Finnegan, *Against the Specter of a Dragon,* 26–30; Clifford, *Citizen Soldier,* 106, 122.

15. Clifford, *Citizen Soldier,* 8.

16. Ibid., 11–12, 14; McCallum, *Leonard Wood,* 256; Kington, *Forgotten Summer,* 2–4.

17. Clifford, *Citizen Soldier,* 16-17, 18; Kington, *Forgotten Summer,* 2–4; Finnegan, *Against the Specter of a Dragon,* 61–62; Chambers, *To Raise an Army,* 79; Reynolds, *General Staff as a Propaganda Agency,* 402–3.

18. Clifford, *Citizen Soldier,* 19–23; Finnegan, *Against the Specter of a Dragon,* 61–62; Pearlman, *To Make Democracy Safe for America,* 83–84.

19. Captain Edwards quoted in Clifford, *Citizen Soldier,* 27, 28–29.

20. Clifford, *Citizen Soldier,* 27–28; Pearlman, *To Make Democracy Safe for America,* 83–84; Millett and Maslowski, *For the Common Defense,* 340. Note: The number of students attending the Military Training Camps is different in various publications.

21. Pearlman, "Leonard Wood, William Muldoon and the Medical Profession," 326.

22. Ibid., 330–31.

23. Dr. Charles Burr quoted in Pearlman, "Leonard Wood, William Muldoon and the Medical Profession," 333.

24. Pearlman, "Leonard Wood, William Muldoon and the Medical Profession," 334.

25. Pearlman, *To Make Democracy Safe for America*, 35–36; Pearlman, "Leonard Wood, William Muldoon and the Medical Profession," 344.

26. Pearlman, *To Make Democracy Safe for America,* 42.

27. Clifford, *Citizen Soldier,* 31–32.

28. "Roosevelt Urges Nation to Prepare: Pacifists, He Tells Exposition Audience, Are Seeking to 'Chinafy America,'" *New York Times,* July 22, 1915, 1; Finnegan, *Against the Specter of a Dragon,* 26.

29. Finnegan, *Against the Specter of a Dragon,* 22–26; Biography of Senator Henry Cabot Lodge and Representative A.P. Gardner, see http://bioguide.congress.gov.

30. Clifford, *Citizen Soldier,* 30–34, 34; Finnegan, *Against the Specter of a Dragon,* 24–28.

31. Biography of Senate, George E. Chamberlain and Representative James Hay, see http://bioguide.congress.gov; Also see Herring, "James Hay and the Preparedness Controversy," 384.

32. Herring, "James Hay and the Preparedness Controversy," 384–85.

33. Finnegan, *Against the Specter of a Dragon,* 34; Herring, "James Hay and the Preparedness Controversy," 385.

34. Clifford, *Citizen Soldier,* 61–63, 63; Koistinen, *Mobilizing for Modern War,* 109.

35. Clifford, *Citizen Soldier,* 65.

36. Ralph Barton Perry, *The Plattsburg Movement: A Chapter of America's Participation in World War* (New York: E.P. Dutton & Company, 1921), 117; Clifford, *Citizen Soldier,* 60–61, 69–80. Although most secondary sources list the number of Plattsburg trainee as 1,200, War Department records indicate 1,800 men trained in the New York camp in 1915, see "Military Training Camps, Eastern Department, U.S. Army," *Correspondence of the War College Division and Related General Staff Offices 1903–1919,* April 1916, *War Department General and Special Staff,* Record Group 165, National Archives and Record Administration, 2. [Hereafter, *Correspondence,* WCD, WDGSS, RG 165, NARA.]

37. Clifford, *Citizen Soldier,* 83.

38. Ibid., 78–80, 80.

39. Ibid., 85.

40. Quoted in Clifford, *Citizen Soldier,* 86.

41. Clifford, *Citizen Soldier,* 87.

42. David Kennedy, *Over Here: The First World War and American Society* (Oxford: Oxford University Press, 1980), 32; Clifford, *Citizen Soldier,* 31–32.

43. "National Defense and the Market," *New York Times,* July 8, 1915, 15.

44. "Bankers Indorse Plans for Defense," *New York Times,* September 9, 1915, 6.

45. Irving T. Bush, "The Business Man and Universal Military Training," *Proceedings of the Academy of Political Science of New York City* 6 (July 1916): 71–73.

46. Albert Shaw, "Problems of the Common Defense," *Proceedings of the Academy of Political Science in the City of New York* 6 (July 1916): 8–9.

47. Mooney and Layman, "Some Phases of the Compulsory Military Training Movement," 641; Robert H. Zieger, *America's Great War: World War I and the American Experience* (New York: Rowman & Littlefield Publishers, 2000), 34.

48. Clifford, *Citizen Soldier,* 195.

49. "Our Prestige Lost, Says David J. Hill," *New York Times,* April 11, 1916, 3; Albert Benham, "The 'Movie' as an Agency for Peace or War," *Journal of Educational Sociology* 12 (March 1939): 416.

50. Koistinen, *Mobilizing for Modern War,* 109; Mooney and Layman, "Some Phases of the Compulsory Military Training Movement," 641; Clifford, *Citizen Soldier,* 49; Finnegan, *Against the Specter of a Dragon,* 27, 31–33.

51. Mooney and Layman, "Some Phases of the Compulsory Military Training Movement," 641; Finnegan, *Against the Specter of a Dragon,* 27, 31–33; Kennedy, *Over Here,* 31.

52. Zieger, *America's Great War,* 34.

53. Benham, "The 'Movie' as an Agency for Peace or War," 416; Mooney and Layman, "Some Phases of the Compulsory Military Training Movement," 640–41; Zieger, *America's Great War,* 34; Clifford, *Citizen Soldier,* 49.

54. William E. Leuchtenburg, "Progressivism and Imperialism: The Progressive Movement and American Foreign Policy, 1898–1916," *The Mississippi Valley Historical Review* 39, no. 3 (December 1952): 495; Clifford, *Citizen Soldier,* 35; Finnegan, *Against the Specter of a Dragon,* 105; "Women Cheer for Defense," *New York Times,* April 27, 1916, 22; "135,000 in Parade for Preparedness," *New York Times,* May 2, 1916, 6.

55. Oswald Garrison Villard, "The Cure-All of Universal Military Service," *Proceedings of the Academy of Political Science,* 6, no. 4 (July 1916): 50.

56. Simeon Strunsky, "Armaments and Caste," *Annuals of the American Academy of Science,* 66, no. 1 (1916): 244; Chambers, *To Raise an Army,* 109.

57. Kennedy, *Over Here,* 146.

58. Ibid., 33–34.

59. Chambers, *To Raise an Army,* 109–110; George Nasmyth, "Universal Military Service and Democracy," reprinted in Chambers, *Draftees or Volunteers,* 221–32; William I. Hull, *Preparedness: The American Verses the Military Programme* (1916; repr., New York: Garland Publishing, 1973), Introduction by Blanche Wiesen Cook, 5–13.

60. Jane Addams quoted in Linda Schott, "The Woman's Peace Party and the Moral Basis for Women's Pacifism," *Frontiers: A Journal of Women Studies* 8 (1985): 20, for information on the Woman's Peace party see 18–24.

61. Charles Chatfield, "World War I and the Liberal Pacifist in the United States," *American Historical Review* 75 (December 1970): 1923.

62. Henry Ford, "Humanity and Sanity," *New York Times,* April 23, 1916, 6.

63. "No Masonic Tenant in Preparedness," *New York Times,* April 17, 1916, 20.

64. Charles E. Jefferson, "Military Preparedness a Peril to Democracy," *Annals of the American Academy of Political and Social Science* 66, no. 1 (1916): 230–31.

65. "Prof. Phelps's Speech: Gives out Text of Anti-War Declaration He Says Was Misquoted," *New York Times,* April 9, 1916, 6.

66. "The Pulpit and War: A Protest Against Preaching a Doctrine of National Preparedness," *New York Times,* July 2, 1915.

67. Wilson, *Maneuver and Firepower,* 37.

68. Finnegan, *Against the Specter of a Dragon,* 48, 53; Mooney and Layman, "Some Phases of the Compulsory Military Training Movement," 636.

69. Mooney and Layman, "Some Phases of the Compulsory Military Training Movement," 635–36.

70. U.S. Congress, *Congressional Records,* 64th Cong., 1st sess., February 4, March 17, 1916–March 30, 1916, vol. 53, pt. 3–5, 4330–37; also see Biographical Directory of the United States Congress, http://bioguide.congress.gov/biosearch/biosearch.asp.

71. Herring, "James Hay and the Preparedness Controversy," 391.

72. Koistinen, *Mobilizing for Modern War,* 111.

73. U.S. Congressional Records, 64th Cong., 1st sess., February 4, 1916–March 30, 1916, vol. 53, pt. 3–5, 4353–54; also see Biographical Directory of the United States Congress: http://bioguide.congress.gov/biosearch/biosearch.asp.

74. Herring, "James Hay and the Preparedness Controversy," 393; Clifford, *Citizen Soldier,* 122–29.

75. Herring, "James Hay and the Preparedness Controversy," 394–95; Clifford, *Citizen Soldier,* 116–30; Chambers, *To Raise an Army,* 74, 122.

76. Millett and Maslowski, *For the Common Defense,* 324.

77. Clifford, *Citizen Soldier,* 147–48; Chambers, *To Raise an Army,* 114–17; Millett and Maslowski, *For the Common Defense,* 324–25.

78. Millett and Maslowski, *For the Common Defense,* 322; "Naval Aviation Chronology, 1898–1916," Naval Historical Center, 1–19. See Official Online Site of U.S. Naval History: http://history.navy.mil/branches/avchr1.htm.

79. "Naval Aviation Chronology, 1898–1916," 19, 16–19.

80. "Wood Confers with Baker," *New York Times,* April 20, 1916, 13; Chambers, *To Raise an Army,* 126.

81. "Military Training Camps, Eastern Department, U.S. Army, 1916," *Correspondence,* April 1916, WCD, WDGSS, RG 165, NARA, 4.

82. Ibid.

83. Clifford, *Citizen Soldier,* 152–56; Committee on Regimental Affairs, *The Plattsburger* (New York: Wynkoop, Hallenbeck, Crawford Company, 1917), see advertisement in back of publicity booklet.

84. "Employers Aid Camps," *New York Times,* April 16, 1916, 19; "Employers for Readiness," *New York Times,* April 21, 1916, 20.

85. Ralph Barton Perry, *The Plattsburg Movement: A Chapter of America's Participation in World War* (New York: E.P. Dutton & Company, 1921); Clifford, *Citizen Soldier,* 152–92; Shapiro, *History of National Service in America,* 6–7.

86. Colonel Chase W. Kennedy, "Memorandum for the Secretary of War: The Federal Training Camps and the War Department," *Correspondence (9226-55),* November 1916, WCD, WDGSS, RG 165, NARA, 1–2.

87. H.P. McCain, "War Department, the Adjutant General's Office, Memorandum," *Correspondence,* undated but stamped April 18, 1917 by the War Department, WCD, WDGSS, RG 165, NARA, 1–3; Shapiro, *History of National Service in America,* 6–7.

88. Clifford, *Citizen Soldier,* 210, 218–19.

89. Ibid., 227.

CHAPTER 2

1. Kennedy, *Over Here,* 145.

2. Ibid.

3. Chambers, *To Raise an Army*, 134–35, 139; Millett and Maslowski, *For the Common Defense*, 349–50.

4. Chambers, *To Raise an Army*, 153–56, 170–71; Millett and Maslowski, *For the Common Defense*, 349.

5. Chambers, *To Raise an Army*, 206–9. Note: For more information on Civil War draft resistance see Grace Palladino, *Another Civil War: Labor, Capital, and the State in the Anthracite Regions of Pennsylvania, 1840–1868* (Urbana: University of Illinois Press, 1990); James W. Geary, *We Need Men: The Union Draft in the Civil War* (DeKalb: Northern Illinois University Press, 1991).

6. Geary, *We Need Men*, 73–74.

7. Ronald Schaffer, *America in the Great War: The Rise of the War Welfare State* (New York: Oxford University Press, 1991), 176.

8. Kennedy, *Over Here*, 150, 153.

9. Ibid., 153; Schaffer, *America in the Great War*, 176.

10. Schaffer, *America in the Great War*, 177; Jennifer D. Keene, *Doughboys, the Great War, and the Remaking of America* (Baltimore, MD: The Johns Hopkins University Press, 2001), 9.

11. "Long Live the Constitution," Socialists Party, Pennsylvania, Records of the United States Attorney, RG 118, National Archives, Mid Atlantic Region, Philadelphia.

12. James B. Jacobs and Leslie Anne Hayes, "Aliens in the U.S. Armed Forces: A Historical-Legal Analysis," *Armed Forces and Society* 7 (Winter 1981): 188, 191. Note: The majority of the information on immigrant soldiers was taken from Nancy Gentile Ford, *Americans All: Foreign-born Soldiers in World War I* (College Station: Texas A&M University Press, 2001) and Nancy Gentile Ford, "Mindful of the Traditions of His Race: Dual Identity and the Foreign-Born Soldiers in the First World War American Army," *Journal of American Ethnic History* 16, no. 2 (Winter 1997): 35–57.

13. *Second Report of the Provost Marshal General to the Secretary of War* (Washington, DC: Government Printing Office, 1918), Government Records Department, The Free Library of Philadelphia, Pennsylvania, 86–88; "Alien Citizenship and the Draft," *Infantry Journal* 15, no. 4 (October 1918): 323.

14. Statements from major newspapers quoted in "To Draft Aliens," *Literary Digest* 55 (September 29, 1917): 14. Additional quotes can be found in "To Get the Alien Slacker," *Literary Digest* 55 (August 4, 1917): 22.

15. *Second Report of the Provost Marshal General to the Secretary of War*, 94.

16. Ibid., 93–94; House Military Affairs Committee, *Drafting Aliens into Military Service*, Hearings, 65th Cong., 1st sess., September 26, 1917, 6–8, 22, 1–43.

17. House Military Affairs Committee, *Drafting Aliens into Military Service*, 1–16; *Second Report of the Provost Marshal General to the Secretary of War*, 93.

18. *Second Report of the Provost Marshal General to the Secretary of War*, 81, 96–98; "Amending Naturalization Laws," *Army and Navy Journal* (April 20, 1928): 1274; *Final Report of the Provost Marshal General* (Washington, DC: Government Printing Office, 1920), Government Records Department, The Free Library of Philadelphia, Pennsylvania, 26–27, table 5.

19. MID 10565-110/28, "Ethnic Bulletin," undated but filed in War Department on April 15, 1919, General Records of the Military Intelligence Divisions, General Correspondence, Records of the War Department General and Special Staff, 1917–1941, Record Group 165, National Archives Records Administration II, College

Park, Maryland. [Hereafter, MID, RG 165, WDGSS, NARA]; MID 10565-81/6, February 2, 1918, RG 165, WDGS, N.A.; MID 10565-26/1, March 4, 1918; MID 10080-964, "77th Division Records of Drafted Men, Camp Upton, New York," October 18, 1917; RG 165, WDGSS, NARA; "'Foreign Legion' Companies," *Infantry Journal* 15, no. 3 (September 1918): 252–54.

20. Vardaman quoted in Chambers, *To Raise an Army,* 156.

21. James Mennell, "African-Americans and the Selective Service Act of 1917," *Journal of Negro History* 84 (Summer 1999): 275–80; Chambers, *To Raise an Army,* 156–57.

22. Paul T. Murray, "Blacks and the Draft: A History of Institutional Racism," *Journal of Black Studies* 2 (September 1971): 60.

23. Murray, "Blacks and the Draft," 58.

24. Chambers, *To Raise an Army,* 225–26; Murray, "Blacks and the Draft," 58–59.

25. Ford, *Americans All,* 5–11.

26. Peter Karsten, *The Military in America: From the Colonial Era to the Present* (New York: Free Press, 1980), 229. Also see John M. Gates, "The Alleged Isolation of the U.S. Army Officers in the Late 19th Century," *Parameters: Journal of U.S. Army War College* 10 (September 1980).

27. Russell Weigley, "The Elihu Root Reforms and the Progressive Era," in *Command and Commanders in Modern Warfare: Proceedings of the Second Military Symposium, U.S. Air Force Academy,* ed. William Geffen (Washington, DC: U.S. Air Force, 1969), 12; Jack C. Lane, *Armed Progressive: General Leonard* (London: Presidio Press, 1978), 107, 149, 155.

28. Raymond B. Fosdick, *Chronicle of a Generation: An Autobiography* (New York: Harper & Brothers, 1958), 184.

29. David C. Shank, *Management of the American Soldiers* (distributed to morale officers in August 1918), see memorandum: MID 80-78/2, August 20, 1918, WDGSS, WDGSS, RG 165, NARA.

30. John Carson, "Army Alpha, Army Brass, and the Search for Army Intelligence," *Isis* 84 (June 1993): 278, 282–84.

31. Baker quoted in Carson, "Army Alpha, Army Brass, and the Search for Army Intelligence," 283.

32. Carson, "Army Alpha, Army Brass, and the Search for Army Intelligence," 279, 209–307.

33. Early twentieth century American society considered Southern and Eastern Europeans as belonging to different "races," and the War Department did likewise. However, the training and treatment of immigrant and native-born white soldiers were far different from their African-American counterparts.

34. Historians do not agree on the definition of Progressivism and emphasize its ambiguous and often contradictory nature. While early twentieth century reformers were not totally unified in ideology, most historians identify one aspect as social welfare Progressivism. These Progressives addressed the prevailing social problems of the day and attempted to "morally uplift" society to the middle-class value system. This social welfare movement joined social workers, settlement house workers, public health reformers, and recreational experts. Social welfare workers participated in a relentless crusade against prostitution, alcohol, social disease, and poor sanitary conditions in the nation's major cities and attempted to replace the negative urban environments with playgrounds, sports fields, and various cultural facilities.

35. "The Committee on Training Camp Activities Report," Records of the War Department, General and Special Staff, War College and War Plans Division, Subordinate Offices Education and Recreation Branch, Record Group 165, National Archives Records Administration II, College Park, Maryland, June 1918, 1. [Hereafter, WDGSS, WCWPD, RG 165, NARA.]

36. Paul Boyer, *Urban Masses and Moral Order in America, 1820–1920* (Cambridge, MA: Harvard University Press, 1978), 221. Also see Frederick Palmer, *Newton D. Baker America at War,* vol. 1 and 2 (New York: Dodd, Mead and Co., 1931); and Fosdick, *Chronicle of a Generation.*

37. "Commission on Training Camp Activities Report," WDGSS, WCWPD, RG 165, NARA, June 1918, 1.

38. Donald Smythe, "Venereal Disease: The AEF's Experience," *Prologue* 9, no. 2 (Summer 1977): 66. This article provides an excellent account of the American fights against venereal disease in the American Expeditionary Forces.

39. Palmer, *Newton D. Baker,* 298, 297.

40. Commission on Training Camp Activities, 18–24; "Memorandum Outlining the Various Activities," CTCA 44140, WDGSS, WCWPD, NARA; Fosdick, *Chronicle of a Generation,* 145–46.

41. "Report from Raymond B. Fosdick to Frederick P. Keppel," February 7, 1919, Committee on Training Camp Activities, 22; "Memorandum Outline the Various Activities," Committee on Training Camp Activities, 24, *Commission on Training Camp Activities,* WDGSS, WCWPD, RG 165, NARA, 20; Fosdick, *Chronicle of a Generation,* 147; Palmer, *Newton D. Baker,* 310.

42. Captain Perkins/Lieutenant Horgan to Intelligence Officer, Camp Meade, August 12, 1918, MID 10565-495A; Perkins/Horgan to Walter C. Clark, July 30, 1918, MID 10565-501/8, WDGSS, RG 165, NARA. Palmer, *Newton D. Baker,* 210; Fosdick, *Chronicle of a Generation,* 144; "Memorandum Outlining the Various Activities," CTCA 44140, WDGS WCWPD, RG 165, NARA, 12.

43. Quoted in Boyer, *Urban Masses,* 110.

44. *Commission on Training Camp Activities,* WDGSS, WCWPD, RG 165, NARA, 25–26; "Fosdick Testimony," *Camp Activities: Hearings before the Committee on Military Affairs,* 1–21, Washington, DC, 191, Raymond Fosdick Collection, Seeley G. Mud Manuscript Library, Princeton University, Princeton, New Jersey.

45. "Report from the War Camp Community Services," Committee on Training Camp Activities, 3–6, 31; "Report from Playground and Recreational Association of America," December 1917, CTCA 27333, WDGSS, WCWPD, RG 165, NARA.

46. Bruce W. Bidwell, *History of the Military Intelligence Division. Department of the Army General Staff: 1775–1941* (Frederick: University Publications of America, 1986), 185, 205. The *Infantry Journal* reported that at Camp Gordon, Georgia, "75 percent had neither learned English nor obtained even the most elementary knowledge of the Art of war." Quoted in: "Foreign Legion Companies," *Infantry Journal* 15 (September 1918): 252, MID 10565-512, Memo from Perkins/Horgan to Intelligence Officer, Camp Devens, Massachusetts, August 20, 1918; MID 10565-562, Memo from Director MID to Intelligence Officer, Camp Beauregard, Louisiana, November 6, 1918, WDGSS, RG 165NARA, MID sent similar memos to all training camps to encourage the reorganization of foreign-born troops.

47. MID 105-110/7, September 7, 1918, WDGSS, RG 165, NARA; Capt. Edward R. Padgett, General Staff, "Camp Gordon Plan," *Infantry Journal* 15

(October 1918): 334; Willis Fletcher Johnson, "Students at Camp Upton," *North American Review* 211 (January 1920): 47.

48. MID 10565-414, "'Foreign Legion' Companies," extracted from M.I.3 Bulletin no. 17, July 15, 1918, WDGS, RG 165, NARA.

49. Ibid.

50. MID 10565-512, Memo from Perkins/Horgan to Intelligence Officer, Camp Devens, Massachusetts, August 20, 1918; MID 10565-562, Memo from Director MID to Intelligence Officer, Camp Beauregard, Louisiana, November 6, 1918; MID 10565-472/3-5, 12, Letters from Director of Military Intelligence to Lt. Louis Zara, November 18, 1918; MID 10565-517/27; Memo from Chief, Military Morale Section to Intelligence Officer, Camp Lee, Virginia, October 16, 1918; MID 10565-468/1, Memo from Director, MID to Commanding Generals at Camp Custer, Michigan; Camp Grant, Illinois; Camp Dodge, Iowa; October 20, 1918 (similar memos to all training camps to encourage the reorganization of foreign-born troops); MID 10565-472, "Personal Report and Statement of Preferences for Reserve Officers," June 10, 1921, WDGSS, RG 165, NARA; Officers with "Accents," MID 10565-506/8, Memo from Perkins/Horgan to all camps, August 30, 1918, WDGSS, RG 165, NARA.

51. MID 10565-515/21, FSS report to Chief of MID, January 23, 1919, WDGSS, RG 165, NARA.

52. Ibid.

53. CTCA 36669, July 30, 1918 and CTCA 36820, 9, 13, August 29 and September 9, 1918, WDGSS, WCWPD, RG 165, NARA; MID 10565-533/1, August 21, 1918; and MID 10565-495A/13, August 24, 1918, WDGSS, RG 165, NARA. Numerous ethnic leaders and organizations assisted the military in their socialization efforts. These advisors also pressured the War Department to retain elements of the soldiers' cultural traditions and pushed for fair and just treatment of the foreign-born troops: the Jewish Welfare Board; leaders of the Greek Orthodox church; the Greek-American Boy Scouts; the Italian Bureau of Information; the Russian-American Bureau of Chicago; the Russian-American Economic Association; the Bohemian National Alliance Council; The National Romanian Society; the Lithuanian National Council; The Czechoslovak National Council; American Scandinavian Foundation; South Slavic National Council; Polish National Committee; Slovak League; American-Hungarian Loyalty League. Assistance also came from a number of foreign-language editors including Alex Syaki, editor of Boston's *Kruyer Bostonski (Polish Daily News)* and Shucri Baccash, editor of the Syrian-American newspaper, *Al-Fatata*; a number of college professors including Dr. A. Arbib Costa from the College of the City of New York and Professor Petrunkevitch, Yale University; Captain Roselli, Consular General, New York City; dozens of prominent ethnic doctors with membership in the American Medical Association including Dr. Bina Seymour and Dr. F.D. LaRochelle from Springfield, Massachusetts, Dr. Bernard Klein of Joliet, Illinois, and Dr. F.J. Lejpak of Duluth, Minnesota; dozens of clergymen including Reverends John Zeltonago, and M. Kotecki of Chicago, Illinois; Reverends Joseph Dzvenchik, F.K. Bader, Vince Janneyzi, Jon Vogel, I.N.W. Irvine, N. Metropolsky of New York; Reverends Rocco Petraca, A.M. Seeholzoe, John M. Ratz of Ohio; and Reverends Leonard Steuger, Louis Spannegel, B. Dembinski, J. Kasakaitis, and L.A. Grynia of Pennsylvania; and dozens of ethnic civilians who acted as intelligence agents (too numerous to list) for the Foreign Speaking Soldier

Sub-section. Most of the agents had college educations, professional status, and high recommendations from native-born and foreign-born organizations. See *The Jewish Welfare Board, United States Army and Navy: Purpose, Scope, Achievements* (New York: Jewish Welfare Board, n.d.); *Jewish Welfare Board Army-Navy Division, 1919–1939*, "Graves," I-180, World War I Collection, *Jewish Historical Society; The War Record of American Jews* (New York: The American Jewish Committee, 1919); Correspondence with ethnic leaders/organizations cited as above see MID 10565243, July 18, 1918; MID 10565243, July 30, 1918; MID 10565-495A/4, August 6, 1918; MID 10565-602/6, January 9, 1918; MID 10565-57/1, January 12, 1918; MID 10565-355, June 7, 1918; MID 10565-523/13 October 19, 1918, 10565-537/1, August 16, 1919; October 19, 1918; MID 10565-500B/28, October 29, 1918; MID 10565-522/22, January 3, 1919; MID 10565-255/14–18 and 73–74, June 1–20, 1918; MID 10565-170/4, April 1, 1918 through September 16, 1918; MID 10565-170/18, July 15, 1918; MID 10565-495A/4, August 6, 1918, WDGS, RG 165, NARA.

54. MID 10565-532D, correspondence between Edith Terry Bremer, executive, Division on Work for Foreign-Born Women, War Work Council, The Young Women Christian Association and Perkins/Horgan, August 19, 1918, August 22, 1918, September 4, 1918, September 9, 1918, WDGSS, RG 165, NARA.

55. Report from "Playground and Recreation Association of America," CTCA 27333, December 1917, WDGSS, WCWPD, RG 165, NARA; MID 10565-532D, correspondence between Edith Terry Bremer, executive, Division on Work for Foreign-Born Women, War Work Council, The Young Women Christian Association and Perkins/Horgan, August 19, 1918, August 22, 1918, September 4, 1918, September 9, 1918, WDGSS, RG 165, NARA.

56. CTCA 44183, "Instruction of Non-English Speaking Men and Native-Born Illiterates," April 29, 1918, June 27, 1918 and CTCA 44183, "Instructions in English of Soldiers Who Have Not Sufficient Knowledge of That Language," July, 1918, WDGSS, WCWPD, RG 165, NARA; *Jewish Welfare Board, Purpose Scope Achievements* (New York: Jewish Welfare Board National Headquarters), 1–7; MID 10565-546/4, Letter from Perkins/Horgan to Bureau of Education, Washington, DC, September 19, 1918, WDGSS, RG 165, NARA; *Camp Music Division of the War Department* (Washington, DC: Commission on Training Camp Activities, June 30, 1919), 10, 22–25.

57. CTCA 36669, July 30, 1918 and CTCA 36820, 9, 13, August 29 and September 9, 1918, WDGSS, WCWPD, RG 165, NARA; MID 10565-533/1, August 21, 1918; and MID 10565-495A/13, August 24, 1918, WDGSS, RG 165, NARA.

58. Raymond B. Fosdick, *Report to the Secretary of War on the Activities of Welfare Organizations Serving with the A.E.F.* (Washington, DC: War Department, n.d.); War Department General Order No. 46 "The Jewish Welfare Board," May 9, 1918, and Bulletin no. 25, "Matzos or Unleavened Bread," May 3, 1918; MID 80-81, Letter from Perkins to Col. Harry Cutler, Jewish Welfare Board, August 20, 1918; MID 10565-500D/2, Memo from Perkins/Horgan to Rev. O'Hearn, Washington, DC, August 7, 1918; MID 10565-500D/5, Letter from Perkins/Horgan to Rev. Louis Ahern, Washington, DC, August 20, 1918, WDGSS, RG 165, NARA: Headquarters, 27th Division, Camp Wadsworth, Bulletin no. 79, reprint of December 6, 1917 letter from Toakeim Georges, Archimandrites and Rector of the Greek Orthodox church, to Commander 27th Division, Bulletins WWI, Records of the

American Expeditionary Forces (World War I), Records of the 27th Division, RG 120, NARA, *The Jewish Welfare Board. United States Army and Navy: Purpose. Scope. Achievements,* unnumbered; Jewish Welfare Board Army-Navy Division, 1919–1939, "Graves," 1–180, World War I Collection, *Jewish Historical Society; The War Record of American Jews,* 10, 14–15; *Prayer Book for Jews in the Army and Navy of the United States* (Philadelphia, Issued for the Jewish Welfare Board), v–vi; *Manual for Speakers in the United States War Work Campaign* (New York: Jewish Welfare Board, November 1918).

59. MID 10901-22, Memo from Capt. E.R. Padgett, General Staff to Perkins, September 7, 1918; MID 10565-517, MID 10565-541 and MID 10565-458, Memos from Perkins/Horgan to Intelligence Officers, Camp Lee, Camp Dix, Camp Meade, Camp Lewis, Camp Gordon, Camp Grant, Camp Sherman, Camp Wadsworth, Camp McArthur, Camp Upton, Camp Sheridan, Camp Pike, Camp Devens, September 12, 17, 18, 1918; MID 10565-532/2, Letter from Dr. Justine Klotz, Division on Work for Foreign-Born Women to Perkins, August 12, 1918, WDGSS, RG 165, NARA.

60. Nancy K. Bristow, *Making Men Moral: Social Engineering During the Great War* (New York: New York University Press, 1996), 139–40.

61. Keene, *Doughboys, the Great War, and the Remaking of America,* 91.

62. Baker quoted in Bristow, *Making Men Moral,* 144.

63. Keene, *Doughboys, the Great War, and the Remaking of America,* 83.

64. Bristow, *Making Men Moral,* 143; Kennedy, *Over Here,* 159–60.

65. Scott quoted in Murray, "Blacks and the Draft," 59.

66. Mennell, "African-Americans the Selective Service Act of 1917," 284, 283–85.

67. Chambers, *To Raise an Army,* 223–25.

68. Hal S. Chase, "Struggle for Equality: Fort Des Moines Training Camp for Colored Officers, 1917," *Phylon,* 39 (1978): 298.

69. Ibid., 299–307.

70. Ibid.

71. Emmett J. Scott, special adjutant to Secretary of War, *Scott's Official History of the American Negro in the World War,* chap. VII, "Treatment of Negro Soldiers in Camp," 1919, 2, http://net.lib.byu.edu/~rdh7/wwi/comment/Scott/ScottTC.htm.

72. Chambers, *To Raise an Army,* 223; Kennedy, *Over There,* 161; Chase, "Struggle for Equality," 309.

73. Quoted in Bristow, *Making Men Moral,* 144–45.

74. Ibid., 145.

75. Keene, *Doughboys, the Great War, and the Remaking of America,* 94.

76. Ibid.; Mennell, "African-Americans and the Selective Service Act of 1917," 283; Bristow, *Making Men Moral,* 137–39, 144–46.

77. Mennell, "African-Americans and the Selective Service Act of 1917," 283; Bristow, *Making Men Moral,* 137–39, 144–46.

CHAPTER 3

1. Kennedy, *Over Here,* 61.

2. Charles Chatfield, "World War I and the Liberal Pacifist in the United States," *American Historical Review,* 75 (December 1970): 1921.

3. Kennedy, *Over Here,* 52.

4. Chatfield, "World War I and the Liberal Pacifist in the United States," 1923, 1926.

5. Ibid., 1923–25.

6. *Constitutional Rights in War-Time* (Washington, DC: American Union Against Militarism, May 1917), Jane Addams Papers, American Peace Society, 1906–1928, Reel 43. Swarthmore College Peace Collection, Swarthmore College Peace Library; Chatfield, "World War I and the Liberal Pacifist in the United States," 1922–26; Kennedy, *Over Here,* 34.

7. Chatfield, "World War I and the Liberal Pacifist in the United States," 1926, 1927.

8. *Long Live the Constitution of the United States,* Socialists Party, Pennsylvania Eastern District Office, Record Group 118, Records of the United States Attorney, National Archives, Mid Atlantic Region, Philadelphia, Pennsylvania; Chatfield, "World War I and the Liberal Pacifist in the United States," 1922.

9. Chatfield, "World War I and the Liberal Pacifist in the United States," 1931–36; *Long Live the Constitution of the United States,* Socialists Party, Pennsylvania Eastern District Office, NA Mid Atlantic Region.

10. Ford, *Americans All,* 17–22.

11. Ford, *Americans All,* 27–44, see chapt. 1, "'In the Family of One Nation:' The Complexity of Ethnic Patriotism During the Great War."

12. Mark Ellis, *Race, War and Surveillance: African Americans and the United States Government During World War I* (Bloomington: Indiana University Press, 2001), 1; Wray R. Johnson, "Black American Radicalism and the First World War: The Secret Files of the Military Intelligence Division," *Armed Forces & Society* 26 (Fall 1999): 30–31.

13. Johnson, "Black American Radicalism and the First World War," 31.

14. John F. Fox Jr., "Bureaucratic Wrangling over Counterintelligence, 1917–1918," *Studies in Intelligence* 49 (2005): 1, https://www.cia.gov/library/center-for-the-study-of-intelligence/csi-publications/csi-studies/studies/vol49no1/html_files/bureaucratic_wrangling_2.html.

15. Theodore Kornweibel Jr., *"Investigate Everything:" Federal Efforts to Compel Black Loyalty During World War I* (Bloomington: Indiana University Press, 2002), 19.

16. Kornweibel, *"Investigate Everything,"* 19.

17. Marvin A. Kreidberg and Merton G. Henry, *History of Military Mobilization in the United States Army, 1775–1945* (Washington, DC: Center of Military History, U.S. Army, 1984), 347.

18. Kreidberg and Henry, *History of Military Mobilization in the United States Army,* 348–49.

19. George Creel, "Public Opinion in War Time," *Annuals of American Academy of Political and Social Science* 78 (July 1918): 185.

20. Ibid., 186.

21. Kennedy, *Over Here,* 59–60.

22. *The Creel Report: Complete Report of the Chairman of the Committee on Public Information* (1920; repr., New York: DaCapo Press, 1972), 2; "Danger of America," Committee on Public Information, Division of Four Minute Men, Bulletin no. 31, May 27, 1918, 1, The Pennsylvania Four Minute Men, Clarence B. Brinton

Collection, World War I Liberty Loan Drive Records, 1917–1918, Historical Society of Pennsylvania, Philadelphia, Pennsylvania.

23. Kennedy, *Over Here*, 61.

24. Creel, "Public Opinion in War Time," 192.

25. *The Creel Report*, 3.

26. Kennedy, *Over Here*, 64–68, Posters directed at Foreign-born see: Library of Congress Web site: http://lcweb2.loc.gov/pp/wwiposquery.html and the Roger N. Mohovic Collection, Georgetown University Library Web site: http://www.library.georgetown.edu/dept/speccoll/n12.jpg.

27. Quoted in Kornweibel, *"Investigate Everything,"* 19.

28. Kennedy, *Over Here*, see chap. 1, "The War for the American Mind," 45–92.

29. Frank C. Barnes, "Shall German Be Dropped from Our Schools?" *Modern Language Journal* 2, no. 5 (February 1918): 192.

30. Barnes, "Shall German Be Dropped from Our Schools?" 188.

31. Ibid., 188–89.

32. *The Creel Report*, 79; Kennedy, *Over Here*, see chap. 1, "The War for the American Mind," 45–92.

33. George Creel, *How We Advertised America* (New York: Harper & Brothers, 1920), 2.

34. Kornweibel, *"Investigate Everything,"* 19.

35. Fox, "Bureaucratic Wrangling over Counter Intelligence," 3; *CI Reader: American Revolution into the New Millennium: A Counterintelligence Reader*, vol. 1, chap. 3, 70, 73, see Office of the National Counterintelligence Executive Web site: http://www.ncix.gov/issues/CI_Reader/index.html.

36. Kennedy, *Over Here*, 53–56, 81.

37. Ibid., 82, 81–83.

38. Fox, "Bureaucratic Wrangling over Counter Intelligence," 5.

39. Ibid., 7.

40. Ibid., 5, 8; Kornweibel, *"Investigate Everything,"* 15.

41. *CI Reader: American Revolution into the New Millennium: A Counterintelligence Reader*, vol. 1, chap. 3, 73, 71.

42. Kornweibel, *"Investigate Everything,"* 24.

43. *The Functions of the Military Intelligence Division*, U.S. General Staff (Washington, DC: The Military Intelligence Division, October 1, 1918), 6, U.S. Army Military History Institute (MHI), Carlisle, Pennsylvania; Ellis, Race, War, and Surveillance, xviii. Note: Although the name of the army's intelligence agency has changed, Military Intelligence Division or MID has been used throughout the rest of this chapter to avoid confusion.

44. *Personnel Directory, Military Intelligence Division*, October 1, 1918, 21–57, U.S. Army Military History Archives, Carlisle, Pennsylvania; Kornweibel, *"Investigate Everything,"* 29.

45. *Personnel Directory, Military Intelligence Division*, October 1, 1918, 21–57, MHI.

46. John Whitclay Chambers II, ed., *The Eagle and the Dove: The American Peace Movement and United States Foreign Policy, 1900–1922* (New York: Garland Publishing, 1975), 53.

47. Chatfield, "World War I and the Liberal Pacifist in the United States," 1934.

48. Ibid., 1932.

49. War Department, "Propaganda in Its Military and Legal Aspects," Military Intelligence Division, Executive Division, General Staff, 1918, 21–57.

50. "Propaganda in Its Military and Legal Aspects," 114–15.

51. Kornweibel, *"Investigate Everything,"* 28, MHI; Chambers, *The Eagle and the Dove,* 53.

52. War Department, "Propaganda in Its Military and Legal Aspects," 119–20.

53. See Ford, *Americans All,* especially Introduction and chap. 4, "Military Moral Uplifting" and Ford, "Mindful of the Traditions of His Race."

54. War Department, "Propaganda in Its Military and Legal Aspects," 119–20.

55. Ellis, *Race, War and Surveillance,* 32–33.

56. Ibid., 48–59, 53, also see chap. 2, "The Wilson Administration and Black Opinion."

57. Johnson, "Black American Radicalism and the First World War," 37.

58. Major Loving quoted in Johnson, "Black American Radicalism and the First World War," 44; Ellis, *Race, War and Surveillance,* 57–65.

59. Kornweibel, *"Investigate Everything,"* 227–229, 269; Ellis, *Race, War and Surveillance,* 141–46, also see chap. 5, W.E.B. DuBois, Joel Spingarn, and Military Intelligence.

60. Kennedy, *Over Here,* 75.

61. Kornweibel, *"Investigate Everything,"* 33.

62. Kennedy, *Over Here,* 76.

63. Ibid.

64. Kreidberg and Henry, *History of Military Mobilization in the United States Army,* 350.

65. Ibid., 369, 370.

66. Ibid., 352; Kornweibel, *"Investigate Everything,"* 27.

67. Kreidberg and Henry, *History of Military Mobilization in the United States Army,* 369.

68. War Department, "Propaganda in Its Military and Legal Aspects," 3, 141.

69. Kornweibel, *"Investigate Everything,"* 16.

70. Fox, "Bureaucratic Wrangling over Counterintelligence," 8.

71. Kornweibel, *"Investigate Everything,"* 20.

72. U.S. Army, *History of the Spruce Division: United States Army* (Washington, DC: United States Spruce Production Corporation/Government Printing Office, 1920), 16.

73. Robert L. Tyler, "The United States Government as Union Organizer: The Loyal Legion of Loggers and Lumbermen," *Mississippi Valley Historical Review* 47 (December 1960): 435.

74. "The Shortage of Essential War Materials in the Lumber Industry and the Handling of the War Problem by the Army in Connection Therewith During World War I" (Spruce Production Division, U.S. Army War College, Historical Section Studies, 13–20, 22–35, file 15, 1942), 1, U.S. Army Military History Institute, Carlisle, Pennsylvania.

75. U.S. Army, *History of the Spruce Division,* Introduction, II.

76. Ibid.

77. U.S. Army, *History of the Spruce Division,* 8–16.

78. Tyler, "The United States Government as Union Organizer," 441; U.S. Army, *History of the Spruce Division,* 16.

79. Tyler, "The United States Government as Union Organizer," 441–42; U.S. Army, *History of the Spruce Division,* 20–21.

80. Brice P. Disque, Colonel Air Service, U.S.A., Commanding, War Department, Headquarters Spruce Production Division, Bureau of Aircraft Production, Yeon Bldg, Portland, Oregon, Bulletin no. 80, September 12, 1918, Spruce Production Corporation, Bulletins, November 1917–November 1918, RG18, Box 1, National Archives and Record Administration II.

81. U.S. Army, *History of the Spruce Division,* 21–25; "The Shortage of Essential War Materials," 6–7, 8.

82. U.S. Army, *History of the Spruce Division,* 21.

83. Quoted in Kornweibel, *"Investigate Everything,"* 19.

84. Kornweibel, *"Investigate Everything,"* 19.

CHAPTER 4

1. Byron Farwell, *Over There: The United States in the Great War, 1917–1918* (New York: W. W. Norton and Company, 1999), 44.

2. David A. Zabecki, *Steel Wind: Colonel George Bruchmuller and the Birth of Modern Artillery* (Westport, CT: Praeger Press, 1994), 8; Farwell, *Over There,* 44.

3. Zabecki, *Steel Wind,* 14, 5–17.

4. Ibid., 11; Major Andrew G. Ellis, "The Birth of Modern American Artillery," *Field Artillery,* August 1988, 1; Major Wallace Jackson Savoy, "The Evolution of the American Modern Light Field Gun" (Masters of Arts Thesis, U.S. Army College, Leavenworth, 1978), 53.

5. Farwell, *Over There,* 43; Zabecki, *Steel Wind,* 1–17; Also see various Web sites with information on World War I artillery, tanks, planes, battleships: http://www.airpower.maxwell.af.mil; www.firstworldwar.com; and http://www.bbc.co.uk/history/worldwars.

6. Farwell, *Over There,* 44–48, 80–86; Benedict Crowell, *The Armies of Industry* (New Haven, CT: Yale University Press, 1921), 200–204.

7. William J. Helmer, *The Gun That Made the Twenties Roar* (London: The Macmillan Company, Collier-Macmillan Ltd., 1969), 7.

8. Ibid., 6–9.

9. Crowell, *The Armies of Industry,* 200–204; Helmer, *The Gun That Made the Twenties Roar,* 7; Farwell, *Over There,* 199.

10. Crowell, *The Armies of Industry,* 204–8, 210.

11. Ibid., 214, 223.

12. Farwell, *Over There,* 189.

13. Michael Spick, "The Fokker Menace," in *The Great War: Perspectives on the First World War,* ed. Robert Cowley (New York: Random House, 2004), 260.

14. Farwell, *Over There,* 189.

15. Ibid., 205.

16. Hugh R. Slotten, "Human Chemistry or Scientific Barbarism? American Responses to World War I Poison Gas, 1915–1930," *Journal of American History* 77 (September 1990): 478.

17. Slotten, "Human Chemistry or Scientific Barbarism?" 476; Edgar F. Raines Jr., "The American 5th Division and Gas Warfare, 1918," *Army History* 22 (Spring 1992):

6; Major Charles E. Heller, "Chemical Warfare in World War I: The American Experience, 1917–1918," *Leavenworth Paper No. 10* (Fort Leavenworth, KS: Combat Studies Institute, U.S. Army Command and General Staff College, September 1984), 7, from http://www-cgsc.army.mil/carl/resources/csi/Heller/HELLER.asp; Farwell, *Over There*, 42.

18. *Records of the Great War,* vol. III, ed. Charles F. Horne *National Alumni 1923,* reprinted on Web site: http://www.firstworldwar.com/diaries/gasattackatypres.htm.

19. Slotten, "Human Chemistry or Scientific Barbarism?" 480.

20. Ibid.

21. Heller, "Chemical Warfare in World War I," 9.

22. Farwell, *Over There,* 43.

23. Heller, "Chemical Warfare in World War I," 17; Major Charles E. Heller, "The Perils of Unpreparedness: The American Expeditionary Forces and Chemical Warfare," *Military Review* 65 (January 1985): 15.

24. Quoted in Gilbert F. Whittemore Jr., "World War I, Poison Gas Research, and the Ideals of American Chemists," *Social Studies of Science* 5 (1975): 141, 141–42.

25. Whittemore, "World War I, Poison Gas Research, and the Ideals of American Chemists," 143–44, 146; Charles L. Parson, "The American Chemists in Warfare," *Science* 48 (October 18, 1918): 379–80.

26. Slotten, "Humane Chemistry or Scientific Barbarism?" 486–87.

27. Heller, "The Perils of Unpreparedness," 22; Parson, "The American Chemists in Warfare," *Science* 48 (October 18, 1918): 379–80.

28. Heller, "The Perils of Unpreparedness," 22; Richard W. Steward, ed., *American Military History, Volume II: The United States Army in a Global Era, 1917–2003* (Washington, DC: Center of Military History, U.S. Army, 2005), 25; Whittemore, "World War I, Poison Gas Research, and the Ideals of American Chemists," 149–51; Slotten, "Human Chemistry or Scientific Barbarism?" 485.

29. Parson, "American Chemists in Warfare," 380; Whittemore, "World War I, Poison Gas Research, and the Ideals of American Chemists," 149–51; Slotten, "Human Chemistry or Scientific Barbarism?" 485; Heller, "Chemical Warfare in World War I," 20.

30. Joel A. Vilensky, "Father Nieuwland and the 'Dew of Death,'" *Notre Dame Magazine,* Winter 2002–2003, 1, 1–2, http://www.nd.edu/~ndmag/w0203/poisongas.html; also see Joel A. Vilensky and Pandy R. Sinish, "The Dew of Death," *Bulletin of the Atomic Scientists,* March/April 2004, 1–2, http://thebulletin.metapress.com/content/?k=sinish+the+dew+of+death.

31. Joel A. Vilensky and Pandy R. Sinish, "Weaponry: Lewiste: America's World War I Weapon of Mass Destruction," *Quarterly Journal of Military History* 17 (Spring 2005): 2, reprinted on The History Net. http://www.historynet.com/wars_conflicts/weaponry/3035881.html; Vilensky and Sinish, "The Dew of Death," 1–2.

32. Amos A. Fries. "Gas in Attack and Gas in Defense," reprinted from *National Service Magazine,* June and July 1919, 1–5.

33. Heller, "The Perils of Unpreparedness," 18; Fries, "Gas in Attack and Gas in Defense," 1–16; Heller, "Chemical Warfare in World War I," 20.

34. Heller, "The Perils of Unpreparedness," 21–22; Heller, "Chemical Warfare in World War I," 18–19.

35. General Robert Lee Bullard quoted in Captain Richard Varela, "Ansauville: A Failure in Training," *Infantry* 73 (January–February 1983): 29–30.

36. Varela, "Ansauville," 29–31; Heller, "The Perils of Unpreparedness," 22.

37. Daniel J. Kevles, "Flash and Sound in the AEF: The History of a Technical Service," *Military Affairs* 33 (December 1969): 374–77.

38. Ibid., 378.

39. Ibid., 377–83; John Patrick Finnegan, *Military Intelligence* (Washington, DC: Center of Military History, U.S. Army, 1998), 36.

40. Carol R. Byerly, *Fever of War: The Influenza Epidemic in the U.S. Army During World War I* (New York: New York University Press, 2005), 15, 20–21, 24.

41. Byerly, *Fever of War*, 45.

42. Ibid., 44, 46.

43. Ibid., 8, 29, 31.

44. The Influenza Pandemic of 1918, http://virus.stanford.edu/uda/.

45. Byerly, *Fever of War*, 5.

46. John Ellis, *Eye-Deep in Hell: Trench Warfare in World War I* (Baltimore: The Johns Hopkins University Press, 1989), 55, 63, 94, 174; Subtitle for this section taken from diary of A.W. Miller from Web site: http://udel.edu/~mm/wwi/intro.html.

47. Ellis, *Eye-Deep in Hell*, 9.

48. Diary of Pvt. Nathaniel Rouse from the Great War Society Web site: http://www.worldwar1.com/dbc/biograph.htm.

49. Diary of Pvt. Mathew Chopin, chap. 6, from the Great War Society Web site: http://www.worldwar1.com/dbc/biograph.htm.

50. Ibid.

51. Diary of Sgt. Albert K. Haas from the Great War Society Web site: http://www.worldwar1.com/dbc/ahaas.htm.

52. Ibid.

53. Diary of Clarence Richmond from the Great War Society Web site: http://www.worldwar1.com/dbc/biograph.htm.

54. Diary of Wilfred H. Allen from the Great War Society Web site: http://www.worldwar1.com/dbc/biograph.htm.

55. Diary of James Pierson from the Great War Society Web site: http://www.worldwar1.com/dbc/biograph.htm.

56. Diary of A.W. Miller from Web site: http://udel.edu/~mm/wwi/ linked from: http://www.lib.byu.edu/~rdh/wwi/memoir.html.

57. Paul Wanke, "American Military Psychiatry and Its Role Among Ground Forces in World War II," *Journal of Military History* 63 (January 1999): 128. Note: Focuses on World War II, but provides background on psychiatry during the Great War.

58. Ellis, *Eye-Deep in Hell*, 116–21; Wanke, "American Military Psychiatry and Its Role Among Ground Forces in World War II," 128; Farwell, *Over There*, 180.

59. Wanke, "American Military Psychiatry and Its Role Among Ground Forces in World War II," 128–29.

60. John E. Talbott, "Soldiers, Psychiatrist, and Combat Trauma," *Journal of Interdisciplinary History* 27 (Winter 1997): 437.

61. Major Andrew G. Ellis, "The Birth of Modern American Artillery," *Field Artillery*, August 1988, 1.

62. Heller, "Chemical Warfare in World War I," 37.

63. Ibid.

64. Whittemore, "World War I, Poison Gas Research, and the Ideals of American Chemists," 156.

65. Ibid., 157–58.

66. Jennifer D. Keene, *The United States and the First World War* (New York: Longman, Pearson, 2000), 59–60.

67. Diary of James Pierson from the Great War Society Web site: http://www.worldwar1.com/dbc/pierson.htm.

CHAPTER 5

1. "An Account of the Work of Colonel Arthur Woods, Assistant to the Secretary of War, in Aiding the Return to Civil Life after the Great War of Soldiers, Soldiers, and Marines, March–September 1919," 2, Records of the War Department General and Special Staff, War College Division, RG 165, National Archives Records Administration II, College Park, Maryland. [Hereafter WDGSS, RG 165, NARA]; Stella Stewart, *Demobilization of Manpower, 1918–1919* (Washington, DC: U.S. Government Printing Office, 1944), 51–54 [U.S. Department of Labor, Bureau of Labor Statistics]; Note: Strikes were reported in Arizona, California, Connecticut, Georgia, Illinois, Indiana, Iowa, Kentucky, Massachusetts, Minnesota, Missouri, Montana, New York, North Carolina, Ohio, Oklahoma, Pennsylvania, South Carolina, Texas, Utah, Virginia, Washington, West Virginia, and Wisconsin.

2. Colonel W.E. Haseltine, "Demobilization, Reparation and Rehabilitation of Army Personnel 1918–1919," (Carlisle, PA: Prepared in the Historical Section, Army War College, 1943), 2.

3. General Peyton C. March quoted in Major John C. Sparrow, *History of Personnel Demobilization in the United States Army* (Washington, DC: Center of Military History, U.S. Army, 1994, original printed by Department of the Army, 1952), 12.

4. "Say Soldiers See World in New Light: Col. Roosevelt and Arthur Woods Discuss Job Finding with Brooklyn Employers," *New York Times,* March 30, 1919, 9.

5. Haseltine, "Demobilization, Reparation and Rehabilitation of Army Personnel," 2.

6. Ibid., 3.

7. Lt. Colonel Mathew C. Smith, "Report of the Activities of the Service and Information Branch for the Year 1919," Report for period from November 11, 1918 to December 31, 1919, Records of the War Department General and Special Staffs, Service and Information Branch, 165.8.2, War Plans Division, Record Group 165, National Archives Record Administration, College Park, Maryland, 7–10. [Hereafter WDGSS, SIB, RG 165, NARA.] Note: On September 20, 1919, Lt. Colonel Mathew Smith and Major General Haan succeeded Woods as the head of the War Department's Emergency Employment Committee; also see Stewart, *Demobilization of Manpower.*

8. Sparrow, *History of Personnel Demobilization in the United States Army,* 16; Colonel Henry Hossfeld and Captain Charles H. Collins, "Demobilization of Manpower in the United States Army, 1918–1919" (Carlisle, PA: Prepared in the Historical Section, Army War College, 1942), 60–61, 119.

9. Stewart, *Demobilization of Manpower*, 28, 33.

10. Woods, "Aiding the Return to Civil Life of Soldiers, Sailors, and Marines," 6.

11. Stewart, *Demobilization of Manpower*, 49.

12. Ibid., 42, 59; "To Get Jobs For Soldiers," *New York Times*, April 17, 1919, 6; Sparrow, *History of Personnel Demobilization in the United States Army*, 17; Stewart, *Demobilization of Manpower*, 59; "Woods's Nine Points: Assistant to Secretary of War Presents His Reasons for Giving Jobs to Soldiers," *New York Times*, June 27, 1919, 1.

13. Woods, "Aiding the Return to Civil Life of Soldiers, Sailors, and Marines," 4, 6.

14. U.S. Congress, *Congressional Record*, 66th Cong., 1st sess., Senate, V.58, pt. 3–5, July 1, 1919, 2154.

15. "Fight Employment Service," *New York Times*, May 8, 1919, 27.

16. "Employment Service Hit," *New York Times*, May 30, 1919, 7.

17. *Congressional Record*, 66th Cong., 1st sess., Senate, July 1, 1919, 2160.

18. Ibid., 2157, 2156–69.

19. Ibid., 2156.

20. *Congressional Record*, 66th Cong., 1st sess., Senate, September 11, 1919, 5240.

21. *Congressional Record*, 66th Cong., 1st sess., Senate, V.58, 2169; Stewart, *Demobilization of Manpower*, 60.

22. "Flood of Bills in New Congress," *New York Times*, May 20, 1919, 4.

23. "Senate Acts to Purge U.S. of Bolshevism," *Chicago Tribune*, February 5, 1919, 1.

24. "Employment of Returning Soldiers and Sailors," *Infantry Journal* 15, no. 7 (January 1919): 589; "Flood of Bills in New Congress," May 20, 1919, 4.

25. Haseltine, "Demobilization, Reparation and Rehabilitation of Army Personnel," 10–11.

26. Colonel Woods, "Aiding the Return to Civil Life of Soldiers, Sailors, and Marines," September 1919, Biographical appendix, 1.

27. "Much Can Be Done by Mayors," *New York Times*, March 15, 1919, 14.

28. See letter to Mayors attached to Woods, "Aiding the Return to Civil Life of Soldiers, Sailors, and Marines," September 1919; "Woods Issues Plea to Employment Soldiers: Sends a Letter to Mayors Asking Active Co-operation in the Movement," *New York Times*, March 14, 1919, 9.

29. Stella Stewart, *Demobilization of Manpower, 1918–1919*, (Washington, DC: U.S. Department of Labor, Bureau of Labor Statistics, May 19, 1944), 51–54. Note: Strikes were reported in Arizona, California, Connecticut, Georgia, Illinois, Indiana, Iowa, Kentucky, Massachusetts, Minnesota, Missouri, Montana, New York, North Carolina, Ohio, Oklahoma, Pennsylvania, South Carolina, Texas, Utah, Virginia, Washington, West Virginia, and Wisconsin; Woods, "Aiding the Return to Civil Life of Soldiers, Sailors, and Marines," 2.

30. George F. Fitzgerald, "Stenographic Report of the Emergency Employment Committee Meeting Report," April 11, 1919, 6 [WDGSS, RG 165, NARA].

31. Woods, "Aiding the Return to Civil Life of Soldiers, Sailors, and Marines," September 1919, 11–12.

32. "Wood Sees Danger in Idle Soldiers: General Says Lack of Work Makes Discharged Men Susceptible to Racial Views," *New York Times*, June 15, 1919, 13.

33. Ibid.

34. *Congressional Record,* 66th Cong., 1st sess., Senate, July 1, 1919, 2156, 2157, 2160.

35. "Bolshevism," *Infantry Journal* 15, no. 7 (January 1919): 604.

36. "Union Affiliation," *Infantry Journal* 15, no. 5 (November 1919): 427.

37. "The Emergency Committee," *New York Times,* March 17, 1919, 14; "Council of Defense to Aid Employment: Agency Formed Under Colonel Woods to Offset Curtailment of Federal Service," *New York Times,* March 15, 1919, 5.

38. "Council of Defense to Aid Employment," 5.

39. Woods, "Aiding the Return to Civil Life of Soldiers, Sailors, and Marines," Biographical appendix, 1–19.

40. Ibid.

41. Ibid.; "The Solder and His Job: Government Has Mobilized Many Agencies to Make Sure They Will Get Together," *New York Times,* June 22, 1919, 11; Woods, "Aiding the Return to Civil Life of Soldiers, Sailors, and Marines," Biographical appendix, 1–19; "To Find Jobs for Soldiers: Woods Organizes Advisory Committee of Ex-Service Men," *New York Times,* June 12, 1919, 18.

42. Smith, "Report of Activities of the Service and Information Branch," November 11, 1918 to December 31, 1919, 21.

43. "All Enlisted Men Allowed to Stay in Army Until They Find Civilian Employments," *New York Times,* January 25, 1919, 1.

44. Woods, "Aiding the Return to Civil Life of Soldiers, Sailors, and Marines," 18.

45. Ibid., 4, 12; "Tell Employment Plans: Governors and Mayors Inform Council of National Defense," *New York Times,* April 16, 1919, 16; "States Aid in Job Hunting: Offer Support to Army Officers Who Are to Help Soldiers Find Work," *New York Times,* April 6, 1919, 14; Haseltine, "Demobilization, Reparation and Rehabilitation of Army Personnel," 13–14; "The Emergency Committee," *New York Times,* March 17, 1919, 14.

46. "Hasten Listing Soldiers for Work: Woods Announces That Applications Will Be Made Out on Transports," *New York Times,* May 27, 1919, 17.

47. Smith, "Report of Activities of the Service and Information Branch," 7, 15, 20, 25–26, appendix 6, 9; Haseltine, "Demobilization, Reparation and Rehabilitation of Army Personnel," 11–15; Edward L. Bernays, "The Soldier and His Job," *New York Times,* June 22, 1919, 11; Woods, "Aiding the Return to Civil Life of Soldiers, Sailors, and Marines," appendix, 1–19.

48. Woods, "Aiding the Return to Civil Life of Soldiers, Sailors, and Marines," 10; Smith, "Report of Activities of the Service and Information Branch," 19.

49. Woods, "Aiding the Return to Civil Life of Soldiers, Sailors, and Marines," appendix, 1–19.

50. Smith, "Report of Activities of the Service and Information Branch," 79.

51. "Call on Business to Furnish Jobs: National Chamber of Commerce, at Wood's Request, Makes Plea for Aid," *New York Times,* March 24, 1919, 3.

52. Letter to the Chamber of Commerce from Arthur Woods, Assistant to the Secretary of War, March 21, 1919, attached to Woods, "Aiding the Return to Civil Life of Soldiers, Sailors, and Marines," also see 27–28 and appendix 16.

53. Woods, "Aiding the Return to Civil Life of Soldiers, Sailors, and Marines," 19.

54. Smith, "Report of Activities of the Service and Information Branch," 31, 41.

55. "Tell the Story of 77th First Fight: Major Weaver Reports 2,000 More Jobs Available for 77th Men—Still Needs 3,600," *New York Times,* March 31, 1919, 6; "Col. Woods's Nine Points: Assistant to Secretary of War Presents His Reasons for Giving Jobs to Soldiers," *New York Times,* June 29, 1919, 1; Smith, "Report of Activities of the Service and Information Branch," 41.

56. Smith, "Report of Activities of the Service and Information Branch," 36. Military posters found on various Web sites: see Library of Congress, http://memory.loc.gov/pp/wwiposquery.html and University of Georgia, Poster Collection, http://fax.libs.uga.edu/wwpost/.

57. Smith, "Report of Activities of the Service and Information Branch," 37.

58. Woods, "Aiding the Return to Civil Life of Soldiers, Sailors, and Marines," 15, 16, 19.

59. "Churches to Aid Soldiers: 150,000 to be Organized for Aiding U.S. Employment Service," *New York Times,* March 23, 1919, 18; "Col. Wood's Nine Points" June 27, 1919, 1; "Wilson Asks Work for Men from War: Churches Have Designated May 4 as Employment Sunday, and He Approves Project," *New York Times,* April 20, 1919, 20; "Churches Help Find Jobs for Soldiers: Pastors Throughout Country to Observe Employment Sunday by Appeals to Employers," *New York Times,* May 4, 1919, 1.

60. "Citation for Giving Fighters' Jobs Back: Woods Announces Government Will Recognize Employers' Patriotism with Certificate," *New York Times,* May 4, 1919, 11.

61. "Citation for Giving Fighters' Jobs Back," 21; Smith, "Report of Activities of the Service and Information Branch," 37–39.

62. Smith, "Report of Activities of the Service and Information Branch," 37–39.

63. Lt. Colonel Jacob C.R. Peadbody, "History of Northeastern District," January 9, 1920, 5. This report attached to Smith, "Report of Activities of the Service and Information Branch."

64. "Appeal for Farm Labor," *New York Times,* June 17, 1919, 9; "Need Men for Farm Work: 2,000 Jobs Open at Good Pay in This State Alone," *New York Times,* June 24, 1919, 25.

65. Woods, "Aiding the Return to Civil Life of Soldiers, Sailors, and Marines," 39; Smith, "Report of Activities of the Service and Information Branch," 87.

66. Smith, "Report of Activities of the Service and Information Branch," 87.

67. Ibid., 11.

68. "Furniture Dealers Dine: Col. Arthur Woods Says Unemployment Problems Are Being Met," *New York Times,* April 9, 1919, 6.

69. Stewart, *Demobilization of Manpower,* 28; Woods, "Aiding the Return to Civil Life of Soldiers, Sailors, and Marines," 6; "Woods Issues Plea to Employ Soldiers," 9.

70. Smith, "Report of Activities of the Service and Information Branch," 26; Woods, "Aiding the Return to Civil Life of Soldiers, Sailors, and Marines," 14–15.

71. Woods, "Aiding the Return to Civil Life of Soldiers, Sailors, and Marines," 14–15.

72. Ibid., 25; Smith, "Report of Activities of the Service and Information Branch," 43.

73. Smith, "Report of Activities of the Service and Information Branch," 39–40; "Rockefellers Give $75,000," *New York Times,* October 8, 1919, 24.

74. Woods, "Aiding the Return to Civil Life of Soldiers, Sailors, and Marines," 21.

75. Ibid., appendix 12.

76. Udo Sautter, "Government and Unemployment: The Use of Public Works Before the New Deal," *Journal of American History* 20, no. 4 (December 1992): 65. Sautter article does not discuss Otto Mallery's 1919 role as head of the War Department's Federal Aid and Works Section.

77. Woods, "Aiding the Return to Civil Life of Soldiers, Sailors, and Marines," 22.

78. Ibid., appendix, 22, 1–28.

79. Ibid., appendix, 1–28; Smith, "Report of Activities of the Service and Information Branch," 47.

80. Smith, "Report of Activities of the Service and Information Branch," 22, 46–48.

81. Woods, "Aiding the Return to Civil Life of Soldiers, Sailors, and Marines," 24.

82. Ibid.

83. Colonel John B. Reynolds, "A History of the Central District," Undated But Probably Submitted in December 1919 or January 1920, 7 and Peadbody, "History of Northeastern District," 4. Both report attached to Smith, "Report of Activities of the Service and Information Branch;" Woods, "Aiding the Return to Civil Life of Soldiers, Sailors, and Marines," appendix, 17, Note: Copies of *Rebel Worker: Organ of Revolutionary Unionism* and *The Melting Pot: An Exponent of International Communism* in file with telegram sent to Colonel Arthur Woods signed by Captain Scott, Cleveland, Ohio, June 13, 1919.

84. Captain Edwin Copely Wemple, "History Western District," December 31, 1919, 2–3, 6–7, 11. This report attached to Smith, "Report of Activities of the Service and Information Branch."

85. Letter from Secretary of War Baker to Colonel Arthur Woods, War Department, August 28, 1919 and Letter to Police Chiefs from Arthur Woods, Assistant to the Secretary, undated, attached to Woods, "Aiding the Return to Civil Life of Soldiers, Sailors, and Marines;" Smith, "Report of Activities of the Service and Information Branch," 22, 92–93; "Bars Uniform to Fakers: Col. Woods Calls Them "Cooties" and Asks Police to Stop Them," *New York Times,* April 29, 1919, 7.

86. Letter to Mayors from Colonel Arthur Woods, March 13, 1919, attached to Woods, "Aiding the Return to Civil Life of Soldiers, Sailors, and Marines," also see 20. For detail on the training and treatment of foreign-born soldiers in the American Army, see Ford, *Americans All,*; Smith, "Report of Activities of the Service and Information Branch," 36.

87. "Churches Help Find Jobs for Soldiers: Pastors Throughout Country to Observe Employment Sunday by Appeals to Employers," *New York Times,* May 4, 1919, 1.

88. Reynolds, "A History of the Central District," 8, Attached to Smith, "Report of Activities of the Service and Information Branch."

89. Ibid.

90. Ibid.

91. Smith, "Report of Activities of the Service and Information Branch," 30.

92. Woods, "Aiding the Return to Civil Life of Soldiers, Sailors, and Marines," 13.

93. Ibid., 3–14; Major Carl Clyde Rutledge, "History of the Eastern District," undated but probably submitted in December 1919 or January 1920, 5, attached to Smith, "Report of Activities of the Service and Information Branch," 30. "Tells How U.S. Aids Disabled Fighters: Col. Woods Urges All Crippled Ex-Service Men to Take Free Courses," *New York Times,* June 8, 1919, 2.

94. Letter to Commanding Officers of Hospitals from Arthur Woods, Assistant to the Secretary, undated, attached to Woods, "Aiding the Return to Civil Life of Soldiers, Sailors, and Marines," also see 13–14; Smith, "Report of Activities of the Service and Information Branch," 25, 30.

95. Smith, "Report of Activities of the Service and Information Branch," 30, 33.

96. Smith, "Report of Activities of the Service and Information Branch," 70, 59–69.

97. Sautter, "Government and Unemployment," 65. Sautter article does not discuss Colonel Authur Wood's 1919 role as head of the War Department's Emergency Employment Committee; Woods, "Aiding the Return to Civil Life of Soldiers, Sailors, and Marines," 35.

Selected Bibliography

PRIMARY SOURCES

Archival and Government Records

Doughboy Center: Story of the American Expeditionary Forces. *The Great War Society*. Letters, Diaries, and Biographies. http://www.worldwar1.com/dbc/biograph.htm.

Historical Society of Pennsylvania, Philadelphia, PA. *Clarence B. Brinton Collection*. World War I Liberty Loan Drive Records, 1917–1918.

House Military Affairs Committee. *Drafting Aliens into Military Service*. Hearings, 65th Cong., 1st sess., September 26, 1917.

Library of Congress. *American Memory*. Online documents, http://memory.loc.gov/ammem/index.html.

National Archives, Mid Atlantic Region, Philadelphia, PA. Record of the United States Attorneys. Pennsylvania Eastern District Office. RG 118.

National Archives Record Administration II, College Park, MD. Records of the American Expeditionary Forces (World War I). Records of the 27th Division. RG 120.

———. Records of the Army Air Forces Records of the Spruce Production Division. RG 18, 1903–1964.

———. Record of the War Department General and Special Staffs. Correspondence of the War College Division and Related General Staff Offices 1903–1919. RG 165.

———. Records of the War Department General and Special Staffs. Records of the Military Intelligence Division (MID-G-2) 1900–50. RG 165.

———. Records of the War Department, General and Special Staffs. Records of the War Plans Division 1910–42, Subordinate Offices Education and Recreation Branch. RG 165.

———. Records of the War Department, General and Special Staffs. Records of the War Plans Division 1910–42, Education and Recreation Branch. RG 165.

Seeley G. Mud Manuscript Library, Princeton University, Princeton, NJ. Raymond
    Fosdick Collection.
Swarthmore College Peace Collection, Swarthmore College Peace Library. *Jane
    Addams Papers.* American Peace Society, 1906–1928.
U.S. Congress. *Congressional Record,* 66th Cong., 1st sess., Senate.

Periodicals from 1916 to 1941

Army and Navy Journal
Chicago Tribune
Infantry Journal
Journal of Educational Sociology
Modern Language Journal
Parameters: Journal of U.S. Army War College
Public Opinion Quarterly
Literary Digest
New York Times
North American Review
Proceedings of the Academy of Political Science
Science

PUBLISHED PRIMARY SOURCES AND GOVERNMENT REPORTS

Barnes, Frank C. "Shall German Be Dropped from Our Schools?" *Modern Language
    Journal* 2 (February 1918).
Creel, George. "Public Opinion in War Time." *Annuals of American Academy of
    Political and Social Science*78 (July 1918): 185–94.
*The Creel Report: Complete Report of the Chairman of the Committee on Public
    Information.* Washington, DC: Government Printing Office, 1920. Reprinted
    New York: DaCapo Press, 1972.
Crowell, Benedict. *The Armies of Industry.* New Haven, CT: Yale University Press,
    1921.
Final Report of the Provost Marshal General. Washington, DC: Government
    Printing Office, 1920. Government Records Department, The Free Library of
    Philadelphia, Pennsylvania.
Fosdick, Raymond B. *Chronicle of a Generation: An Autobiography.* New York:
    Harper and Brothers, 1958.
Fries, Amos A. "Gas in Attack and Gas in Defense." Reprinted from *National Service
    Magazine* (June and July 1919): 1–55.
The Functions of the Military Intelligence Division. U.S. General Staff. Washington,
    DC: The Military Intelligence Division, October 1, 1918. U.S. Army Military
    History Institute, Carlisle, Pennsylvania.
Hull, William I. *Preparedness: The American Verses the Military Programme.*
    London: Fleming H. Revell Company, 1916.
Organization and Personnel Directory. U.S. War Department, *Military Intelligence
    Division,* General Staff, October 1, 1918. U.S. Army Military History Institute,
    Carlisle, Pennsylvania.

Palmer, Frederick. *Newton D. Baker America at War*. vol. 1 and 2. New York: Dodd, Mead, 1931.

Parson, Charles L. "The American Chemists in Warfare." *Science* 48 (October 18, 1918): 377–86.

Perry, Ralph Barton. *The Plattsburg Movement: A Chapter of America's Participation in World War*. New York: E.P. Dutton & Company, 1921.

Committee on Regimental Affairs, *The Plattsburger*. New York: Wynkoop, Hallenbeck, Crawford Company, 1917.

"Propaganda in Its Military and Legal Aspects." Washington, DC: Military Intelligence Division Branch, Executive Division, General Staff, 1918, U.S. Army Military History Institute, Carlisle, Pennsylvania.

Reynolds, Mary T. "The General Staff as a Propaganda Agency, 1908–1914." *Public Opinion Quarterly* 3 (July 1939): 391–408.

Scott, Emmett J, Special adjutant to Secretary of War. *Scott's Official History of the American Negro in the World War*, 1919, http://net.lib.byu.edu/~rdh7/wwi/comment/Scott/ScottTC.htm.

Second Report of the Provost Marshal General to the Secretary of War. Washington, DC: Government Printing Office, 1918, Government Records Department, The Free Library of Philadelphia, Pennsylvania.

Stella Stewart, U.S. Department of Labor, Bureau of Labor Statistics. *Demobilization of Manpower, 1918–1919*. Washington, DC: Government Printing Office, May 19, 1944.

U.S. Army. *History of the Spruce Division: United States Army*. Washington, DC: U.S. Spruce Production Corporation/Government Printing Office, 1920. U.S. Army Military History Institute, Carlisle, Pennsylvania.

Books and Articles

Baldwin, Fred Davis. "The American Enlisted Man in World War I." PhD diss., Princeton University, 1965.

Beckett, Ian F.W. *The Great War 1914–1918*. New York: Longman Press, 2001.

Benham, Albert. "The 'Movie' as an Agency for Peace or War." *Journal of Educational Sociology* 12 (March 1939): 416.

Bidwell, Bruce W. *History of the Military Intelligence Division. Department of the Army General Staff: 1775–1941*. Frederick, MD: University Publications of America, 1986.

Boyer, Paul. *Urban Masses and Moral Order in America, 1820–1920*. Cambridge, MA: Harvard University Press, 1978.

Bristow, Nancy K. *Making Men Moral: Social Engineering During the Great War*. New York: New York University Press, 1996.

Byerly, Carol R. *Fever of War: The Influenza Epidemic in the U.S. Army During World War I*. New York: New York University Press, 2005.

Carson, John. "Army Alpha, Army Brass, and the Search for Army Intelligence." *Isis* 84 (1993): 278–309.

Chambers II, John Whiteclay. *Draftees or Volunteers: A Documentary History of the Debate over Military Conscription in the United States, 1787–1973*. New York: Garland Publishing, 1975.

————, ed. *The Eagle and the Dove: The American Peace Movement and United States Foreign Policy, 1900–1922*. New York: Garland Publishing, 1975.

————. *To Raise an Army: The Draft Comes to Modern America*. New York: Free Press, 1987.

Chase, Hal S. "Struggle for Equality: Fort Des Moines Training Camp for Colored Officers, 1917." *Phylon* 39 (1978): 297–310.

Chatfield, Charles. "World War I and the Liberal Pacifist in the United States." *American Historical Review* 75 (December 1970): 1920–37.

CI Reader: American Revolution into the New Millennium: A Counterintelligence Reader. vol. 1, chap. 3, 70, 73, see Office of the National Counterintelligence Executive Web site: http://www.ncix.gov/issues/CI_Reader/index.html.

Clifford, John Garry. *The Citizen Soldier: The Plattsburg Training Camp Movement, 1913–1920*. Lexington: University Press of Kentucky, 1972.

Clifford, John Garry, and Samuel R. Spencer, Jr. *The First Peacetime Draft*. Lawrence: University Press of Kansas, 1986.

Cowley, Robert, ed. *The Great War: Perspectives on the First World War*. New York: Random House, 2004.

Crowell, Benedict. *The Armies of Industry*. New Haven, CT: Yale University Press, 1921.

Ellis, Major Andrew G. "The Birth of Modern American Artillery." *Field Artillery* (August 1988): 26–30.

Ellis, John. *Eye-Deep in Hell: Trench Warfare in World War I*. New York: Pantheon Books, 1976.

Ellis, Mark. *Race, War and Surveillance: African Americans and the United States Government During World War I*. Bloomington: Indiana University Press, 2001.

Farwell, Byron. *Over There: The United States in the Great War, 1917–1918*. New York: W.W. Norton and Company, 1999.

Finnegan, John Patrick. *Against the Specter of a Dragon: The Campaign for American Military Preparedness, 1914–1917*. Westport, CT: Greenwood Press, 1974.

————. *Military Intelligence*. Washington, DC: Center of Military History, 1998. Online book: http://www.army.mil/CMH/books/Lineage/mi/mi-fm.htm.

Ford, Nancy Gentile. "Mindful of the Traditions of His Race: Dual Identity and the Foreign-Born Soldiers in the First World War American Army." *Journal of American Ethnic History* 16, no. 2 (1997): 35–57.

————. *Americans All: Foreign-Born Soldiers in World War I*. College Station: Texas A&M University Press, 2001.

Fosdick, Raymond B. *Chronicle of a Generation: An Autobiography*. New York: Harper and Brothers, 1958.

Fox, John F., Jr. "Bureaucratic Wrangling over Counterintelligence, 1917–1918." *Studies in Intelligence* 49 (2005): https://www.cia.gov/library/center-for-the-study-of-intelligence/csi-publications/csi-studies/studies/vol49no1/html_files/bureaucratic_wragling_2.html.

Gates, John M. "The Alleged Isolation of the U.S. Army Officers in the Late 19th Century." *Parameters: Journal of U.S. Army War College* 10 (1980): 35–45.

Geary, James W. *We Need Men: The Union Draft in the Civil War*. DeKalb: Northern Illinois University Press, 1991.

Heller, Major Charles E. "The Perils of Unpreparedness: The American Expeditionary Forces and Chemical Warfare." *Military Review* 65 (1985): 12–25.

Helmer, William J. *The Gun That Made the Twenties Roar*. London: The Macmillan Company, Collier-Macmillan Ltd, 1969.

Herring, George C., Jr. "James Hay and the Preparedness Controversy, 1915–1916." *The Journal of Southern History* 30 (1964): 383–404.

Hewes, James E., Jr. *From Root to McNamara: Army Organization and Administration*. Washington, DC: Center of Military History, U.S. Army, 1975. Online book: http://www.army.mil/cmh/books/root/index.htm#contents.

Higham, John. *Strangers in the Land: Patterns of American Nativism 1860–1925*. New York: Athenaeum Press, 1969.

Jacobs, James B., and Leslie Anne Hayes. "Aliens in the U.S. Armed Forces: A Historical-Legal Analysis." *Armed Forces and Society* 7 (1981): 187–208.

Johnson, Wray R. "Black American Radicalism and the First World War: The Secret Files of the Military Intelligence Division." *Armed Forces & Society* 26 (Fall 1999).

Karsten, Peter. *The Military in America: From the Colonial Era to the Present*. New York: Free Press, 1980.

Keene, Jennifer D. *Doughboy, the Great War, and the Remaking of America*. Baltimore, MD: The Johns Hopkins University Press, 2001.

———. *The United States and the First World War*. New York: Longman, Pearson, 2000.

Kennedy, David. *Over Here: The First World War and American Society*. Oxford: Oxford University Press, 1980.

Kevles, Daniel J. "Flash and Sound in the AEF: The History of a Technical Service." *Military Affairs* 33 (1969): 374–84.

Kington, Donald M. *Forgotten Summer: The Story of the Citizen Military Training Camps, 1921–1940*. San Francisco: Two Decades Publishing, 1995.

Koistinen, Paul A.C. *Mobilizing for Modern War: The Political Economy of American Warfare, 1865–1919*. Lawrence: University Press of Kansas, 1997.

Kornweibel, Theodore, Jr. *"Investigate Everything:" Federal Efforts to Compel Black Loyalty During World War I*. Bloomington: Indiana University Press, 2002.

Kreidberg, Marvin A., and Merton G. Henry. *History of Military Mobilization in the United States Army, 1775–1945*. Washington, DC: Center of Military History, U.S. Army, 1984.

Lane, Jack C. *Armed Progressive: General Leonard*. London: Presidio Press, 1978.

Leuchtenburg, William E. "Progressivism and Imperialism: The Progressive Movement and American Foreign Policy, 1898–1916." *Mississippi Valley Review* 39 (1952): 483–504.

McCallum, Jack. *Leonard Wood: Rough Rider, Surgeon, Architect of American Imperialism*. New York: New York University Press, 2006.

Mennell, James. "African-Americans and the Selective Service Act of 1917." *Journal of Negro History* 84 (1999): 275–87.

Millett, Allan R., and Peter Maslowski. *For the Common Defense: A Military History of the United States of America*. New York: Free Press, 1984.

Mooney, Chase C., and Martha E. Layman. "Some Phases of the Compulsory Military Training Movement, 1914–1920." *Mississippi Valley Historical Review* 38 (1952): 633–56.

Murray, Paul T. "Blacks and the Draft: A History of Institutional Racism." *Journal of Black Studies* 2 (1971): 57–76.

"Naval Aviation Chronology, 1898–1916." Naval Historical Center, 1–19. See Official Online Site of U.S. Naval History: http://history.navy.mil/branches/avchr1.htm.

Palladino, Grace. *Another Civil War: Labor, Capital, and the State in the Anthracite Regions of Pennsylvania, 1840–1868.* Urbana: University of Illinois Press, 1990.

Pearlman, Michael. "Leonard Wood, William Muldoon and the Medical Profession: Public Health and Universal Military Training." *New England Quarterly* 52 (1979): 326–44.

———. *To Make Democracy Safe for America: Patricians and Preparedness in the Progressive Era.* Urbana: University of Illinois Press, 1984.

Raines, Edgar F, Jr. "The American 5th Division and Gas Warfare, 1918." *Army History* 22 (1992): 6–10.

Sautter, Udo. "Government and Unemployment: The Use of Public Works before the New Deal." *Journal of American History* 20, no. 4 (1992): 65.

Savoy, Major Wallace Jackson. "The Evolution of the American Modern Light Field Gun." Masters of Arts Thesis, U.S. Army College, Leavenworth, 1978.

Schaffer, Ronald. *America in the Great War: The Rise of the War Welfare State.* New York: Oxford University Press, 1991.

Schott, Linda. "The Woman's Peace Party and the Moral Basis for Women's Pacifism." *Frontiers: A Journal of Women Studies* 8 (1985): 18–24.

Shapiro, Peter, ed. *A History of National Service in America.* College Park, MD: University of Maryland, Center for Political Leadership and Participation, 1994. Online book: http://www.academy.umd.edu/publications/NationalService/index.htm.

Slotten, Hugh R. "Human Chemistry or Scientific Barbarism? American Responses to World War I Poison Gas, 1915–1930." *Journal of American History* 77 (1990): 476–98.

Smythe, Donald. "Venereal Disease: The AEF's Experience." *Prologue* 9, no. 2 (1977): 65–74.

Sparrow, Major James C. *History of Personnel Demobilization in the United States Army.* Department of the Army, 1952.

Talbott, John E. "Soldiers, Psychiatrist, and Combat Trauma." *Journal of Interdisciplinary History* 27 (Winter 1997): 437–54.

Tyler, Robert L. "The United States Government as Union Organizer: The Loyal Legion of Loggers and Lumbermen." *Mississippi Valley Historical Review* 47 (December 1960): 434–51.

Varela, Captain Richard. "Ansauville: A Failure in Training." *Infantry* 73 (Janaury–February 1983): 28–31.

Vilensky, Joel A. "Father Nieuwland and the 'Dew of Death.'" *Notre Dame Magazine* (Winter 2002–03), http://www.nd.edu/~ndmag/w0203/poisongas.html.

———. "Weaponry: Lewiste: America's World War I Weapon of Mass Destruction." *Quarterly Journal of Military History* 17 (2005): 1–4.

Vilensky, Joel A., and Pandy R. Sinish. "The Dew of Death." *Bulletin of the Atomic Scientists* (March 2004), http://thebulletin.metapress.com/content/?k=sinish +the+dew+of+death.

Wanke, Paul. "American Military Psychiatry and Its Role among Ground Forces in World War II." *Journal of Military History* 63 (January 1999): 127–46.

Weigley, Russell. "The Elihu Root Reforms and the Progressive Era." In *Command and Commanders in Modern Warfare: Proceedings of the Second Military Symposium, U.S. Air Force Academy*, edited by William Geffen, Washington, DC: U.S. Air Force, 1969.

Whittemore, Gilbert F., Jr. "World War I, Poison Gas Research, and the Ideals of American Chemists." *Social Studies of Science* 5 (1975): 135–63.

Wilson, John B. *Maneuver and Firepower: The Evolution of Division and Separate Brigades*. Washington, DC: Center of Military History, U.S. Army, 1998. Online book: http://www.army.mil/CMH-pg/books/Lineage/M-F/index.htm.

Zabecki, David A. *Steel Wind: Colonel George Bruchmuller and the Birth of Modern Artillery*. Westport, CT: Praeger Press, 1994.

Zieger, Robert H. *America's Great War: World War I and the American Experience*. New York: Rowman & Littlefield Publishers, 2000.

Index

Abbott, Lyman, 58, 134
Addams, Jane, 18, 52
Advisory Board of University Presidents, 7, 23
Aeronautical Board, 23
African Americans: domestic surveillance of, 61–62; establishment of NAACP, 17; fighting with French Army, 48, 128–29; German propaganda efforts, 63–65; loyalty and support of war, 55; military training, 46–47, 151 n.33; military units, 47–48; national draft of, 34–35; officer training, 126–28; prewar Great Migration, 34, 55, 63, 113; summer training camps, 24; veteran reemployment, 113–14
Agriculture: anti-immigrant debate and, 32–33; conscription and, 29; veteran reemployment in, 107–8
Ainsworth, Fred C., 5
Aircraft/air warfare: censorship on production, 65; chemical warfare and, 81; labor union problems, 67–70; Marlin Machine Gun, 75; Naval Act of 1916 and, 23; U.S. limitations in, 76
Alcohol: enforcement efforts, 60; prohibition, 97; social activities and entertainment for, 42; social reform campaigns, 38–42

Alien Act of 1918, 56, 70
Alien Property Custodians, 61
Aliens. See Immigrants/immigration
Allen, Wilfred H., 88–89, 135–36
Allied Powers, 27–28
"America" (music), 45
American (magazine), 109
American Academy of Political and Social Science, 110
American Academy of Political Science, 14, 16–17, 19
American Ambulance Service, 84
American Anti-imperial League, 17
American Association for Labor Legislation (AALL), 110
American Banker's Association, 14
American Chemical Society, 79
American Civil Liberties Union (ACLU), 53
American Expeditionary Forces: aircraft limitations, 76; armament limitations, 72–76; arrival in France, 75; censorship, 65; chemical warfare losses, 80, 83; deaths and casualties, 86–89, 92; demobilization, 93–95; gas defense training, 82–83; venereal disease rate, 40
American Federation of Labor (AFL), 96–99
American League to Limit Armament, 18

American Legion, 95, 112
American Legion Magazine, 105
American Library Association, 40, 45, 69, 106
American Medical Association, 85
American Peace Society, 52
American Protection League (APL), 58–60
American Psychopathic Association, 37
American Red Cross, 62, 69, 95, 105
American Scandinavian Foundation, 153 n.53
American School Peace League, 52
American Social Hygiene Association (ASHA), 40
American Socialists Party, 30–31, 53–54, 124–25
American Society of Sanitary and Moral Prophylaxis, 40
American Union Against Militarism (AUAM), 17–18, 52–53, 65
American University, 80–81, 134
American-Hungarian Loyalty League, 153 n.53
Anti-immigration debate, 31–33
Antimilitary opposition: to *Land Forces* report, 4–5; politics of, 122–23; to Preparedness Movement, 16–19
Anti-Saloon League, 40
Antitrust legislation, 2–3
Antiwar movement, 53–54, 62–63, 66
Argonne Forest, 88–89, 137
Armstrong, James, 110
Army Appropriations Act of 1912, 4
Army command structure, 9
Army League, 6, 15
Army-Navy Board, 23
Artillery: chemical weapons for, 77–78, 80–81; flash and sound ranging, 83–84; as "King of Battle," 91; shell shock and postwar trauma, 89–90; soldier's stories of bombardment, 86–89, 135–37; types and use of, 72–73
As You Were (soldier journal), 105
Asheville, NC, 7

Ashurst, Henry Fountain, 96
Auld, S. J. M., 83
Australian Army, 88, 136–37
Austro-Hungarian Empire, 33–34, 54

Baccash, Shucri, 153 n.53
Bader, F. K., 153 n.53
Baekeland, L. H., 59, 133
Baker, Newton D., 22–23, 28, 30, 34–38, 41–44, 47, 93, 97, 102, 106, 112
Baker, Ray Stannard, 57
Baldwin, Roger, 53
Barbusse, Henri, 86
Baruch, Bernard, 12–13, 118
The Battle Cry of Peace (motion picture), 16
"Battle Hymn of the Republic," 45
Battle of Gettysburg, 7
Battle trauma, 89–90
Battles, Great War. *See individual place names*
Berger, Victor, 63
Berkman, Alexander, 63
Bielaski, A. Bruce, 60, 64
Birmingham, AL, 50
Blanton, Thomas Lindsay, 96–97
Bohemian National Alliance Council, 153 n.53
Bolshevik Revolution of 1917, 99
Bourne, Randolph, 52
Boy Scouts of America, 107, 153 n.53
Boyce, William, 90
Bremer, Edith Terry, 44
British Army, 55, 77
Browning, John Moses, 74
Bull, Henry T., 6
Bullard, Robert Lee, 83
Burleson, Albert Sidney, 64–65
Burlington, VT, 7
Burr, Charles, 8
Burrell, George, 80, 82
Bush, Irving T., 14
Butler, Benjamin, 74

Camp Devens, MA, 50, 85, 137–38
Camp Funston, KS, 50
Camp Gordon, GA, 43, 45
Camp Grant, IL, 45

Camp Jackson, SC, 49–50
Camp Lee, AL, 50
Camp Logan, TX, 47
Camp McPherson, GA, 45
Camp Meade, MD, 50
Camp Merritt, NJ, 50
Camp Travis, TX, 50
Camp Upton, NY, 45, 50
Camp Wheeler, GA, 10, 45
Canadian Army, 77
Carnegie Endowment for International
   Peace, 52
Catholic Church/organizations, 40,
   44–46, 95, 106
Catholic University, 80–81
Catt, Carrie Chapman, 18, 52
Censorship, 56–59, 65–66, 129
Central Committee of Negro College
   Men, 49
Central Powers. *See* Austro-Hungarian
   Empire; Germany
Chamberlain, George E., 11, 20, 32
Chambers of Commerce, 15–16, 96,
   104–6
Champagne, France, 87
Chateau-Thierry, France, 84, 87
Chemical warfare: Allied and Central
   Powers use of, 77–78; defense
   against attacks, 82–83; gas mask
   development, 81–82; postwar
   backlash, 91–92; soldier's stories of
   attacks, 86–89, 135–37; U.S.
   development of, 78–80, 134–35;
   U.S. losses from, 80, 84–86; U.S.
   production, 80–81
Chicago Daily Tribune, 32
Chicago Tribune, 14, 78
Choate, Joseph H., 15
Chopin, Mathew, 87–88
"Christian Pathology," 8–9
Church Peace Union, 52
Churches and clergy: antipreparedness
   efforts, 19, 118–19; Lutheran
   Church, 61; peace movement, 52;
   veteran reemployment efforts, 106.
   See also Religion/religious groups
Churchill, Marlborough, 61
Citizen Army, 20–22

Citizen Cadet Corps, 20–22
Citizen Training Camps, 25
Citizen-army, 1–4
Citizen's Preparedness Parades, 16
Citizenship: military obligations of, 12;
   naturalization process for, 31–34;
   newspapers and, 14; socialization
   and "Americanization" for, 45
Civil liberties: as casualty of war, 51–
   53, 62; CPI assault on, 70; domestic
   surveillance and, 60; Post Office
   assault on, 64–65
Civil rights, 47, 64. *See also* Racial
   discrimination; Racial segregation
Civil War: adequacy of training in, 3;
   Battle of Gettysburg, 7;
   demobilization, 94; development of
   "Gatling Gun," 74; freedom and
   civil rights failures, 55; wartime
   draft, 29–30
Civilian preparedness organizations,
   13–16
Clark, Grenville, 11–12, 15, 24
Clarke, Walter C., 41
Cleveland *Plain Dealer,* 14
Collier's (magazine), 109
Columbia University, 7, 14, 80
Commission on Training Camp
   Activities (CTCA), 39–40, 49–50
Committee of Ladies, 49
Committee of One Hundred, 12, 49
Committee on Public Information
   (CPI), 56–59, 129–31
Communism (Red Scare), 56, 58, 98–
   100, 112
Compulsory military training. *See*
   Universal Military Training (UMT)
Conant, James, 80–81, 81
Congressional Medal of Honor, 2
Conscientious objectors: criticism of,
   123–24; domestic surveillance, 62;
   draft registration, 30; employment
   discrimination, 107; peace
   movement and, 52–53; "slacker
   raids," 60;
Conscientious Objectors Bureau, 53
Conscription: African American, 34–
   35, 46–50, 127–28; Camp Gordon

Plan, 125–26; Civil War problems,
    29–31; criticism of, 124–25;
    immigrant, 31–34, 42–46, 125–26;
    peace activist objections, 31, 53–54,
    124; Selective Service Act of 1917,
    27–29; UMT and, 1, 27. *See also*
    Draft exemptions
"Continental Army Plan," 20–22;
Cook, George W., 49
Cornell University, 7, 23, 80
Costa, A. Arbib, 153 n.53
Council of National Defense, 4
Counterintelligence measures, 51,
    66–67
Creel, George, 56–59
Crowder, Enoch H., 30, 32
Crowell, Benedict, 75–76, 94
Crumpacker, M. E., 69
Cuba, 2, 10
Cultural customs: Americanization
    campaign, 54–55; CPI propaganda
    and, 57–58; foreign-born soldiers,
    45–46, 153 n.53. *See also* Religion/-
    religious groups
Czechoslovak Legion, 54–55
Czechoslovak National Council, 153
    n.53

Damaged Goods (motion picture), 41
Daniels, Josephus, 22–23
Deaths and casualties: AEF, 80; air
    warfare, 76; chemical warfare, 77,
    83–84; Influenza Epidemic of 1918,
    85–86, 137–38; shell shock and
    postwar trauma, 89–90; soldier's
    stories of, 86–89, 135–37; total
    Great War, 71, 92
Debs, Eugene, 30, 63
Dembinski, B., 153 n.53
Demobilization: challenge of postwar,
    93–95, 140–41; labor unions and
    politics of, 95–97; labor unrest and
    strikes, 97–98, 162 n.1; soldier
    anticipation of, 139. *See also*
    Emergency Employment Committee
Democracy, militarism as threat to, 19
Democratic Party, 4–5
Des Moines News, 96

Desertions, Civil War, 29
Devine, Edward T., 18
Disabled veterans, 114–15
Disque, Brice P., 68–70, 133
Domestic surveillance: of African
    Americans, 55; antiwar movement,
    62–65; civilian-military conflicts,
    66–67; counterintelligence mea-
    sures, 51, 59–62
Draft. *See* Conscription
Draft Act, 53
Draft exemptions: African American,
    34–35; immigrant, 31–34; racial and
    ethnic, 30; Selective Service Act of
    1917, 29
Drinker, Henry Sturgis, 7
DuBois, W. E. B., 55, 126
Duluth *News Tribune,* 14
Dzvenchik, Joseph, 153 n.53

Eastman, Crystal, 18
Eastman, Max, 63
Economic Advisory Committee, 110,
    116
Edgewood Arsenal, MD, 80
Education: foreign-born soldiers, 42–
    46; intelligence testing, 38; muck-
    raking as, 57; promoting patriotism,
    58; social justice reform, 18; social
    welfare, 39; teaching German lan-
    guage, 58–59, 133–34; university
    support of war, 7, 14, 23, 37, 80, 84;
    venereal disease, 40–41
Edward, Oliver, 8
Emergency Employment Committee:
    creation of, 100–102, 140–41;
    outreach to returning soldiers, 102–
    3; programs with businesses, 104–7;
    public works projects, 109–11;
    soldier relocation program, 107–8;
    soldier retraining, 108–9
Enemy aliens, 31–34, 56
Enrollment Act of 1863, 29
Environmental conservation, 2
Erman, Frank D., 68
Espionage: arrests for, 63; domestic
    surveillance and, 59–62; English and
    German efforts at, 55–56

Espionage Act of 1917, 56, 65–66
Estabrook, Henry D., 14
Ethnic groups. *See*
 Immigrants/immigration
Europe: Hague Peace Conference of
 1899, 77; Hague peace conference
 of 1915, 52; military reservist
 model, 3–4; rise of militarism in, 11,
 17. *See also* War in Europe

Fellowship of Reconciliation (FOR),
 52
Fifth Avenue Association, 107
Final Report (Pershing), 91
First aid and sanitation, 24. *See also*
 Health care and medicine
Fiske, Bradley A., 10
Flynn, William J., 60
Ford, Henry, 19
Foreign policy: isolationism, 11, 27–
 28; neutrality, 52–55
Fort Benjamin Harrison, IN, 24
Fort Douglas, UT, 56
Fort Oglethorpe, GA, 24, 56
Fort Sam Houston, TX, 24
Fort Sheridan, IL, 24
Fosdick, Raymond, 39–41
Fosdick, Raymond B., 125
Foster, Reginald L., 104
Foulkes, Charles H., 91
Four-Minute Men, 57–58, 102, 104,
 129
France: lack of racial prejudice, 64;
 production of U.S. aircraft, 76;
 production of U.S. artillery, 73;
 production of U.S. gas masks, 82;
 rise of militarism in, 17; war death
 toll, 92
Franz Ferdinand (Archduke), 9
Free Masonry, 19
Freifield, George, 19
French Army: African American
 soldiers with, 48, 128–29; chemical
 warfare use by, 77; flash and sound
 ranging, 84; U.S. immigrant legions
 in, 54–55
Frick, Henry C., 15
Fries, Amos A., 82

Gambling, social reform campaigns,
 38–42
Gardner, Augustus Peabody, 10–11
Gardner, Edward S., 103
Garrison, Lindley M., 5–6, 9–10, 13,
 20–22
Garrison, William Lloyd, 17
Gary, Elbert H., 115
Gas warfare. *See* Chemical warfare
Gatling, Richard Jordan, 74
German War Practices, 129
Germany: African American
 propaganda by, 63–65; chemical
 warfare use by, 77–78; immigrant
 draftees from, 33–34; media
 portrayal as enemy, 16; military
 preparedness of, 11; propaganda
 efforts by, 55–56; propaganda
 efforts toward, 58–59; rise of
 militarism in, 17; U.S. declaration of
 war on, 28; war death toll, 92
Geronimo (Apache chief), 2
Gettysburg, PA, 6–7
Giddings, Franklin H., 133
Gimel Brothers, 24
Global arms race, 18
Goldman, Emma, 63
Gompers, Samuel, 97
Granger, Alfred Hoyt, 109–10
Great Britain: American cultural ties
 to, 28; production of U.S. gas masks,
 82; propaganda efforts in U.S., 55–
 56; war death toll, 92
Great Migration, prewar black, 34, 55,
 63, 113
Great War. *See* War in Europe
Greek Orthodox Church, 46, 153 n.53
Greek-American Boy Scouts, 153 n.53
Greene, Frank Lester, 20, 120
Greer, David H., 106
Gregory, Thomas Watt, 59–60, 67
Grynia, L. A., 153 n.53
Guggenheim, Simon, 15
Gunpowder Neck, MD, 80
Gutowski, Stanislaw A., 43

Haan, William George, 115–16, 141,
 162 n.7

Haas, Albert K., 88, 136–37
The Hague, 52, 77
Hallinan, Charles T., 18
Hammond, John Hays, 115–16
Harding, Warren G., 116
Harvard Club, 12
Harvard University, 7, 23, 37, 80, 84
Hay, James, 4–5, 11, 21–22
Hay Bill (National Defense Act of 1916). *See* National Defense Act of 1916 (Hay Bill)
Haywood, "Big Bill," 63, 68
Health care and medicine: army advances in, 84–85; chemical warfare, 79–80; disabled veterans, 114–15; Influenza Epidemic of 1918, 85–86, 137–38; psychiatry and shell shock, 89–90; Scientific Management Movement, 36–37; social reforms for, 18, 38–42; UMT and, 8–9
Hibben, John Geir, 58, 134
Hill, David Jayne, 15
Hindenburg Line, 89
Holl, Edward Leo, 114
Holloway, Edwin L., 103
Holmes, John Haynes, 18
Hoover, Herbert, 110
Horn, Robert O. Van, 6–7
The Houston Freeman (newspaper), 47
How the War came to America, 129
Howard University, 49, 126–27
Howe, Frederic C., 18
Huidenkoper, Frederick L., 15
Hull, William I., 18

Immigrants/immigration: Camp Gordon Plan, 125–26; domestic surveillance of, 62–63; drafting of, 31–34, 151 n.33; language training, 42–44; National Origins Act of 1924, 70; patriotism and support of war, 54–55; postwar restrictions on, 97; socialization and "Americanization," 15, 28, 45–46, 153 n.53; U.S. wartime restriction on, 56; veteran reemployment, 113; vigilantism and xenophobia, 57–60

Independent (magazine), 109
Indian Wars, 10, 74
Industrial Revolution, impact on warfare, 71–72, 86, 91
Industrial Workers of the World (IWW), 61–63, 65, 67–70, 99, 112
Industry (magazine), 109
Infantry Journal, 100
Influenza Epidemic of 1918, 84–86, 137–38
Integration, 43–44, 50
Intelligence collection: civil-military conflicts, 66–67; counterintelligence measures, 59–62; domestic surveillance, 51, 62–65; ethnic civilians in domestic, 153 n.53
Intelligence testing, 36–38, 90
International Congress of Farm Women, 18
International peace movement, 18–19
International Women's Congress for Peace and Freedom, 52
Irish Ancient Order of Hibernians, 54
Irvine, I. N. W., 153 n.53
Irwin, Will, 57
Isolationism, U.S. policy of, 11, 27–28
Italian Bureau of Information, 153 n.53

Janneyzi, Vince, 153 n.53
Jefferson Charles E., 19
Jewish Building Fund, 109
Jewish community, 45
Jewish Legion, 55
Jewish Welfare Board (JWB), 40, 44–46, 50, 95, 106, 153 n.53
Jobs for Soldiers, 113
John Hopkins University, 80
Johnson, Bascon, 40–41

Kaiser Wilhelm Institute, 77
Kasakaitis, J., 153 n.53
Keeping Fit to Fight (motion picture), 41, 44
Kelley, Florence, 18
Kellogg, Paul U., 18
Kennedy, Chase W., 25

Keppel, Frederick, 45
Keys, Edward A., 110
Kimball, Henry Hudson, 110
Kirchway, George W., 18, 142
Kitchen, Claude, 20
Klein, Bernard, 153 n.53
Knights of Columbus, 40, 44, 50, 69, 106
Kobbe, William Hoffman, 102
Kotecki, M., 153 n.53

Labor unions: domestic surveillance of, 61–63; labor unrest and strikes, 97–98, 163 n.29; postwar demobilization and, 95–97; public works projects and, 111; Red Scare and, 98–100; sabotage, 67–68; veterans organizing as, 99
Land Forces report of 1912, 4–5
Lane, Franklin K., 101
Lansing, Robert E., 32–33
LaRochelle, F. D., 153 n.53
Lavelle, M. J., 106
Lee, Joseph, 39
Lehigh University, 7, 23
Lejpak, F. J., 153 n.53
Leslie's (magazine), 105, 109
Lewis, I. N., 75
Lewis, Winford Lee, 81
L'Hommendieu, Robert, 110
Liberty Loan Campaign, 54, 57–58
Life (magazine), 105, 109
Literacy: American soldier, 37–38; foreign-born soldiers, 42–45, 113
Literary Digest, 32, 79, 96
Lithuanian National Council, 153 n.53
Lodge, Henry Cabot, 10–11
London, Meyer, 20
Lovejoy, Owen, 18
Loving, Walter Howard, 64
Loyal Legion of Loggers and Lumbermen, 68–69, 132–33
Loyalty: African American, 55, 64; domestic surveillance of, 62–65; foreign-born soldiers, 33–34; immigrant, 54–55, 58; music to instill patriotism and, 45; as quality of a soldier, 105, 113, 143–44;

Sedition Act of 1918 and, 56, 66, 131–32; vigilantism in enforcement of, 60
Ludington, MI, 7
Lyman, Theodore, 84, 135
Lynch, Frederick, 19

MacArthur, Douglas, 6
Machine guns, 74–76
Macon Telegraph, 32
Madden, Martin B., 49
Madison, James, 17
Mahan, Alfred Thayer, 1, 77
Mallery, Otto T., 110
The Management of the American Soldiers (Shank), 36–37
Manhattan Project of WWII, 80
Manning, Van H., 80, 135
March, Peyton C., 91, 94
Marlin, John M., 75
Marlow, Francis Smith, 109–11
Marne, France, 84
Massachusetts Institute of Technology, 80
Maxim, Hiram, 74
McAdoo, William, 59–60
McCain, H. P., 25
McClure's (magazine), 105, 109
McKinley, William, 2
Media. See Motion pictures; Newspapers and print media
Medicine/medical technology, 8–9. See also Health care and medicine
The Melting Pot: An Exponent of International Communism, 112
Menken, S. Stanwood, 15
Methodist Episcopal Church, 106
Metropolitan (magazine), 109
Metropolsky, N., 153 n.53
Mexico: immigrant labor from, 32–33; U.S. involvement in, 5, 9; Villa cross-border raids, 22; Zimmerman telegram, 28
Military Intelligence Division (MID), 59, 61–68
Military leadership, Scientific Management and, 36–37
Military posts/facilities: Camp A. A.

Humphrey, 83; Camp Devens, MA, 50, 85, 137–38; Camp Funston, KS, 50; Camp Gordon, GA, 43, 45; Camp Grant, IL, 45; Camp Jackson, SC, 49–50; Camp Lee, AL, 50; Camp Logan, TX, 47; Camp McPherson, GA, 45; Camp Meade, MD, 50; Camp Merritt, NJ, 50; Camp Travis, TX, 50; Camp Upton, NY, 45, 50; Camp Wheeler, GA, 10, 45; Edgewood Arsenal, MD, 80; Fort Benjamin Harrison, IN, 24; Fort Oglethorpe, TN, 24; Fort Sam Houston, TX, 24; Fort Sheridan, IL, 24

Military reform: "Continental Army Plan," 20–22; National Defense Act of 1916, 22; political lobbying for, 15–16; Preparedness Movement and, 2–6; preparedness politics and, 9–11; public health and morality in, 8–9; reserves military training, 6–8, 11–13; Scientific Management Movement in, 35–38

Military training: African American soldiers, 46–50; foreign-born soldiers, 42–46, 151 n.33; health and morality, 8–9; inadequacy of, 91; intelligence and psychological testing, 37–38; Plattsburg Movement, 11–13, 23–25, 119–20; preparedness politics and, 14; reserve forces and summer camps, 3–8; Scientific Management Movement in, 36–37; social reform campaigns, 38–42

Military Training Camp Association (MTCA), 15, 22–25

Military training camps: health and disease control, 85–86; integration efforts, 50; segregation, 47–49; social activities and entertainment for, 41–42, 125; vice and morality enforcement near, 39–41, 60

Military units: 1st Division, 75, 82–83; 5th Marine Regiment, 2nd Division, 88; 18th Infantry Division, 83; 24th Infantry Division, 47; 27th Division, 95; 27th Engineers, 89; 29th Engineers, 84; 65th Infantry, 42nd Division, 87; 77th Division, 95; 92nd Combat Division, 48–49; 93rd Division, 48; 108th Infantry, 89; 308th Infantry, 27th Division, 88–89, 135–36; 309th Infantry, 78th Division, 88, 136–37; 356th Infantry, 89th Division, 87–88; African American, 47; Development Battalions, 43–44; Military Intelligence Division, 43; "Rough Riders" Volunteer Cavalry Regiment, 2; Sanitary Corps, Social Hygiene Division, 40–41. *See also* American Expeditionary Forces

The Military Unpreparedness of the United States (Huidenkoper), 15

Militia. *See* National Guard

Miller, A. W., 89

Mitchel, John Purroy, 12–13

Mobilization, 4, 22

Monteagle, Paige, 102

Monterey, CA, 6–7

Morale: foreign-born soldiers, 43–45, 63; influence of vice and morals on, 38–42; postwar demobilization and, 94; propaganda impact on, 66–67

Morality: of chemical warfare, 77, 81, 91–92; Scientific Management Movement and, 36–37; social reforms and, 18, 38–42; UMT and, 8–9; of veteran reemployment, 97–98

Motion pictures: army training, 41, 44; entertainment, 42; preparedness, 16

Mott, John, 39

Muckraking, 57

Music: censorship, 59; instilling patriotism with, 45–46; Philippine Constabulary, 64

Nash, Paul, 86

Nash, Roy, 49

National Academy of Sciences, 79, 84

National Association for the Advancement of Colored People (NAACP): domestic surveillance of, 64; establishment of, 17; military racial policy and, 48–49, 126–28; position on national draft, 34–35

National Association of Colored Women, 18–19

National Association of Manufacturers, 142–43

National Catholic War Council, 95, 106

National City (magazine), 109

National Conference of Catholic Charities, 18

National Council of Jewish Women, 18

National Defense Act of 1916 (Hay Bill), 22, 28, 79

National draft. *See* Conscription

National Federation of Settlements, 18

National German-American Alliance, 54

National Guard: African American units, 48; National Defense Act of 1916, 20–22; postwar strike suppression, 99; press criticism, 14; race riots of 1917, 64; state control, 3–5; summer military camps, 23–24; in a two-army system, 9; wartime "federalization," 28–29;

National Guard Association, 21

National League of Teachers, 18

National Origins Act of 1924, 70

National Research Council (NRC), 84

National Reserve Corporation, 7

The National Romanian Society, 153 n.53

National Security League (NSL), 15, 19, 118–19

National Service (soldier journal), 105

National Weekly News, 112

Naturalization, citizenship, 31–34

Naval Act of 1916, 22–23

Naval Reserve Corps, 23

Navy League, 15, 119

Neutrality: African American support of, 55; ethnic group support of, 54–55; peace movement and, 52–53; U.S. policy of, 27–28

New York Evening Globe, 105

New York Evening Sun, 78

New York Furniture Exchange Association, 108

New York Globe, 32

New York Journal of Commerce, 96

New York Sun, 32

New York Times, 10, 13–14, 19, 20–22, 24, 32, 78, 105

New York *Tribune*, 14

New York World, 105

Newspapers and print media: African American, 47, 55, 64; anti-immigrant sentiment, 32; censorship, 56, 65–66, 129; chemical warfare reporting, 78; ethnic group, 54; for foreign-born soldiers, 44–45; Post Office assault on, 65; postwar demobilization reporting, 96–97; postwar unemployment reporting, 104–5; Preparedness Movement attention in, 14; "Spruce-up Campaign," 109; *Trench and Camp*, 42

Nieuwland, Julius Aloysius, 81

"No man's land," 72, 86, 136–37

Nobel Peace Prize, 2

Office of Naval Intelligence (ONI), 59–61, 66–67

Officer training: African American, 48–50, 126–28; bilingual immigrant, 43–44; *Land Forces* report and, 4–5; National Defense Act of 1916, 20–22; Plattsburg Movement, 23–25; ROTC, 22; summer military camps, 6–8, 11–13, 48; training manual, 119–20

O'Hare, Kate Richards, 63

The Old Colony Magazine, 105

"open door" policy, 28

Organized Militia System, 1–4. *See also* National Guard

O'Ryan, John F., 24

Our Military History: Its Facts and Fallacies (Wood), 2

The Outlook, 58, 134

Pacifism, 52, 62

Padgett, Edward R., 125

Palestine, 55
Palmer, Frederick, 40
Palmer, John McAuley, 4
Panama-Pacific Exposition of 1915, 10, 117
Parker, John, 110
Patriotism: conscription and, 30; escalation to mass hysteria, 51; ethnic group demonstration of, 54–55; foreign-born soldiers, 45; Four-Minute Men speeches, 57–58, 102, 104, 129; obligatory military service and, 14; preparedness politics and, 17–18; scientific research and, 79; veteran reemployment and, 106–7, 143–44; war as source of, 11; war bonds and, 58. *See also* Loyalty
Peace Movement, 51–53, 62
Peadbody, J. C. R., 100–101, 107
People's Council of America for Peace and Democracy, 53–54
Perkins, Francis Orville, 109, 114
Pershing, John J., 4, 22, 76, 83–84, 91
Petraca, Rocco, 153 n.53
Petrunkevitch, Alexander, 153 n.53
Phelps, William Lyon, 19
Philadelphia *Inquirer,* 14
Philippine Constabulary, 64
Philippines, 2–3, 10
Pickens, William, 126
Pierson, James, 89, 92
Pinchot, Amos, 17
Pinchot, Gifford, 17
Plattsburg, NY, 24
Plattsburg Movement, 11–13, 23–25, 48, 119–20, 126
Playground and Recreational Association, 39–40, 42, 45
Polish Legion, 54–55
Polish National Committee, 153 n.53
Polish Press Bureau, 43
Politics: antipreparedness efforts, 16–19; gas warfare research, 79; military reform, 4–5, 21–23; preparedness debate, 9–11, 120–23; preparedness lobbying, 15–16; Southern white racial, 34–35

Poole, Ernest, 57
Postwar trauma and casualties, 89–90
Prayer Book for Jews in the Army and Navy, 46
Preparedness Movement: "Christian Pathology" and, 9; opposition politics, 4–6; public debate opposed to, 16–19; public debate supporting, 13–16; Roosevelt on, 117; U.S. Congress and, 9–11, 120–23; UMT and the, 1; Wood as proponent of, 2–3
Preparedness: The American Versus the Military Programme (Hull), 18
Presidio, CA, 6–7
Princeton University, 23, 80
"Problems of the Common Defense" (Shaw), 14
Progressive Era: definition and ideology, 151 n.34; influence on peace movement, 51–53; muckraking, 57; objections to militarism, 16; public service philosophy, 79; social justice reform, 35–36, 95; social welfare philosophy, 38–42
Progressive Party, 5, 13, 16
Prohibition, 97
Propaganda: civil-military conflicts, 66–67; creation of CPI for, 56–57, 129–31; creation of war hysteria, 57–59; English and German efforts at, 55–56; to instill patriotism, 45; postwar radicalism, 111–12; preparedness efforts as, 17–18; preventing enemy, 51; "selling the draft," 30; "selling" the war, 51, 57; veteran reemployment, 104–7
Prostitution, 38–42, 60
Providence *Journal,* 14
Psychological testing, 37–38
Public health, 8–9, 18. *See also* Health care and medicine
Public opinion: muckraking and, 57; newspapers and, 14; preparedness politics and, 9–11; summer camp publicity and, 12–13; wartime definition for, 130–31

Public works projects, 109–11
Punitive Expedition to Mexico, 22

Quakers (Society of Friends), 16, 52,
    62

Racial discrimination: black soldier,
    49–50; officer training, 126–28;
    solving the "race question," 47;
    support of war effort and, 55; U.S.
    military, 34–35
Racial integration, 50
Racial segregation: military racial
    policy, 34–35, 46–48; officer
    training, 49–50
Racial violence: 1917 race riots, 46–
    47, 55, 63–64; 1919 Chicago riots,
    114; lynching, 64; U.S. prewar, 34
Radio transmissions, censorship,
    65–66
Randolph, A. Philip, 35, 55
Ratz, John M., 153 n.53
Rebel Worker: Organ of
    Revolutionary Unionism, 112
Red Scare (Communism), 56, 58, 98–
    100, 112
Regular Army: Land Forces report of
    1912, 4–5; National Defense Act
    of 1916, 20–22; in a two-army
    system, 9
Religion/religious groups: Catholic,
    40, 44, 46, 106; Greek Orthodox
    Church, 46, 153 n.53; integration
    efforts, 50; Jewish, 40, 44–46;
    Knights of Columbus, 45–46, 106;
    Methodist Episcopal, 106; Quakers
    (Society of Friends), 16, 52, 62. See
    also Churches and clergy
Republican Party, 4–5
Reserve forces: in the "Continental
    Army Plan," 20–22; European
    model of, 3; National Defense Act of
    1916, 20–22; Naval Reserve Corps,
    23; seven-year enlistment plan, 4;
    summer military training, 6–8; in a
    two-army system, 9
Reserve Officers' Training Corps
    (ROTC): African American

exclusion, 48; establishment of, 22;
    recruitment of trainees for, 24
Review of Review (magazine), 109
Revolutionary War, 31
Reynolds, John Bateson, 101, 112–13
Richards, Theodore W., 58, 133
Richmond, Clarence, 88
RMS Lusitania, 12–13
Rockefeller, John D., Jr., 109
Roosevelt, Franklin D., 10, 22–23
Roosevelt, Theodore, 2, 5, 10–11, 13,
    94, 117, 123–24
Root, Elihu, 1, 3, 12, 36
Rouse, Nathaniel, 87
Russia: Bolshevik Revolution of 1917,
    99; German gas attacks on, 77; rise
    of militarism in, 17; U.S.
    propaganda toward, 58; war death
    toll, 92
Russian Revolution of 1917, 53
Russian-American Bureau of Chicago,
    153 n.53
Russian-American Economic Associa-
    tion, 153 n.53
Russo-Japanese War, 2
Rutledge, Carl Clyde, 100, 114

Sabiston, Harry, 110
Sabotage: domestic surveillance and,
    59–62; German campaign of U.S.,
    55–56
Sabotage Act of 1918, 56
Salmon, Thomas, 90
Salvation Army, 39–40, 95
San Francisco Chronicle, 78
Sassoon, Siegfried, 90
Saturday Evening Post, 109
Schenck, Charles, 63
Schwab, Charles M., 115
Scientific American, 109
Scientific Management Movement,
    35–38
Scott, Emmett J., 47–49
Scott, Hugh L., 10, 23
Secretary of War: Baker as, 22;
    Garrison as, 5–6, 9–11; Stimson as,
    3–5
Sedition Act of 1918, 56, 66, 131–32

Seeholzoe, A. M., 153 n.53
Selective Service Act of 1917, 28–29, 41
Selective Service System: enforcement, 60; foreign-born classifications, 31–32; local draft boards, 30; quota system, 32–33; racial discrimination, 49
Settlement House Movement, 18
Sexual transmitted disease, 38–42
Seymour, Bina, 153 n.53
Shank, David C., 36
Shaw, Albert, 14
Shell shock and postwar trauma, 89–90
Simmons, Roscoe Conklin, 55
Slovak League, 153 n.53
Smith, Dan, 105
Smith, Mathew, 116, 141, 162 n.7
Social justice reform: dealing with vices and morals, 38–42; expanded government role, 2; peace movement and, 51–53; Progressivism and, 151 n.34; Settlement House Movement, 18; UMT and, 8–9; women's peace efforts and, 18–19
Society of Experimentalists, 37
Society of Friends (Quakers), 16, 52, 62
Soldiers, Sailors, and Marine Union, 99, 112
South Slavic National Council, 153 n.53
Spanish-American War, 2, 17, 74
Spannegel, Louis, 153 n.53
Springarn, Joel E., 48, 64, 126
"Spruce-up Campaign," 109–10
Spry, Bryon Philip, 104
St. Louis Globe Democrat, 32
St. Louis Star, 14
St. Mihiel, 84, 87–88
Standing army: defense of, 121; James Madison warning on, 17; Meyer London warning on, 21; as threat to freedom, 1, 3; in a two-army system, 9; U.S. unpreparedness of, 73
Standord-Binet intelligence scale, 37

Stanford University, 7
"Star-Spangled Banner," 45
State militias. See National Guard
Stearns, Cuthbert P., 68
Steuger, Leonard, 153 n.53
Stevens Institute of Technology, 23
Stimson, Henry L., 3–4
"Stimson Plan" (Land Forces report of 1912), 4–5
Stokes, Rose Paster, 63
Straley, John A., 110
Strunsky, Simeon, 17
Submarine warfare: attacks on American ships, 28; sinking of RMS Lusitania, 12–13; U.S. Navy modernization and, 23; as weapon of war, 73–74
Summer Military Instruction Camps, 6–8, 23–25, 48
Syaki, Alex, 153 n.53

Taft, William Howard, 2, 4–5, 11
Tanks/tank warfare, 73
Tarbell, Ida, 57
Taylor, Harry, 104
Telephone/telegraph, censorship, 65–66
"The Business Man and Universal Military Training" (Bush), 14
Thomas, Jesse O., 113
Thomas, Norman, 65
Thompson, John T., 74
Toledo Blade, 14
Torossian, Gregory, 59, 134
Trading-with-the-Enemy Act of 1917, 56, 65, 129
Treat 'Em Rough (soldier journal), 105
Trench and Camp (newspaper), 42
Trowbridge, Augustus "Gus," 84
24th Infantry Division, 47
Two-army system, 9

U.S. Air Service, 76
U.S. Army: African American soldiers in, 46–50; chemical warfare development, 78–81; foreign-born soldiers in, 42–46; integration efforts, 50; limitations on men and

weapons, 72–74; Plattsburg Movement, 6–8, 11–13, 23–25; Scientific Management Movement in, 36–37; Wood-Garrison reform efforts, 5–6; Wood-Stimson reform effort, 3–5. *See also* American Expeditionary Forces; Military units; National Guard; Regular Army

U.S. Army American Ambulance Service, 84

U.S. Army Chemical Warfare Service, 80–81, 91–92

U.S. Army Chief of Staff: Hugh L. Scott as, 10; Leonard Wood as, 2–11, 36; Peyton C. March as, 91, 94

U.S. Army Corps of Engineers, 83

U.S. Army Gas Defense Service, 82–83

U.S. Army General Staff: call for national draft, 28; censorship policy, 56; "Continental Army Plan," 20–22; racial policies, 47; Wood-Ainsworth conflict, 5

U.S. Army Medical Department, 84–85

U.S. Army Military Intelligence Division (MID), 59, 61–68

U.S. Army Ordnance Department, 74–75

U.S. Army Signal Corps, 84

U.S. Army Surgeon General, 40–41, 83

U.S. Army War College, 79

U.S. Bureau of Aircraft Production, 68

U.S. Bureau of Cartoons, 57

U.S. Bureau of Education, 45, 58

U.S. Bureau of Intelligence, 63

U.S. Bureau of Investigation, 59–62

U.S. Bureau of Mines, 79, 82, 134–35

U.S. Bureau of Returning Soldiers, 112

U.S. Bureau of Vice and Liquor Control, 41

U.S. Bureau of War Photographs, 57

U.S. Congress: postwar demobilization and, 95–97; postwar hearings, 91; preparedness debate, 9–11, 120–23; public works projects, 109–11

U.S. Congress, legislation: Alien Act of 1918, 56, 70; Army Appropriations Act of 1912, 4; Conscription Act, 124–25; Draft Act, 53; Enrollment Act of 1863, 29; Espionage Act of 1917, 56, 65–66; National Defense Act of 1916, 22, 28, 79; National Origins Act of 1924, 70; Sabotage Act of 1918, 56; Sedition Act of 1918, 56, 66; Selective Service Act of 1917, 28–29; Trading-with-the-Enemy Act of 1917, 56, 65, 129

U.S. Constitution, 124–25

U.S. Department of Justice, 59–62, 66

U.S. Department of Labor, 93–99, 105, 108–10

U.S. Department of State, 33, 64

U.S. Department of Treasury, 59–62

U.S. Employment Service, 95–96, 140–43

U.S. Law Enforcement Division, 41

U.S. Navy: limitations on ships, 73–74; Naval Act of 1916, 22–23; Office of Naval Intelligence (ONI), 59–61, 66–67; preparedness politics and, 10; radio censorship, 66; reserves military training, 6; summer training camps, 24

U.S. Post Master General, 62, 64–65, 129, 132

U.S. Railroad Administration, 106

U.S. Secret Service, 59–60, 67

Unemployment: African American veterans, 113–14; award programs to combat, 106–7; disabled veterans, 114–15; Emergency Employment Committee, 100–106, 140–41; ethnic civilians in domestic, 153 n.53, 163 n.29; growing radicalism, 111–12; immigrant veterans, 113; labor and the Red Scare, 98–100; panhandling and begging, 112–13; postwar demobilization and, 93–95, 142–43; relocation programs to end, 107–8; retraining programs to end, 108–9; War Department efforts, 97–98

Uniforms/clothing: chemical warfare, 82; summer military camps, 7, 24

United Press Association (UPA), 66

United States Spruce Production
Corporation, 68–70, 132–33
*Universal Military Service and
Democracy* (Nasmyth), 18
Universal Military Training (UMT):
Anti-preparedness Movement and,
16–19; Army Appropriations Act of
1912, 4; "Continental Army Plan"
and, 20–23; *Land Forces* report and,
4–6; National Defense Act of 1916,
20–22; national draft for, 27; peace
movement and, 52–53; Preparedness
Movement and, 1; as public health
project, 8–9; summer training
camps, 6–8, 23–25, 48
University of Alabama, 23
University of California, Berkeley, 7,
23
University of Illinois, 23
University of Michigan, 23
University of New York, 23
University of Notre Dame, 81
University Presidents, Advisory Board
of, 7
U.S. Bulletin, 109

Van Deman, Ralph H., 61
Vanderbilt, Cornelius, 15
Vanderbilt University, 23
Vardaman, James, 34
Venereal disease (VD), 40–41
Veterans: disabled, 114–15;
employment and wages, 108;
employment preference program,
104, 143–44; growing radicalism,
111–12; immigrant, 113; labor
union organizing by, 99;
panhandling and begging, 112–13;
shell shock and postwar trauma, 90.
See also Demobilization; Emergency
Employment Committee;
Unemployment
Vickers Company, 74
Vigilantism, 57–60
Villa, Pancho, 22
Villard, Oswalt Garrison, 16
Virginia Military Institute, 23
Vogel, Jon, 153 n.53

War/warfare: to end all wars, 121–22;
humane death in, 77, 81, 91–92;
industrialization of, 71–72, 86, 91;
inevitability of, 123; soldier's stories
of, 86–89, 135–37; trauma and
casualties, 89–90
War bonds, 54, 57–58
War Camp Community Service
(WCCS), 42, 45, 69, 106
War in Europe: assassination of Franz
Ferdinand, 9; deaths and casualties,
71–72, 76–77, 92; impact on U.S.
economy, 118; sinking of RMS
Lusitania, 12–13; U.S. declares war
on Germany, 28. *See also* Europe
War Message and Facts behind It, 129
War of 1812, 3
War Trade Board, 61
Washington, Booker T., 47
Washington Times, 96
Weapons of war: aircraft/air warfare,
76; artillery, 72–73; chemical
warfare, 77–83; flash and sound
ranging, 83–84; grenades and
flamethrowers, 73; machine guns,
74–76; mass production and
mechanization, 71–72, 86; Naval
Act of 1916 and, 23; submarine
warfare, 73–74; tanks/tank warfare,
73
Webster, Daniel, 124
Welsh, Charles, 110
Wemple, Edwin Copely, 101, 112
West Point Military Academy, 10
Western Frontier, 10
Wheeler, Harry, 104
Whitney, Leonard H., 110
Wickersham, George W., 115
Wilkins, Ernest H., 44–45
Williams College, 23
Wilson, James H., 10–11
Wilson, William B., 95
Wilson, Woodrow, 20–21, 25; African
American conscription, 34–35;
antipreparedness efforts, 5–6;
chemical warfare and, 80, 134–35;
domestic surveillance and, 60, 62;
foreign policy shifts, 28; postwar

crises, 95, 106; preparedness politics and, 9–10, 13; wartime propaganda, 56
Wise, Stephen S., 18–19
Womanhood: The Glory of a Nation (motion picture), 16
Woman's Christian Temperance Union (WCTU), 18–19
Woman's Peace Party (WPP), 18–19, 52
Women: in government, 109; peace and anti-military efforts, 18–19, 52; portrayal in propaganda, 58; preparedness politics and, 10; prostitution, 40–41; right to vote, 97; social welfare programs, 44; summer training camps, 24
Women's Home Companion, 105, 109
Women's Peace Party (WPP), 65
Women's Suffrage Movement, 18–19
Women's Trade Union League, 18

Wood, Leonard, 2–3, 5–6, 36, 99–102, 142
Woods, Arthur D., 98–106, 109, 112, 115, 140–41
World Peace Foundation, 52
World's Work (magazine), 109
Wright, Orville, 76

Yale University, 7, 23, 80
Yerkes, Robert M., 37
As You Were (soldier journal), 105
Young, Charles, 126
Young Men's Christian Association (YMCA), 39–42, 44–45, 50, 52, 69, 95
Young Women's Christian Association (YWCA), 39–40, 44
Ypres, Belgium, 78

Zeltonago, John, 153 n.53

About the Author

NANCY GENTILE FORD is Professor of History at Bloomsburg University of Pennsylvania. She is the author of *Issues of War and Peace* (Greenwood, 2002) and *America's All! Foreign Born Soldiers in World War I* (2001).

Recent Titles in in War and in Peace: U.S. Civil-Military Relations

Military Necessity: Civil-Military Relations in the Confederacy
Paul D. Escott

Civil-Military Relations on the Frontier and Beyond, 1865–1917
Charles A. Byler

A Clash of Cultures: Civil-Military Relations during the Vietnam War
Orrin Schwab

James K. Polk, Presidential Power, and Political Ambition: Civil-Military
Relations in the Mexican War
John C. Pinheiro